ELEANOR OF AQUITAINE

Curtis Howe Walker

Illustrated by M. S. Nowicki

F NORTH CAROLINA PRESS

To the Memory of

LAWRENCE BUTLER BRAMAN

Who suggested the Writing of this Book

Preface

A GENTLEMAN who had traced his family line back to 55 B.C. with *two breaks,* once remarked to me that the greatest word in history was "probable." Though I agree with him I have, nevertheless, eliminated it from this book and must ask the reader, gentle or otherwise, to understand that much of what I have written about Eleanor and her experiences is only *probable.* All the dialogues and some of the speeches are imaginative reconstructions representing what I believe the characters would have said, judging by what the records show them to have been. In the text I have not attempted to distinguish between the fictional and the recorded speeches—all alike are given in quotation marks. Anyone who desires to check on a speech or incident may do so by turning to the section of Explanatory Notes and Source References, in the back of the book. Here will be found references by page numbers to matters mentioned in the text, as well as an account of the general nature of my research. In the Chronicles there are explicit references to Eleanor's character, to her beauty and charm, but not a single word to tell what she looked like. The only hint as to her appearance is given by the representations of her figure found on the seals reproduced on the jacket and half-title page of this book.

In working up the material for this volume I have been assisted by a Carnegie Grant-in-Aid secured through the University Center Research Council at Vanderbilt University. The publication of the book has been made possible through a loan granted by the Institute of Research and Training in the Social Sciences of Vanderbilt University to whose energetic Director, Dr. George W. Stocking, I am deeply indebted.

For my knowledge of the sites associated with Eleanor's activities I am much indebted to the kindness of my hostess at Poitiers, Mme. Georges Valette. To M. François Eygun, also of Poitiers, I owe the photographic reproductions of Eleanor's seals.

In making the revisions of the original draft of the manuscript my friend, Dr. William Bridgwater, gave me an unremitting assistance for which I shall never cease to be grateful. Nor have I words fitly to express my gratitude to Miss Peggy McComas, for assistance in the same work of revision far beyond the call of duty.

My friends in the Departments of History and English at Vanderbilt University, William C. Binkley, Richmond Croom Beatty, Clarence Nixon, Walter Clyde Curry, and above all Frank Lawrence Owsley, have given me constant encouragement through the years. For this and for their aid in finally securing the publication of the book I shall ever bear them in grateful memory.

Much of this book was written at Hadlyme, Connecticut, in "Eleanor's Bower." Its owner, the Squire of Stonehenge, contributed more to the completion of the manuscript than he can possibly imagine. For his many kindnesses I wish here to express my deepest gratitude.

CURTIS HOWE WALKER
August 1, 1949
Vanderbilt University

Introduction

ROMANCE offers no more brilliant picture than does the story of Eleanor of Aquitaine, wife of two powerful medieval monarchs, and mother of two more—one of them a villain, the other, the most famous warrior of his time. Her life was entwined with the great ones of her age. It plunged her into adventure after adventure, and led her from one extremity of the known world to the other. And hers was a long life. She made her first entrance on the public stage as a bride at the age of fifteen, and held her place upon it for three score years. After her last dramatic act, the defense of a besieged castle, she made her exit at the age of eighty-two.

Eleanor played a passionate part in a passionate age. For the twelfth century seethed with creative force. Its men and women brought forth the pageants of the Crusades, the wonder of the Cathedrals, the busy hives of the Universities, the Scholastics' acutely reasoned orderings of knowledge, the sonorous Latin hymns which ring down the ages, the songs of the troubadours, the magic fantasy of Arthurian tale.

And all the ordered turmoil of this age thrived in an atmosphere of emotional conflict, contradictory yet consistent. An ideal goal, eternal happiness in the world to come, had been for hundreds of years held before these childlike, half-barbaric peoples with an unparalleled insistence by an organization unique in human history. For six centuries medieval society had been drilled and led upward by the Church. To their wondering imaginations, Jehovah in all his majesty had been presented with authority. Before their terror-stricken eyes, the Church had held up the consequences of sin, the eternal penalties of a burning Hell. They trembled before the dreadful realities of the Judgment Day. But they also heard of redemption and the ways of redemption; of Christ's pitying and sacrificial life, of the gracious Virgin-Mother with her all-embracing love, of the kindly Saints incessantly interceding for sinful man. Born and bred in its ritual, they were part and parcel of the Church. They gave abundantly to it of their possessions, they supported and feared its priests, they clung lovingly to its promises.

But they were human; they lived in this world and they found it a confusing business. In the struggle for existence, passions were aroused that drove them into courses that perilled their souls: they did what they pleased and seized what they wanted. But when cooler moments came, the perils of Hell burst vividly upon their imaginations. Then atonement must be made, and that quickly. So, abandoning worldly ambition, they feverishly sought the surest way of salvation. Some endowed and built churches; others donned pilgrim garb and travelled to the Holy Land; while others gave up all their possessions and entered the monastery.

In this world of the twelfth century Eleanor played no minor part. And yet her position has never been properly evaluated. According to that careful historian, Bishop Stubbs, "few women have had less justice done them in history than Eleanor."

That Eleanor's was a striking personality is testified to by the legends that accumulated about her name. These stories were started by her conduct at Antioch, where she succeeded in compromising herself with the scheming, vindictive, but utterly fascinating Prince Raymond of Antioch. When one considers that Eleanor was Raymond's niece and that, in addition to being one of the most beautiful women of the day, she was also the most highly placed woman in French society, it is easy to realize why the affair made such a stir among the gossips. Though her marriage with Louis was annulled on the ground that they were too nearly related, contemporaries recorded their belief that the real cause for the divorce was adultery.

As the accounts of Eleanor's indiscretions trickled back from the East, they were seized on by popular story tellers and exaggerated through the years until they lost all semblance of reality. One of the English ballads represents Eleanor in her last illness as sending for two confessors from France. On learning of the summons, King Henry resolved to hear in person his wife's confession. He compelled William Marshal to accompany him, though the cautious William first exacted an oath that whatever the queen might confess, King Henry would not harm him. Disguised as friars, the two entered the queen's chamber where the quaking Marshal heard Eleanor confess that she had had a son by him.

> The King Pulled off his fryar's coat,
>   And appeared all in red;
> She shrieked, she cry'd, and wrung her hands
>   And said she was betrayed.

> The King look'd over his left shoulder,
>   And a grim look looked he;
> And said, "Earl Marshal, but for my oath,
>   Or hanged shouldst thou be."

In a popular account of French history written by a minstrel about thirty years after the queen's death, Eleanor is represented as being courted by the famous Saracen ruler, Saladin. She was about to set foot on a vessel sent by the Sultan to carry her away when the enraged Louis, having had warning of her design, rushed up just in time to snatch her from the gangplank. Unfortunately for the story, Saladin was barely ten years old when this escapade supposedly took place. Another French writer in the thirteenth century quotes Eleanor as saying to her own barons after her divorce from Louis: "Voyez, seigneurs: Mon corps n'est-il pas délectable? Le Roi disait que j'étais diable."

Finally, a bit of flotsam and jetsam from the twelfth century shows how widespread was Eleanor's reputation as a wanton. A wandering student, one of those Bacchic poets of the Middle Ages sang of Eleanor:

> Were the world all mine
> From the sea to the Rhine,
> I'd give it all
> If so be the Queen of England
> Lay in my arms.

While these references show that Eleanor's personality, whatever else it might have been, was at least a striking one, they have a further significance. They created a mist of romance which has befogged the vision of historians from the seventeenth century on down to the twentieth. Considering Eleanor as a gay, careless creature, they have failed to take her seriously, neither assessing properly her significance in the field of politics nor in that of cultural developments.

Eleanor first made herself a significant historical figure when, largely through her own initiative, she secured her divorce from Louis and married the young count of Anjou, later to become, as Henry II, king of England. By these acts she transferred direct control of one quarter of modern France from the French king to the king of England. She thus delayed the centralization of France and helped prolong for generations the wars between the French and the English. Had she been a different sort of person, had she been merely "one of those foolish women," as William of Tyre calls her, neither her separation from Louis nor her marriage with Henry would have taken place. But when her mind was once made up, she carried through her purpose with persistence, courage, and skill. Hers is a clear case of the influence of personality upon history.

Eleanor showed the same daring when she attempted to wrench her territories free from Henry by taking a leading part in the conspiracy which led up to the general revolt against him after the murder of Becket. The long isolation at Salisbury castle which followed the failure of the revolt might have broken the spirit of a person with fewer mental resources and less strength of will, but Eleanor survived the test. At the age of sixty-two she emerged to coöperate with Henry during the last five years of his reign and to play an important role throughout the whole of Richard's reign and during the early years of John's.

The failure to give Eleanor her due is nowhere more evident than in the accounts of Richard's reign. To her more than to anyone else is due the credit for blocking John's efforts to displace Richard during his absence in the Holy Land and during his captivity. Her forceful personality, coupled with her prestige as Queen Mother, enabled her to hold Archbishop Hubert Walter and the other barons firmly together in their opposition to John. Her drive and force made her also the central figure in the collection of Richard's ransom. At the emperor's court it was her commanding presence that sustained Richard in the last trying scenes leading to his liberation. Following Richard's death she helped make good his wish that John, rather than Arthur, should succeed to the throne. Her death robbed John of the one person who might have inspired him to foil Philip's efforts to conquer Normandy.

Eleanor's cultural and social significance can scarcely be overestimated. A product of the most socially advanced court of the day, her rich personal endowments and her force of character, coupled with high social position, enabled her to make effective her conceptions of refined intercourse and her interests in artistic matters.

When marriage brought her from Poitiers to Paris, she linked up the creative musical and literary activities of the South with those of the North. She thus became a chief means at the French court in familiarizing the trouvères of the North with the work of the troubadours of the South. As a result, the themes of courtly love, courtesy and the idealization of women fused with those of the feudal epic to produce the more elevated ideal of knighthood exhibited in the Romances of Adventure. Dedications of works to her by contemporary writers indicate the value they placed upon her interest and patronage.

Eleanor's influence was not confined to shaping ideals of conduct in literature. On the contrary, she must be regarded as one who by personal example led the way in the refinement of manners and helped advance women to a position of steadily increasing influence in society. She strove to inculcate her ideas by the practice of her own court, which became a school of manners both for the old and the young wherever she might be. And its influence was widespread and continuing. Especially important in this connection was the influence exerted by her daughters through their courts. Most notable of these daughters were the cultured Marie, Countess of Champagne, and her sister, Adele, Countess of Blois. Then in Spain there was Eleanor's namesake, Eleanor, Queen of Castile, whose daughter Blanche married an heir to the French throne and became the mother of that great king, Saint Louis, one of the grandest gentlemen of all time. Eleanor's eldest daughter by Henry, Matilda, Duchess of Saxony, returned from Germany to England and brought her children for some years directly under the influence of her mother's court. Otto, one of these grandchildren of Eleanor's, later ruled in Germany as emperor. Eleanor's niece, Isabella, also shared in and continued the influence of the great queen. Of all Eleanor's sons, Richard most clearly followed in her footsteps, for he inherited from her an intense interest in ecclesiastical music and a gift of poetry and song.

From a mere suggestion of her life story, Eleanor's personality flashes: spirited, beautiful, and clever; self-willed and courageous; gifted and intelligent; rashly imprudent in early life, wise in later years. Her life is an epitome of the century in which she lived. How its points of view became her own, how she was shaped by, and helped to shape, its interests and activities, it will be the object of the following pages to unfold.

Contents

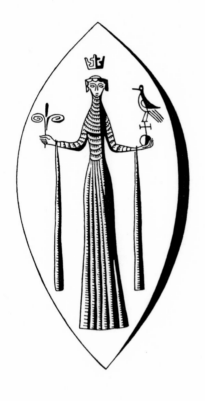

ELEANOR OF
AQUITAINE

The Young Duchess
1122-1137

ELEANOR OF AQUITAINE WAS SEVEN YEARS OLD WHEN SHE MADE her first recorded entrance on the stage of history. It was on a July morning of the year 1129 in the great hall of her father's castle at Poitiers on the river Clain.

Her father, William the Toulousan, gigantic Count of Poitou and Duke of Aquitaine, was holding court. He was seated in a chair placed on the dais at one end of the hall, and the members of his family, the chief officials of the household, ecclesiastics, nobles, and others were gathered around him to witness a charter. Seated beside the count was his wife, Aénor of Châtellerault; behind her stood her father, Vicomte Aimeri. Cuddled in Aénor's embrace was her youngest child, William Aigret, scarcely a year old, and standing by her side were her two daughters, little Pétronille and the Lady Eleanor.

The especially interested parties were the abbot and monks of nearby Montierneuf, for to that abbey the countess was transferring her right to certain exactions. The deed of gift, written out by Pierre, the family chaplain acting as chancellor, lay spread out on the table before her. Pierre first asked his Lady if she were making the grant freely and willingly. She replied that she was. He then handed her a quill pen, with which she made a cross after her name, already written at the end of the charter. The count did the same. Then, as the eldest child, it was Eleanor's turn. She took the pen from Pierre's hand and made a clear cross after her name. Little William presented a problem. But the resourceful Pierre found a way out of this difficulty. Assisted by Aénor, he took the baby's right hand and, dipping the fingers lightly in ink, pressed them carefully down upon the parchment. When the hand was removed, the clear pattern of the child's finger prints was revealed—an indisputable signature. When the chaplain added a cross, the ceremony was ended.

Neither little William Aigret nor his mother was ever to be called on later to confirm the grant which they had witnessed: death soon claimed them both. William's death left Eleanor the prospective heir of her father's domains; Aénor's left her motherless. Eleanor, naturally self-willed, tended to become more so under these conditions. Ladies-in-waiting could not exert over their future duchess the restraint that Aénor might have imposed. Without motherly guidance, the girl was thrown on her own resources and developed self-reliance and decisiveness, qualities which had been possessed in the highest degree by two of her ancestors, her paternal grandfather and her maternal grandmother, two dashing individuals who had figured in a notorious escapade.

The man in the case (Eleanor's grandfather) as Count of Poitou, bore the title "William VII"; as Duke of Aquitaine, the title "William IX." His genius as a poet won him the title "William the Troubadour," and he was described as "a vehement lover of women." This Troubadour Count eloped with Eleanor's grandmother, his own vassal's wife, the Vicomtesse de Châtellerault, who had been aptly christened "Dangereuse."

Châtellerault, near the junction of the Clain with the larger stream of the Vienne, was only a day's ride from Poitiers. Count William found no difficulty in making himself agreeable to the vicomtesse. He was not only one of the greatest nobles of France, but also a raconteur with a satirical wit, described by a contemporary as a gifted amateur surpassing in brilliancy of mind all the artists whose profession it was to entertain others. Dangereuse exerted her charm with such effect that the count soon found himself writing such impassioned stanzas as:

> If my beloved her love will grant,
> I am prepared to thank and take
> And to dissemble for her sake,
> And say and do what e'er she want;
> Of her nobility I'll chant,
> And all my songs for her I'll make.

> To send no message do I dare,
> Fearing her anger, nor do I
> —So fear I to do wrong—draw nigh
> To her, my passion to declare,
> Yet she indeed for me should care,
> Knowing my cure in her doth lie.

Dangereuse, enjoying her power over him, tried to keep the count in the role of pleading suitor. But William, accustomed to having his way quickly in such matters, decided to take things into his own hands. Awaiting a favorable occasion when Dangereuse's husband, Aimeri, was absent, and his own wife, Philippa, was far away in Toulouse, he set his horse off at a gallop along the Clain to Châtellerault. He dismounted at the castle, made his way to Dangereuse's bower, seized the lady in his arms, bore her, faintly protesting, to his horse and carried her off to Poitiers.

William cared little what the world might say or do. The world, indeed, said a great deal but did very little. The papal legate, Girard, threatened excommunication and demanded that William give up his illicit amour. The count, staring at Girard's head, which was as smooth as a billiard ball, insolently replied that the bishop's pate would sprout a crop of curls before he would give up the vicomtesse. William was as good as his word, for, until the day of his death, Dangereuse remained undisputed mistress of both tower and hall, untroubled by the Troubadour's lawful wife, Philippa. This pious woman, who while at Toulouse had presented a second son to her husband, withdrew from the world and took the veil. At the double monastery of Fontevrault, fifty miles north of Poitiers, she soon passed away.

Dangereuse's husband, Vicomte Aimeri, also quietly accepted the situation. The clever Dangereuse, who came to be known as "La Maubergeonne" or simply "Maubergeonne," from the name of William's recently built tower in which she had her residence, determined to capitalize on the influence which her tact enabled her to exert over the passionate count. She herself could not legally become countess of Poitou and duchess of Aquitaine, but she determined that her daughter, Aénor, should. She finally succeeded in obtaining Count William's consent to a marriage between his elder son and heir, the gigantic William, and the slender Aénor of Châtellerault. From this union was born in 1122 the girl, Eleanor, in whose veins thus flowed the blood of both William and Dangereuse. Nor was their bequest to Eleanor merely physical and temperamental: the social environment which they had created survived their death.

The court of Poitiers, under William the Troubadour and his mistress, was a center of culture almost unique at the time. William's political position, his wealth, his literary endowment, his social gifts, enabled him to bring together the most talented men and women of southwestern France. All were interested in the theme of courtly love and manners. The creative artists discussed with William new forms of verse or sang their own latest compositions which celebrated the love of woman and its ennobling effects.

After the deaths of Count William and Dangereuse, these gatherings declined in brilliance, even though the new count and countess, Eleanor's parents, carried on to the best of their ability. They at least continued to attract troubadours and jongleurs to their court by their liberal patronage. And they took care that their children were trained as they themselves had been. Eleanor, in particular, took an eager interest in both poetry and music. She listened to tales of knights battling for their ladies and to the spring-love songs of the troubadours. One tale fascinated her above all. Once a wandering minstrel stopped, like many others of his kind, to enjoy the hospitality of her father's castle. The minstrel was a Welshman; Bleheris was his name. He told of the loves of a certain Tristan and Iseult. The story burned itself into the mind of the young girl. Indeed, Eleanor, as she developed, was to show such a widening interest in cultural influences of her time that she stimulated a similar interest in others wherever she moved.

Eleanor's environment was otherwise no different from that which formed the outlook and habits of other girls of her class. She learned the arts of spinning, weaving, and embroidery, as well as the supervisory duties of the feminine head of a great baronial household. She was trained in the courtesies to be extended to the newly arrived traveller and in the treatment to be accorded to the knight wounded in tournament or battle. She acquired a knowledge of the use of herbs for healing and cooking, and a love for the garden. One of her earliest associations with the old castle at Poitiers was the fragrance floating down from the linden trees when their boughs were thick with blossoms in July.

Eleanor lived in a world permeated with religious belief and practice. Mass was said daily in the little chapel adjoining the great hall. Familiar sights were the churches of the town: Notre Dame la Grande, visible just down the hill from the castle; the ancient abbey church of St. Hilaire, a mile away along the hill's crest. In the opposite direction was the monastic church of Montierneuf, her grandfather's burial place. One reached this church by the narrow roadway leading downward along the edge of the hill to the meadows held in a fork made by the junction of the Boivre with the Clain at the end of the Clain's encircling sweep around the town.

The tedium of daily attendance at service was relieved for the child by the figures from Biblical stories in the windows and the outlandish beasts carved on doorway and pillar. She would stare absorbedly at a window where Adam, reclining at ease with head propped on hand, calmly observed Eve as she emerged from his side in response to the touch of the Creator. Sometimes the fascination of horror would draw her eyes to a scene from the Last Judgment where grinning demons with long tails pitchforked sinners into the flames of hell.

On feast days, the family would ride out from the castle, down the sloping hill, and through narrow streets to the cathedral of St. Pierre, where the special attraction was the music: sonorous anthems chanted in unison by a well-trained choir. After a visit with the bishop, they would sometimes ride on to the near-by church of Ste. Radegonde, patron saint of Poitiers. After vespers, Eleanor would be led down dark steps to a dank chamber. Here, dimly lighted by a half-dozen long tapers, stood a great stone coffin containing the miracle-working remains of the holy Radegonde. The ghostly darkness of the crypt never frightened Eleanor, for she knew that Ste. Radegonde, like the Blessed Virgin Mary, was a friend always ready to help in time of trouble. Maidens who left here by the tomb a lighted candle and a little waxen heart went away sure of having their dearest wishes granted. And outside, the sick found healing power in the leaves of a laurel tree

planted by the saint herself. The child loved to hear tales of Radegonde's life, and her mother had to tell again and again how, centuries ago, the holy queen, fleeing near Poitiers from the wrath
of her husband, the Frankish King Clothaire, turned her horse
aside into a field just recently sown with oats, and how the oats,
by the mercy of God, immediately sprang up and concealed her as
her cruel husband rode by.

Stories about miracles are one thing, but to see one happen
before one's eyes is another. Eleanor, before she was ten years
old, was to see a miracle wrought on her father by a man of God
filled with spiritual fire. The incident occurred in 1130, the year
following the charter ceremony, when William the Toulousan had
become involved in an ecclesiastical quarrel. Two men, Innocent
II and Anaclete, were fighting for recognition as pope. Division
threatened the Church. Fortunately there appeared, in response
to the occasion, a remarkable man, both mystic and politician:
Bernard of Clairvaux, known to later ages as Saint Bernard. Bernard, whose persuasive personality burned with love for his Saviour and his Saviour's Church, first satisfied himself that Innocent's cause was just, then came forward as its champion. His
advice was accepted by the able King of France, Louis VI, known
as Louis the Fat, who swung the influence of the French royal
house to Innocent. Louis's action was decisive for most of his vassals. But the duke of Aquitaine, whose authority in one-fourth of
the kingdom rivalled that of his sovereign, was persuaded by
Girard, Bishop of Angoulême, to decide for Anaclete. In the struggle which followed, Girard, supported by the duke, replaced the
bishop of Poitiers by another man.

Bernard sought by letters and other means to bring pressure
on Duke William, but without effect. Finally a man well liked
by the duke, an ecclesiastic named Geoffrey du Lauroux, won William's consent to an interview with Bernard. The meeting took
place thirty miles west of Poitiers at the monastery of Parthenay
le Vieux, near the town of Parthenay, which lay huddled around
its castle on a rocky tongue of land cut out by the river Thouet.
Here Geoffrey du Lauroux brought William. With the widowed
duke came his two daughters, Eleanor and Pétronille.

In the conference William declared his willingness to renounce Anaclete but stubbornly refused to reinstate the bishop
whom he had displaced. His persistent refusal led to a deadlock.
But at this juncture, Bernard, during a celebration of mass in the

priory's vast church, was inspired to an act which literally brought William to his knees. As he turned around after the consecration of the Host, the priest caught a glimpse of the duke who, as an excommunicate not allowed to enter the holy temple, was standing in the church porch. The sight of the obstinate duke inflamed Bernard. He took the sacred Elements, now become the Body and Blood of the Saviour, placed them on a silver salver and, raising them on high, marched straight down the aisle toward William. Bernard arrived at the porch. His slight figure confronted the towering bulk of the duke. Grimly the saint-to-be dared the duke to scorn his God as he had scorned His servants. The holy man seemed to the amazed warrior the very flame of the Spirit of God. William began to tremble, slowly fell to his knees, then sank to the ground. Eleanor gazed with terrified eyes upon the senseless form of her father. She saw him, however, slowly recover consciousness and struggle upright, assisted by those around him. She watched him, still half dazed, listen submissively while Bernard commanded him to submit to Pope Innocent, to reconcile himself to the deposed bishop of Poitiers, and to compel the subjects whom he had drawn into schism to follow his example. The deposed bishop, William Alleaume, stepped forward when Bernard ceased, and approached the duke who tremulously gave him the kiss of peace. William then led the bishop into the church and conducted him to the episcopal chair. Thus was Bernard shown to be an instrument in the hands of the Lord, and thus did he perform his miracles. For it was as a miracle that this triumph of fiery determination was regarded by all witnesses and by William himself. Eleanor bore away a vivid memory of Bernard of Clairvaux.

The adherents of Anaclete, as a consequence of Bernard's triumph, gradually disappeared from the scene, leaving the field clear for Innocent's followers, among whom Geoffrey du Lauroux rose to a commanding position as archbishop of Bordeaux. His talents were soon to find opportunity for their fullest exercise as a result of Duke William's determination, announced toward the end of the year 1136, to go on a pilgrimage to Compostella in the far northwestern corner of Spain. Here he wished to worship at the all-healing shrine of St. James, called the brother of the Lord Jesus. The duke had been influenced to make this decision chiefly by the memory of his sinful defiance of Pope Innocent. The more he reflected on it the more he felt the necessity of forsaking for a while the pleasures of this world to make surer of happiness in the next. He planned to time his journey so that he might join the throngs that every Lenten season crowded the Pilgrims' Way to the shrine of St. James. He also planned to take his daughters with him as far as Bordeaux and place them in the care of Archbishop Geoffrey du Lauroux during his absence.

Soon the castle at Poitiers was filled with the bustle of preparations. Eleanor and Pétronille, both in their early teens, were delighted at the prospect of this long journey which would carry them into country they had never before seen. Chests were gotten out, and finery for both the girls and their women attendants was assembled and packed. At last, the happy confusion over, the whole party—the duke and his knights, squires and men-at-arms, the women and the baggage train—was ready to start. They left about the middle of February in time to cover the eight hundred miles or so that lay between Poitiers and Compostella and arrive at St. James's shrine by Easter.

From Poitiers the Pilgrims' Way led through pleasant country to the next great shrine, that of St. Jean d'Angély, where the chief attraction was the head of John the Baptist. The Way continued southward to Saintes and then on and on until the stream of the Garonne was reached. There on the other side, as the duke's party paused for embarkation, stood Bordeaux, its cathedral towers high above the town's dwellings, which were still for the most part crowded within its Roman walls. The travellers, after being ferried across in boats whose crews had to fight the river's downward current, made a safe landing. They passed through a fortified gateway and found themselves facing the duke's castle. Their goal, however, was the archbishop's castle adjoining the cathedral which, like the duke's residence, was just within the wall, but at some distance from the city's entrance gate. Here they were warmly welcomed by Archbishop Geoffrey and the members of his court. Duke William, however, scarcely had time to see his daughters installed in their quarters before it was necessary to give them a parting embrace.

William went on his way toward Compostella, passing first through a barren country of pine woods where the travellers were pestered by stinging flies. Next the party journeyed through the country of the Gascons whom they found to be "great talkers, jesters, drunkards and gourmands but hospitable." As William and his men approached the foothills, two treacherous streams had to be crossed in wretched boats, each hollowed out of a single tree. After passing through the country of the Basques, "who deserved excommunication for demanding excessive tolls," the party began the tortuous climb to the pass of Roncesvalles. At the summit they saw a forest of crosses planted by the thankful thousands who had achieved the climb before them. The descent took them to the plain where the great battle had been fought, and then through the country of the Navarrese "who greatly resembled the Basques, though having darker complexions and a language still more barbarous, sounding like the barking of dogs." The party came at last to Pampeluna and a more civilized land. The chief danger here lay in the numerous streams crossing their path. Though the party had been warned of the deadly effects of these waters and their fish, William scorned the danger. The duke was a giant with a giant's appetite, and one evening after a day of hard riding he could not resist making a meal of fish from the nearest stream. He was taken violently ill before the party reached Compostella, but he lived to be carried into the cathedral. There, at the feet of the Blessed St. James, on Good Friday, April 19, 1137, as the Host was being consecrated, William, Count of Poitou and Duke of Aquitaine, breathed his last. He was buried beside the saint's tomb and it was inevitable that he should share in the sanctity of James. The Lord had so ordered it by permitting him to reach the shrine and die at the most sacred moment of the service. Henceforth the worshipers at St. James's shrine knelt also at William's tomb, imploring the aid of both. This popular canonization of Duke William was confirmed by the Church and a special service in commemoration of his anniversary was incorporated in the missals of southwestern France.

William's death effected two transformations: it transformed him into a saint, his daughter into the countess of Poitou and duchess of Aquitaine.

On their return to Bordeaux, the companions of Duke William brought word of his dying wish that the king of France be asked to take Eleanor under his protection until her marriage. Archbishop Geoffrey immediately dispatched an embassy to inform King Louis of the duke's request. The Aquitainians found the king at Béthisy near Compiègne, a few leagues north of Paris. Louis could scarcely conceal his joy when he heard of this unexpected piece of good fortune. He asked its bearers to retire, in order that he might consult with his counselors about the matter. The Aquitainians retired and then Louis the Fat gave way to the thanksgiving that flooded his heart. Aquitaine extended from the Pyrenees almost to the Loire and to the boundaries of Anjou and Touraine. By marrying his son to the heiress he could obtain control of this land and thus block the ruler of England from the further expansion he had been threatening.

Louis the Fat and his counselors lost no time in deciding to accept the offer and to marry the duke's daughter, "a most nobly born girl," to Louis the Young. The bearers of the duke's plea were recalled and informed of the king's gracious acceptance and of his determination that the duke's daughter be given in marriage to his own son.

King Louis at once plunged into plans for Young Louis's journey. The stir created by his activities was unprecedented. Both the king's eagerness and the magnificent scale of his preparations indicated the importance he gave to the whole undertaking.

First he sent messengers to the direct vassals of the crown announcing the approaching marriage and bidding them come with appropriate forces to assist in the expedition. The townsmen on the royal domain received similar messages. The necessary funds came from resources already in hand, supplemented by a special levy. The armed forces soon began arriving in large numbers: "barons and knights, the noblest in the kingdom," among them the influential Thibaud, Count of Champagne who, arms in hand, had time and again bitterly opposed Louis the Fat; and Ralph, Count of Vermandois, Louis's cousin. Each lord brought a train of knights to swell the king's forces. The inhabitants of the towns also came in goodly numbers.

King Louis placed in joint command of this army of five hundred and more, representing the elite of the land, the rival counts Thibaud and Ralph who, under pressure from the king, had momentarily buried their hostility. Yet Louis depended for the army's real guidance not so much on these noblemen as on a churchman, a man of the humblest birth. This man was Suger, the clever abbot of the monastery of St. Denis.

The diminutive abbot and the stout king were friends and associates of long standing. Their acquaintance began in boyhood when they found themselves thrown together as pupils in the school for novices in the cloisters of St. Denis. The prince and the poor man's son, both boys of exceptional capacity, formed a firm friendship in this intimate and democratic association. When

Prince Louis had taken up the responsibilities of the kingship and when the ambitious Suger's talents had advanced him to the headship of the great abbey, the king called his old friend to help in the administration of the realm. The masterful little abbot, once having taken his place in the royal council, soon made himself the king's right-hand man by his energy and wisdom. It was therefore upon his *alter ego,* the skillful Suger, that King Louis mainly relied for the carrying through of this mission to Aquitaine.

One matter particularly engaged the attention of the king: he was greatly concerned lest his Frenchmen on their march should arouse hostility among the Aquitainians by plundering. To prevent this, Louis supplied an abundance of money and provisions and commanded Suger to make free distribution of rations daily so that temptations to harry the countryside would be slight.

When the army was on the point of departure, King Louis spoke a few words of farewell to his son. They were recorded by Suger:

May the powerful hand of almighty God, through whom kings reign, protect thee and thine, my dear son, because, if by some misfortune I should lose thee and those I am sending with thee, from that day forth I should care no longer either for myself or for the realm.

The father did not live to see the son's return.

The Duchess Becomes a Queen 1137-1144

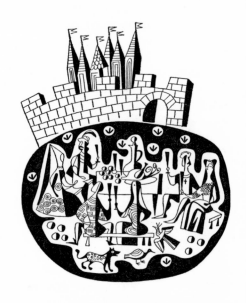

THE EXPEDITION RODE SOUTHWARD FROM PARIS, CROSSED THE Loire at Orleans, and drew near the Limousin. On the first of July the vanguard sighted the towers of Limoges outlined on a hill above the sparkling Vienne. Soon the host had forded the river and was encamped along its banks below the walled town. Within the hour, Prince Louis and Abbot Suger were leading a cavalcade around the base of the hill toward the episcopal city. They were received within its gates by Bishop Eustorgius, his clergy, and a gathering of eminent ecclesiastics and nobles from the southern region. These had come both to join the prince's party and to attend the feast of St. Martial which had taken place the day before. The remains of this saint, regarded as the apostolic founder of Christianity in that region, were buried under the abbey church's altar in the town on the hill overlooking the episcopal city. The following day the devout prince, with the whole throng, eagerly climbed the hill to worship at the shrine of this saint.

Abbot Suger, too, was a lover of saints, but he was also a statesman with a mind alert to the interests of the monarchy. He seized every opportunity to study these men of the South, noting their temperaments, interests, and relationships—everything that would assist in the design of bringing these regions more closely under the influence of the king. In particular, the little abbot urged the most important lords of the Limousin to attend, as in duty bound, the wedding of their young duchess. So it was with increased numbers that, after a day or two, the royal host set out for Bordeaux.

A halt was called when the Garonne blocked their advance. A swarm of small craft immediately began putting out from the opposite shore. For hours boats plied back and forth. As their cargoes were discharged, there began, amidst much running about and shouting, the work of pitching hundreds of tents in which the major part of the host were to be quartered during the visit. Many of the more important personages were provided with lodgings in different parts of the town: some at the ducal castle, some at monastic establishments, some at inns or at houses of substantial citizens. Prince Louis, Abbot Suger, the counts of Champagne and of Vermandois with their attendants, were entertained by Geoffrey du Lauroux at the archiepiscopal residence.

It was here that the fifteen-year-old Eleanor and the sixteen-year-old Louis met for the first time. Both had anticipated this moment with curiosity. The "nobly appearing" boy whom Eleanor now saw approaching pleased her exacting feminine eye. But her delight was as nothing compared to the magnetic attraction which her own vivacious beauty exerted on Louis. He was immediately infatuated with her—and even after more than a decade of marriage the king's love for his queen was to be still "almost foolishly boyish." When the formal greetings were over, both gave themselves up to the gorgeous festivities of the next fortnight, rendered doubly enjoyable to each by the other's company.

Guests continued to pour in not only from nearby Saintonge but also from the far south. Nobles from Eleanor's own Poitou answered the king's summons in such numbers that it seemed "as though they had entered into a conspiracy to empty the royal purse." They were not disappointed in their expectations of being splendidly entertained.

On their arrival, they found the most elaborate preparations in progress for the wedding. "Scarcely the tongue of Cicero," says a contemporary, "could do justice to the munificence of the multiform expenditures that had been made, nor could the pen of Seneca fully describe the variety of meats and rare delicacies that were there." The tables were loaded with roasts, fowl of all kinds, and highly spiced messes, as well as fish, crabs, and broiled eels with delicious sauce. Along with these were served rice cooked in milk of almonds with powdered cinnamon, lettuce salad, fresh figs and other fruits, all accompanied by excellent wines. The eye was entertained by the feats of jugglers, and the ear by the tale and song of the jongleur with his harp or lute. Braces and quartets of trumpets heralded the comings and goings, while in the meadows beyond the walls the young men and girls of the town caroled as they circled in the dance.

The merrymaking continued till the last Sunday of July, 1137, when the royal marriage was celebrated in the Romanesque cathedral of St. André. In the stifling air, suffused with candlelight and the fragrance of incense, the crowd strained to see the climax of the ceremony: the double coronation. Archbishop Geoffrey, surrounded by high Aquitainian clergy, placed golden diadems on the heads of the young couple kneeling before him. They arose not only as man and wife but as the formally recognized duke and duchess of Aquitaine.

Suger and the other leaders, under the pressure of urgency, marshaled the host for departure as soon after the wedding as possible. They marched on guard for the first few days, ready for a surprise attack which they had some reason to expect. None took place, however, and tension gradually relaxed as, passing through Saintes, they crossed the Charente and accepted the hospitality of Geoffrey de Rancon, lord of Taillebourg. Here the young couple spent their first night together.

From Geoffrey's castle, the road led back to St. Jean d'Angély, and, skirting the green marshes so refreshing to the eye in the boiling heat of that summer, passed on to Niort where the ducal castle overlooked the Sèvre's cool stream. Through Poitou the way led to the great abbey of St. Maixent and, farther along, wound close under the sharp hill which was crowned by the rocky nest of the pestiferous de Lusignans. This time, however, all was peaceful, and a half-day's ride brought the party to a clear view of Poitiers where the Clain cuts sharply into the plateau and sweeps out to half-encircle the city. News of the cavalcade's approach spread like wildfire through the town, and men, women, and children poured into the streets. They welcomed their young countess and her royal husband with cheers and the waving of pennons. And so "amidst the exultation of the whole land" they rode on along the crest of the hill till they dismounted at the cream-white castle. Poor Suger and the older members were thankful to reach a place of rest, since they were "completely exhausted because of the remorseless heat."

During these early days of August, Eleanor took delight in playing hostess. One evening, as Louis was about to take his place at the nightly feast, she surprised him with a gift—a beautifully proportioned goblet, carved from a single piece of rock crystal and mounted in jewel-set gold. Eleanor had always prized it even more for its mystery than for its richness. The cup had belonged to her father, and before that to his father, yet all anyone could tell her was that it had been sent to Count William the Troubadour by a certain "Mitadolous" about whom nothing was known.

Festivity followed festivity until the honeymooning was brought to an abrupt end. "Because night presses on day," says the philosophical chronicler of Morigny, "and the lots of human happiness change quickly, Fortune, which had so gaily and joyously smiled upon him in this glorious hour, at last changed the color of its deceptive countenance and cut off the extremes of joy by importunate grief." A messenger, "flying along with pernicious haste," brought to Louis the news of his father's death. Louis the Fat, having suffered a recurrence of the dysentery that had plagued him so long, had died on the first of August at Paris.

Louis was overwhelmed by the news of his father's death; yet the thought of wrenching himself away from his bride was almost unendurable. But on this point his counselors were inexorable. Paris, they said, was no place for his bride until Louis had made sure of his throne. He must proceed there at once without his bride and at all possible speed to prevent the "plunderings, deviltries and uprisings" which Abbot Suger and the others knew only too well were wont to occur when death struck the scepter from a hand which had long held the riotous in check. Reluctantly Louis yielded to this decision, but he was determined that his love should have the best protection possible. So it was to the care of experienced Geoffrey de Lèves, Bishop of Chartres, that he entrusted Eleanor.

Abbot Suger and the other counselors, in the meantime, were making arrangements for the safety of the duchy. They introduced royal garrisons into Poitiers and other strategically placed castles. Louis, when all such matters had been attended to, finally tore himself from his bride and, at the head of an imposing array, rode down the hill and set out alongside the Clain for Paris.

Eleanor, bereft thus abruptly of Louis's devotion, had time to linger on the memories of the last weeks, crowded as they had been with one novel experience after another. Seated in the cool hall of the old castle or in the garden under the shade of the linden trees, she and her ladies talked of the gaieties at Bordeaux, called to mind details of the wedding, and laughingly recalled the odd ways of the Northerners whom they had met. When Eleanor's fourteen-year-old sister, Pétronille, remarked that she had not found these Northerners at all queer, the others in the circle exchanged knowing smiles. The charming and vivacious girl had quickly caught the eye of the middle-aged Ralph de Peronne, Count of Vermandois and Seneschal of France. On the long journey from Bordeaux he had sought every occasion to ride beside Pétronille and beguile the way with banter or with stories drawn from his own adventurous life. These attentions had not escaped the eyes of Pétronille's companions, but at that time neither they nor Eleanor had attached any great significance to them.

So the days passed. Yet if tongues were busy, so were fingers. The women worked incessantly at the task of making clothes and finery both for themselves and the men. Their hours of diversion were whiled away in company with the squires and pages attendant on Bishop Geoffrey. Devotees of chess and checkers did not lack for opponents. The music of voice and lute sounded as of old through the castle's great hall. Eleanor herself took the lead, being skilled not only in singing but in the composition of rondeau and pastorelle. Nevertheless, the time of waiting seemed long. It was terminated at last by the news that the king was safely in possession of the royal authority and was anxious that Eleanor join him with the least possible delay.

Eleanor and Bishop Geoffrey gave orders for an early start the following morning and within three days the cavalcade sighted Paris. Just as the capital came into view, crowded on its island in the Seine, a group of horsemen crossed the bridge and rode quickly toward them. One rider soon began to outdistance the rest, and Louis came up at a gallop to welcome his bride and escort her to the old Capetian castle, occupying with its various buildings, garden, and enclosing wall, a third of the island at its western end. There Eleanor, after a somewhat cold reception from her husband's mother, the Dowager Queen Adelaide, was introduced to her own quarters. These included a bower ensconced in a tower rising directly from the water's edge. Its thick walls were pierced with window openings, broad on the inside but narrowing on the outside to long narrow slits, through which one could see a bit of the river and catch a glimpse of the quadrangular keep guarding the bridgehead on the northern side. The apartments were less commodious than those in Maubergeonne's Tower, and Eleanor resolved to have them made more comfortable at the earliest opportunity.

The dowager queen found life with her daughter-in-law difficult. The management of household affairs was no longer hers. Her son had slipped almost entirely from her control. The dress and manners of the strange young women who had accompanied Eleanor from the south were not to her taste. The young couple spent the royal treasure like water in feasting and entertaining. Adelaide, not content with hectoring them, complained to the council. Abbot Suger and the other counselors, however, feeling that the queen dowager was a dangerous nuisance, induced her to retire to her dower lands near Compiègne. She was escorted there by Ralph of Vermandois on his way home after an absence of six months, three of them spent in the society of Pétronille.

Eleanor, relieved of Adelaide's presence, began making changes. Her own chamber, with only a brazier for heat and narrow slits for light, was to be made more livable: the slits should be widened and provided with tightly fitting shutters, and a chimney and fireplace constructed. She ordered linen for table cloths and napkins, and persuaded the squires and pages attendant at table to have more regard for their attire and the cleanliness of their hands. She increased the number of minstrels, provided better stringed instruments, and introduced some of the more recent songs of the troubadours.

The choir-singing in the castle chapel was unsatisfactory: the cantor was old and not receptive to suggestions for change. But to her delight Eleanor found at Notre Dame a talented canon by the name of Leonin who, not satisfied with the unison of plain song and the unvarying fifths of organum, was experimenting with counterpoint to secure more agreeable effects. Eleanor told him of the pioneering work being done along the same line by the monks of St. Martial's abbey at Limoges and of a manuscript volume of their compositions which they had recently given her. Leonin, fired by this news, begged so for a chance to copy it and showed such understanding of the new chants that the queen presented it to him outright. She never had cause to regret her generosity, for under Leonin and his gifted successor Perotin the school of Notre Dame became the leader in musical development not only in France but in the whole of Europe.

These activities of Eleanor were interrupted by the court's constant travelling, occasioned by a decline in the food supply, the change of season, a desire for better hunting, or the outbreak of trouble. The royal cortège was always followed on these occasions by a horde of other persons—litigants or seekers after one concession or another. Eleanor, through her association with Louis in the hearing of trials and the granting of charters, began her initiation into the burden of ruling.

Typical of the petitioners was Eleanor's persistent aunt, Agnes de Barbezieux, Abbess of Saintes. She appeared before Louis and Eleanor, either in person or by a representative, three times in one year as they progressed from Paris to Orleans, to Aquitaine, and back to Paris. Each time she secured charters granting coinage rights to her abbey, judicial privileges of one sort or another, and exemptions from the obligations to furnish knights in time of war and from interference by royal agents. One of these grants bore not only Eleanor's customary cross, but the impression of her seal as queen of France and duchess of Aquitaine.

Eleanor's influence during these early years was shown by Louis's attempt to win for the crown the control over the city and county of Toulouse. Eleanor had a claim to them through William the Troubadour's wife Philippa, heiress to the rights of one of two brothers between whom had been divided the possessions of the counts of St. Gilles and Toulouse. Eleanor's father had been born at Toulouse and had designated himself in his charter signatures as "William the Toulousan," but had never attempted to make good his claim to the city and county, now held by one of Eleanor's cousins, Alphonse Jourdain.

Eleanor finally fired Louis's pride by repeatedly suggesting that he enhance his reputation through the capture of Toulouse. By the Easter feast, 1141, all was in readiness, save that the count of Champagne had neither put in an appearance nor sent any contingent of knights. Louis was at last obliged to start without him, though furious at this, the second defalcation of his great vassal. The king led his ill-organized army to Limoges, whence he pushed on to the upper Garonne and arrived before the walls of Toulouse on the twenty-fourth of June, the feast of St. John the Baptist. Count Alphonse Jourdain, warned of their approach, was prepared to offer a vigorous defense. Louis had counted on surprise and was in no position to undertake a prolonged siege. He was forced to withdraw by way of Angoulême to Poitiers, where he had agreed to meet Eleanor and take her with him through western Poitou.

One of the reasons for turning in this direction was Eleanor's desire to visit the monastery of Nieuil-sur-l'Autise, where her mother was buried. They halted for a day or two on the way at the abbey of St. Maixent, and again at the castle of Niort where Aunt Agnes importuned successfully for further favors. The next morning Eleanor, Louis, and a few others set out for Nieuil, reaching there in time for mass. Eleanor rewarded the abbot and his monks for their care of her mother's tomb by donations and the confirmation of their charters.

Resuming the journey, the court arrived at Talmond, long held in high favor by the counts of Poitou as a hunting and fishing resort. The original structure had been a small stone hall and chapel set on a rounded hill whose base was washed by an inlet of the ocean. This unpretentious building had in the course of two centuries grown into an impressive fortress dominated by a great quadrangular keep which had been built over and around the hall and chapel. The whole sandstone structure was tinted a rose-pink by the setting sun as Louis and Eleanor approached. Eleanor's earliest memories of the place were of the great ocean which she had here seen for the first time, and of the orange sunsets cut by the contrasting deep blue of the sea.

Louis's memories were of another sort. It was at Talmond, shortly after his accession, that he had had his baptism of fighting. He had been compelled to go there by the conduct of William de Lezay, its castellan. The scheming baron had refused to give up the castle and its precious gerfalcons except to the king in person. Abbot Suger, suspicious of de Lezay's intentions, had counselled caution, but Louis and the younger men had been eager for the hunting and fishing.

Accordingly, the whole court had gone off in holiday mood.

Many of the knights had even sent their heavy swords and chain mail on ahead under the charge of sergeants with the baggage. The first nobles to cross the drawbridge into the castle had been made prisoners. De Lezay had been planning to hold them and the king for ransom. Warned by the shouts of the captives, Louis and his companions had had time to seize their swords and repel De Lezay's sudden rush, killing or wounding all but the few who regained the keep and escaped by an underground passage to the ocean shore.

Eleanor found Louis's excitement when he now recounted this fierce hand-to-hand struggle much more to her liking than his humbleness in the presence of all men of religion and the profound devotion he showed before the relics of saints.

The royal couple, after days of sport at Talmond, returned to Paris where, through their interests in Pétronille's affair with Count Ralph of Vermandois, they soon became involved in a contest with the Church. Count Ralph's absence from court, begun when he escorted the Dowager Queen Adelaide from Paris, had not lasted long. After his return he sought every opportunity to be with Pétronille. Their mutual attraction led to a desire for marriage, but Ralph was encumbered with a wife, the niece, unfortunately, of the powerful Count Thibaud of Champagne. The distressed couple turned in their dilemma to Eleanor, whose sympathy was at once enlisted in their cause. As ground for annulment of his marriage, Ralph claimed that he and his wife were too nearly related to consider themselves lawfully married. It was necessary in order to dissolve such a marriage to secure three bishops who would swear to the relationship. Secrecy was desirable lest Count Thibaud get wind of the matter and use his influence to have the procedure blocked. Eleanor determined to do all in her power to assure Pétronille's happiness.

She easily secured Louis's support, for he esteemed Count Ralph and still nursed a grudge against Count Thibaud for refusing to aid in the expeditions against Poitiers and Toulouse. Three bishops—of Noyon, Laon, and Senlis in the royal domain—readily agreed to the annulment. Count Ralph returned his wife's dower and sent her back to her uncle, Count Thibaud. Pétronille and her mature lover were shortly after married in the royal chapel. It was neatly done, but the reckless matchmakers had counted without Thibaud.

The count of Champagne, outraged at this treatment of his niece, began cudgelling his brains to determine how best to seek revenge. The way opened to him when he realized that the rash young king and queen had neglected to secure papal consent. He resolved, therefore, to rouse up the irascible Innocent II against them. And then there was the case of Pierre la Chatre: by befriending him, he would at one stroke infuriate Louis and please the pope.

The case of Pierre la Chatre was a sore one for Louis. He had become involved in it through the solicitations of one Cadurce, an intriguer who had hungered for the income attached to the archbishopric of Bourges and had urged Louis to secure his election to the vacant see. Louis yielded to the extent of granting to the canons freedom to elect anyone they wished with the exception of Pierre la Chatre, whom they all wanted. Innocent, outraged at the king's attempt to interfere with ecclesiastical elections, had declared Cadurce unfit for any kind of church preferment and straightway consecrated Pierre, then at Rome, as archbishop. Calling the king of France a child who needed to be educated and kept from forming bad habits, he sent Pierre off to Bourges to take possession of his office.

Louis was stung to the quick. He leaped up in the midst of his court, strode over to a reliquary, placed his hand upon its sacred relics, and swore that Pierre la Chatre should never set foot within the city of Bourges. Innocent's rejoinder was to place an interdict on any castle or town where Louis might reside. Thus he converted Louis into a travelling pest whose presence would paralyze the hand of every priest in his neighborhood, suspending the performance of mass, the hearing of confession, the marriage of lovers, the baptism of the newly born, the burial of the dead. Such a sentence bore heavily on a man as devoted to religious observance as Louis. Even if his own chaplain ignored the pope's decree, the court would still carry trouble and discomfort everywhere it went.

At this moment, Count Thibaud delivered a double blow: he invited Pierre to enjoy the hospitality of the court of Champagne, and sent to Innocent a statement of his niece's case, emphasizing the hasty nature of the annulment, the neglect to secure papal sanction, and the intrusion of the secular power upon ecclesiastical jurisdiction. The news of Louis's offensive conduct aroused Innocent. He commissioned as legate to hear the case Cardinal Yves of St. Laurent. Yves summoned a council to meet at Lagny-sur-Marne within Thibaud's territory. The validity of Count

Ralph's first marriage was affirmed by the council before June, 1142; his contumacy in refusing to give up Pétronille was punished by excommunication; and the three bishops who had agreed to the annulment were suspended from their functions.

Louis, when he learned the council's action, needed no urging from Eleanor to strike back. He gathered what forces he could, rushed into Champagne, and set fire to a castle belonging to Thibaud at Vitry-sur-Marne. The flames spread to the villagers' huts and then to the church in which the inhabitants had taken refuge. The roof of the church fell with a crash, imprisoning the victims. Their shrieks made Louis burst into tears and seared into his memory the horrors of Vitry-the-burned.

Eleanor and Pétronille welcomed the return of Louis and Ralph from their triumph over Thibaud. The four of them felt certain they had gained the upper hand. With the county of Vitry in their grasp they were sure they could bring Thibaud to terms. Accordingly, they offered to return his possessions, provided he would bestir himself to secure the removal of Count Ralph's excommunication through the mediation of Bernard of Clairvaux, whose aid, they thought, would be half the victory.

This appeal brought Bernard into a case which had already caused him serious concern. He loved Louis but he loved the Church more, and to its service he devoted himself with all the intensity of his gifted nature. He was now placed in a difficult position: he wished to restore peace and yet support the pope in his condemnation of Count Ralph's second marriage. The solution he proposed was ingenious, if ingenuous. He felt that one was entirely justified in attempting to outwit a sinner like Ralph of Vermandois. He urged the pope, therefore, to remove the excommunication long enough for Louis to restore to Count Thibaud his lands, and then renew it. The count of Champagne consented to this scheme with reluctance, but Saint Peter's successor welcomed the proposal and immediately ordered Ralph's excommunication removed.

Bernard's saintly stratagem was only partially successful. Eleanor and the others of the family group were overjoyed at what seemed the complete success of their diplomacy. The lifting of the excommunication was one triumph, and they felt certain it would be followed by another: the legitimation of Pétronille's and Ralph's union. Louis, faithful to his promise, at once restored the count's territory. Then he determined, so confident was he of papal favor, on making an effort to have the interdict removed. He commissioned the abbot of Morigny to beg the pope with prayers and gifts to lift the interdict, but to do so without asking the king to break his oath never to admit Pierre la Chatre within the precincts of Bourges. Innocent, provoked by such naïveté, not only bluntly refused, but threatened to reëxcommunicate Count Ralph if he did not immediately give up Pétronille.

This news confounded and angered the royal circle. Bernard's stratagem seemed to them the basest kind of duplicity. Louis dictated a biting letter upbraiding Bernard for his tactics and warning him that he would again attack Thibaud if Count Ralph were reëxcommunicated. Bernard replied, protesting vehemently. Innocent launched against Ralph the threatened reëxcommunication. Thereupon Louis once more invaded Thibaud's lands, pillaging and burning even more extensively than before. He also threw down another challenge to the Church by attempting to block episcopal elections at Châlons and Paris. He seized church revenues, and from Châlons, his brother, Count Robert de Dreux, plundered church lands across the countryside almost to Rheims.

Count Thibaud put up only a feeble resistance. His vassals, disgusted with the once warlike count, ridiculed his prayers and alms. "Now he is getting his deserts," said they; "instead of knights he has monks, in place of cross-bowmen, lay brothers; he sees now to what end such actions lead." His clergy could see no help unless God intervened. They finally appealed to Bernard, asking him if he had yet had any prophetic vision regarding the outcome of the affair. At first the holy man only referred them to the trials of Job. At last, however, his mind was illumined by a light from heaven, and he cried out, "Within five months peace will be made." And so it was.

Innocent II died September 24, 1143, and two days later the conciliatory Celestine II was elected pope. To him both Louis and Thibaud sent off messengers, requesting him to act as arbitrator between them. Bernard also wrote, begging Celestine to give peace to his children in France. When Louis's ambassadors arrived before the pope, he rose and, extending his hand toward France, raised the interdict. Since Louis had already given proof of his pacific intentions by returning liberty of election to the churches of Paris and Châlons, the time seemed propitious for the settlement of his other difficulties.

Eleanor herself began, indeed, to perceive that her championship of Pétronille's cause was placing Louis and herself in an impossible position. She saw that public opinion was against the course which she had rashly urged Louis to pursue. In chastened mood, she was ready to listen to Abbot Suger. Under his expert guidance, the way was prepared, with Bernard's aid, for an almost complete surrender to the pressure of the Church. Yet the decisive blow was struck only when Eleanor was confronted by Bernard himself.

A council, under the joint leadership of Suger and Bernard, was first held at Corbeil. The conference had scarcely begun when one speaker bluntly told Louis that he had been only a tool in the hands of the count of Vermandois. Louis hotly denied the charge, jumped to his feet, uttered an angry denunciation, and stalked from the hall. The disconcerted prelates slowly followed him out. But Suger and Bernard were not to be thus easily cheated of victory. They finally soothed Louis's pride and made arrangements for a second council, to be held this time at Suger's own abbey on the festival of St. Denis. Louis and Eleanor arrived on the appointed day, the eleventh of June. Bernard, when he heard of Eleanor's arrival, asked for a private interview with her in the cloisters.

Eleanor had intended at the beginning of their interview to make some stinging allusion to Bernard's duplicity, but somehow the words faltered on her tongue as Bernard spoke of the welfare of the kingdom and of the divinely ordained cooperation of Church and State. He so won her confidence, he spoke so directly to her inmost being that, forgetting Pétronille, she began in a gush of long-suppressed feeling to pour out her anxiety to him as a father confessor. She was childless, and what availed it to be queen if she could not give her husband an heir to his throne? She had given birth to one child, only to have it laid in her arms, still-born. The Lord, since that time, had closed her womb to offspring. She implored the man of God to intercede for her at the throne of heaven that she might bear an heir to the crown of France.

Such a transformation in the bearing of the queen might have astonished Bernard had he not before this seen stubborn wills suddenly bow before his. Nevertheless he saw with joy that the long prayed for victory was in his hands, and that the spirit of the Lord, working through him as an humble instrument, had once more wrought a miracle. Then he said gently to the young queen, "Seek, my child, those things which make for peace. Cease to stir up the king against the Church and urge upon him a better course of action. If you will promise to do this, I in my turn promise to entreat the merciful Lord to grant you offspring."

Eleanor bent in gratitude before the man of God. Then she hurried away to tell Louis the good news and to urge upon him a complete surrender to the Church upon all points. It was worth any sacrifice, she said, to secure what they had so long desired, an heir to the throne. Ralph and Pétronille must fend for themselves. Louis was quite prepared to agree with this advice: he was ready both to make peace with Thibaud and to recognize Pierre la Chatre as archbishop, but he still had scruples on one point. How could he be at full peace with Pierre without a breach of his oath never to admit him into Bourges? Here was an unlooked-for difficulty, but it proved not insuperable to Suger. The Church was fully empowered, he said, to relieve the king of his oath, but to show repentance for his contumacy the king must swear an oath to go on a pilgrimage to Jerusalem.

Louis, as soon as a full peace had been made, sought out the holy man of Clairvaux and in strict privacy urged him, now that he and Eleanor had discharged their side of the bargain, to keep his. Bernard was as good as his word, for Eleanor soon confided to her husband that she was pregnant. The queen was safely delivered of a child within less than a year; but since the baby was a girl, Bernard had worked only half the desired miracle. Nevertheless, the birth of Marie brought comfort to Eleanor, who was convinced that her fertility was restored. She could now cherish the hope of eventually giving birth to a future king of France. But Eleanor cherished this hope in vain.

Eleanor Takes the Cross
1145-1147

ELEANOR TOOK UN-
FEIGNED DELIGHT
IN HER BABY EVEN
THOUGH SHE HAD
longed for a boy. She was so interested in this novel possession
that she failed to notice for some
time her husband's increasing absorption in religious observances.
Naturally devout, Louis had
been trained for the Church and
would gladly have entered it had
he not become heir to the French
throne when his elder brother,
Philip, was thrown from his
horse and killed. Louis now worshipped daily not only at mass and
vespers but also at the other canonical hours, besides spending
much time at prayer in his private chapel. Eleanor soon discovered
that the cause of Louis's absorption was a longing to make a
pilgrimage to the Holy Land. He had vowed to go there, he said;
furthermore, he could not forget Vitry, and felt, as Bernard had
often told him, that he could never be sure of forgiveness until he
had sought pardon at the Saviour's tomb. He hesitated though, vital
as his soul's salvation was, to leave the kingdom; and the thought
of the long separation from Eleanor was almost unbearable.

These revelations of her husband's feelings did not come to Eleanor wholly as a surprise, since he had often shown how the atrocity at Vitry weighed on his conscience. She had also seen him make the pilgrimage vow and she knew how much such an act meant to him. It was not certain of course that Louis would go; but if he did, and she were to be left as the sole representative of the monarchy, ought not she and Louis to be formally crowned once more? Louis agreed that such a step would be highly desirable, and it was decided that the double coronation should take place at the Christmas court to be held that year at Bourges.

Before that time, however, the pilgrimage question had become a burning one. News came that the great outpost of Edessa had been retaken by the infidels, opening a new threat to the Christian states in Syria and Palestine. The pope had issued a call to the men of the West to assist their brothers in the East. Louis was greatly moved and Eleanor awaited anxiously the outcome.

She was not left long in doubt, for Louis soon opened his mind to her. He had decided, he said, that he would immediately fulfill his pilgrimage vow, but he would go to the sepulchre of the Lord at the head of as many crusaders as he could gather around him. Eleanor, though momentarily stunned by the announcement, rejoiced at one thing: if her husband was to make the pilgrimage to the Holy Land, she much preferred to have him march as a warrior-king at the head of a great host than go as an humble pilgrim accompanied by only a small band of followers. Her imagination glowed with the excitement of adventure; she wished she could share in it. Her distaff duties at home seemed dull by comparison.

Louis, as though reading her thoughts, told of the pain it gave him to leave her behind and to be constantly anxious of her welfare. "And I too, my lord," replied Eleanor. "Do you not realize that I would be anxious about your safety, exposed to the dangers of the way as well as to the blades of the cursed infidels? If you were wounded, who would tend you? My place is by your side." Louis wished with all his heart that this were possible, but felt she would not be able to endure the long rides and the hardships of the journey. "Think not of these things, my lord. What are long rides to a daughter of Poitou? Have I not been used to them from childhood? And can I not, if need were, ride astride as well as any man? Have not women made the journey before this? Did not many of them accompany their husbands on the last great crusade? I, too, long to kneel at the birthplace of Our Lord and seek forgiveness at the

Saviour's tomb." Louis was moved by Eleanor's impassioned words to take her in his arms and seal his consent with a kiss. And so the great decision was made—a decision that Louis, before he ever reached Jerusalem, had cause bitterly to regret. The future, however, was fortunately hidden from the young king and he was as happy as Eleanor at the prospect of her accompanying him on the long journey.

For the time, the king kept secret his determination to lead a crusade, but he planned to make announcement of his purpose during the Christmas festivities at Bourges. He took pains, nevertheless, before that time, to seek the counsel of his most intimate advisers. He found Suger cool toward the idea. The clear-headed abbot saw too plainly the risks for the monarchy. Who in the king's absence, he asked, could put down violence? There was as yet no direct male heir to the throne. If Louis should die on the expedition, who would succeed him? The pious Bernard, on the other hand, was all encouragement: the whole thing was clearly the work of the Lord. This was also the conviction of Bernard's friend, Godfrey de la Roche, Bishop of Langres, an ardent spirit. It was arranged to have Bishop Godfrey come to the support of the king when he made his appeal to the barons.

Clergy and nobles from all the land came in great numbers to Bourges in answer to their king's summons. The king and queen, when the double coronation ceremony had been completed, led the way to the great hall of the castle and seated themselves on the dais. Eleanor, more nervous than her husband, waited for him to begin.

Louis spoke first of his personal reasons for going, of his urgent desire to seek forgiveness and absolution at the Lord's sepulchre for his sins. He then spoke of the need of the Christians in the East and of his determination to lead an army to their support, and called on all men to follow him. He urged them to forget bodily comfort, fleshly pleasures, and desire for this world's goods, and to win eternal happiness by fighting for the Saviour who died to save them. It was a simple speech, but delivered with such intensity of feeling that, as Eleanor noted, the audience was deeply impressed. Godfrey de la Roche immediately arose to second the king's appeal. The bishop of Langres, a skilful orator, brought tears to the eyes of his listeners when he painted the sufferings of the Christians at the hand of the Saracens, but he did not move his audience as had the impassioned young king.

Yet the speakers elicited no burst of enthusiasm for the crusade. Neither bishop nor baron, much as they deplored the lot of their brothers in the East, was moved to forsake his worldly pursuits to draw sword against the Infidel. There was clearly much work yet to be done. The king announced, accordingly, that he would call them together again, three months later at Vézelay during the season of the Lord's Passion and Resurrection. Louis, assisted by Bernard's counsel, worked hard in the interval to insure the success of his heart's desire.

Louis sought first to obtain the support of Pope Eugenius. He immediately sent messengers to beg for assistance in carrying through a design so dear to the pope's own heart. Eugenius sent back letters "sweeter than honey" commanding obedience to the king, regulating the kind of arms, the form of vestments, and promising, to all who should go, remission of sins and protection for their wives and children. Eugenius, since he could not himself come to France because of the turbulent citizens of Rome, delegated supervision of the affair to Bernard, "the holy abbot of Clairvaux." Louis and Eleanor took care that the pope's commands should be published as widely as possible in the few weeks that remained before Easter.

Passion Week fell at the end of March and the beginning of April in the year 1146 of the Incarnation of the Word. Scattered groups of riders and people on foot could be seen during the last week of March making their way along the winding roads leading towards the town of Vézelay perched on its conical hill. Louis and Eleanor were lodged in the castle fronting the lovely western façade of the new church of St. Mary Magdalene. Bernard's quarters were in the monastery near-by. Eleanor, assured that many would follow the king on the crusade, had prepared a great bundle of crosses, cut as the pope had prescribed and ready to be sewn on the garments of all those who should take the vows.

The royal couple, early on Sunday, the thirty-first of March, descended to the castle hall where their investiture was to take place. Bernard's hand, as he approached Louis, held an embroidered silken cross, blessed by Pope Eugenius. Louis was overcome by this attention of his Holiness. Eleanor next assumed the cross. She was followed by Godfrey de la Roche; Arnoul, Bishop of Lisieux; Count Robert de Dreux, the king's brother; and Count Amadeus II, the king's uncle. Archambaud de Bourbon and Enguerrand de Coucy also took the cross. Last came Henry of Blois, eldest son of the king's old enemy, Count Thibaud of Champagne. In sign of his sympathy with Louis in this undertaking, Thibaud had sent a mass of hyacinths to decorate the altar of the abbey church.

Bernard and the king, after the completion of this private investiture, led the prelates and magnates from the castle. The procession passed around the abbey wall, which encircled the edge of the hill, and moved part way down the slope to where a platform had been erected. Eleanor and the others grouped themselves around the base of this while the abbot and the king mounted a platform at the back of which had been erected a huge cross. The fragile man of God and the tall king, with this gaunt symbol behind them, took their stand before the multitude of beholders which stretched down the slope as far as the eye could see. Then the "heavenly orator spread abroad the dew of the divine word" with such power that, when he had finished, there welled up from the throats of the multitude one mighty roar: "The crosses! The crosses!" Bernard seized the bundle of crosses, plucked out handful after handful, and scattered them like seed amidst the outstretched hands of the crowd. When the supply had been exhausted, Bernard seized a knife and began cutting from his gown crosses which he scattered about in the same manner. Soon other material was provided and Bernard continued laboring at his task hour after hour. Nor did the Lord fail to set the seal of His approval on the proceedings of that day. For the sick and halt crowded around the inspired monk beseeching his healing touch and blessing. Eleanor marvelled anew at the mysterious power of the man as she saw the petitioners depart rejoicing. She and Louis, uplifted by the day's experiences, withdrew to the castle only after the sun had set.

The problem of financing the expedition was discussed on the following day. The ecclesiastical and lay magnates empowered the king to levy a tax upon all his vassals, and agreed that each of the great men who were going should provide for himself and his men in whatever way possible. It was thought best, in order to leave time for these preparations, to put off the time of departure a whole year, until the spring of 1147.

Bernard, while the others turned their attention to the material side of things, turned his to the continuance of the work begun at Vézelay. His task was to touch the springs of action, to fire the religious emotions of the peoples of western Europe. His divinely energized will drove him on ceaselessly to the accomplishment of this purpose. Letters dictated to his secretaries served to carry on the work in France. He brought in person his message to the peoples of Flanders and the Rhineland, travelling with a few companions on muleback or afoot. His work met with overwhelming success, attended by the miracles at which he himself never ceased to wonder.

One of the king's first cares, after the royal couple had returned to Paris, was to seek aid from abroad. He wrote to the rulers of Germany and Hungary asking permission to pass through their countries and to trade at their markets. He sent deputies for the same purpose to the Greek emperor at Constantinople, and also to Roger, king of the Norman realm in southern Italy and Sicily. Financial matters next claimed Louis's attention. While his ministers were engaged in gathering the money granted at Vézelay, the king and queen made a series of progresses in order to stimulate donations. Eleanor's presence was especially valuable in Aquitaine because of her intimate knowledge of the local people and resources. Her appeals stimulated particularly the enlistment of crusaders. Many a baron and knight who otherwise might have remained at home took the cross at the behest of his hereditary ruler.

The securing of money gifts, however, was a different matter. Monk and nun were ready to pray for the crusaders' success, for this was their peculiar function; but to make outright gifts of money without receiving something tangible in return was contrary to the habit of businesslike bishop and abbot. They were responsible for their corporations' properties and revenues; it behooved them to be watchful in their generosities. The king and queen, in order to secure contributions, were compelled to promise in return perpetual rights to revenues from markets and fairs, to wood or pasturage, and to income from mills. Thus the sovereigns, at the expense of permanent revenue, procured the sums for which they had immediate need. The procedure was a costly one both for them and for the many nobles who resorted to the same method.

Eleanor and Louis, on their return to the capital, found it the scene of intense activity: preparations of all sorts were going forward. Reports came in of increasing numbers enlisting for the crusade. Even in England, it was said, men were preparing vessels to follow after the king. The royal couple were especially elated to find awaiting them deputies with favorable responses from all to whom the king had written. Louis received from Manuel, the emperor at Constantinople, an adulatory letter in which the Greek ruler promised him a great deal more than he actually ever gave him. The kings of the Germans and Hungarians welcomed him to their lands, promising to supply the provision markets. Roger, King of Apulia, sent an embassy promising Louis that if he would make the journey by ship from southern Italy he should have everything he needed, and that in addition either he himself or his son would accompany the expedition.

King Roger's invitation to travel by sea brought division among the king's counselors. The notion of the sea voyage appealed strongly to some. It would eliminate the difficulties of the march down the Danube and through unknown Asia Minor where the crusaders would be exposed to attack from the infidels. Furthermore, they would be allied with King Roger, a Frenchman by blood, a man known to several of the king's followers. Others preferred the Danube—Asia Minor route travelled by the army of the First Crusade. That expedition had foiled the treacherous Greeks at Constantinople, beaten off the Turks in Asia Minor, and recovered the Lord's sepulchre. The dangers of the sea route were untried and unknown. This question of routes was so important that Louis decided to refer it to a fuller assembly; so he sent out, to all prelates, barons, and other vassals of the crown, a summons to meet at Étampes on the day of *Circumdederant Me*, Septuagesima Sunday.

It was an immense throng that came together at Étampes on the sixteenth of February, 1147. Scarcely had the chivalry of France crowded into the great hall than they were thrown into a frenzy by the entrance of Bernard of Clairvaux. The abbot had just returned from Germany bringing great news: Conrad, King of the Germans, had taken the cross! The Holy Roman emperor who had long stubbornly resisted Bernard was at last overcome at Mainz by the abbot's burning spirit. Conrad had fallen to his knees and vowed coöperation in the warfare for the Cross of Christ. His nephew, Frederick of Hohenstaufen, and many others had done the same. No wonder that the warriors of France thundered in acclaim as Bernard made his way through their dense mass to the dais where, with Louis and his counselors, sat the deputies of Emperor Manuel and King Roger.

One of the king's secretaries read to the assembly the letters from Manuel and Roger. Then in turn the deputies of the two rulers rose and, speaking directly to the assembly, urged the advantages of the offers made by their respective monarchs. The majority of the nobles favored the Danube route, the natural one for the Germans, and felt it desirable that both armies should travel the same way. Many spoke against this route, emphasizing the perfidy of the Greeks which they well knew both from what they had read and from their own experiences. In spite of these objections, the final decision was to follow the Danube route. The ambassadors of King Roger were disappointed: they had hoped to gain the crusaders' aid in their king's struggle against Manuel. The Greek representatives were elated: their master, however little he might wish to have a hoard of western barbarians passing through his empire, had no desire to have them bring aid to King Roger who, he suspected, had designs on the empire's territory opposite southern Italy.

Louis, on the last day of the assembly, delegated to his council the choice of regents to govern the kingdom in his absence. The council chose for this responsibility two men, Abbot Suger and the count de Nevers, but the latter refused to accept the appointment, saying that he had vowed to become a monk at Chartreuse. The king and the others begged him to defer his entrance into the monastery but they were unable to turn him from his purpose. The burden of government, in consequence, fell wholly upon the abbot's shoulders. The assembly's final act was to fix the time of departure for three months hence on the day of Pentecost and the place of rendezvous as Metz.

The succeeding weeks were busy ones for both Louis and Eleanor. New arrivals kept pouring into Paris. The men of Aquitaine came in numbers. Geoffrey de Rancon and the other leaders remained near the royal court while their men-at-arms and foot soldiers were directed to march on to Metz. Eleanor devoted herself to the entertainment of these guests while Louis, his counselors and clerks, were docketing and packing in chests and bundles the money, clothing, and tents required for the journey. These were stored in carts or tied on mules and sent off guarded by men-at-arms. Most distinguished of the new arrivals was Pope Eugenius who reached Paris shortly before Easter, in time to officiate at Louis's consecration.

On the day appointed for this ceremony Louis, dressed in black and accompanied by Eleanor, his mother Adelaide, Odo de Deuil, his chaplain-confessor, and other close associates, set out from the royal castle to make the rounds of all the city's monasteries. The king first led the way across the Seine to the abbey church of St. Germain des Prés. He humbly begged from its monks their blessings and their prayers for the success of his undertaking. He next visited the monks at the abbey of Mont Ste. Geneviève, and so continued on until, crossing the river again, he passed outside the city's gates and approached the dwelling places of the lepers. Here the king commanded Eleanor, Adelaide, and the procession following them to walk on to St. Denis and await him at the abbey. Then the king bade his immediate associates remain behind and, followed by only two attendants, went to meet the astonished lepers huddled in front of their dwellings. Louis, borne up by the exaltation of his spirit, unhesitatingly embraced and kissed each in turn and then humbly asked of them their prayers for the success of the expedition. Odo the chaplain says of this scene which he witnessed that it was a praise-worthy action, but one which few men would have imitated.

An hour's dusty walk brought to the eyes of Louis and his companions the western front of the new abbey church dedicated three years before. It was the pride of Suger's life. As a young man he had seen people so densely jammed into the small church on the feast days of the saint that women fainted and children almost smothered. He had resolved that some day, if God granted it to him, he would remedy these conditions. At last he had become abbot, and, having control of the abbey's resources, he had been able to realize his dream. He had planned and worked for many years. He had summoned the best masons and artists-craftsmen from all quarters. Since Suger had in the first place desired a larger building, it had been decided to make use of a new structural principle, a pointed instead of a rounded arch. This, the master builder and others had argued, would give both greater height and greater breadth. Furthermore, they had determined to tell in sculpture more vividly than ever before the story of the Saviour's salvation-bringing death and resurrection. They would show him as an unyielding judge, but they would also depict his merciful mother. They would, as the crowning touch, picture the miraculous act of the martyred Denis. Louis and Eleanor had come with a great throng when the building was completed to witness the dedication. Something of this recent history flashed across Louis's mind as he now approached the church, where he was to receive consecration for his holy undertaking.

The wait at St. Denis seemed interminable to Eleanor and Adelaide, wearied after their long walk. But all weariness was forgotten the instant their attention was caught by the stir occasioned by the king's approach to the entrance. The dense throng parted only with difficulty, so eager were the people to catch sight of their revered king whose visit to the lepers had invested him with an aura of special sanctity. They crowded forward, eager to touch his robe, as Louis, his eyes fixed on Christ's crucified figure in the chancel, walked slowly on toward the altar.

Pope Eugenius, Abbot Suger, and his monks stood grouped in the chancel, awaiting the king. The queen mother and the queen were close by them, both tensely watching Louis as he came nearer and nearer. He paused at last before the statue of St. Denis, then prostrated himself before his patron. The crowd's pent-up emotions, at the sight of their sovereign's form upon the pavement, found relief in an outburst of sobbing and groaning. Eleanor saw her husband rise and then kneel before the altar as Eugenius and Suger opened a golden door and took out a silver chest which they placed in the king's hands. Louis was overwhelmed by the touch of this reliquary containing the remains of the Blessed Martyr. He covered the holy receptacle with kisses and pressed it convulsively to his heart. When he had recovered himself, he held the reliquary before him, and, according to usage, humbly asked from the Blessed Denis both his banner and his leave to depart. The king then rose, after restoring to Suger the strength-giving relics, and, extending himself to his full height, reverently took down from above the altar the scarlet and gold banner of Saint Denis, the oriflamme of France. The king's black figure stood out in stark contrast against the banner's brilliant background as it fell in folds from its staff, the butt of which Louis had rested beside him on the pavement. Eleanor then saw Pope Eugenius step forward and, hanging the pilgrim's scrip by its strap over Louis's shoulder, stretch out his hands in blessing over the king's bent head.

Louis, thoroughly exhausted by the labors and emotions of the day, turned and slowly made his way toward the dormitory of the monks. Eleanor and Adelaide, almost suffocated by the heat and the crowd, were glad to make their escape from the church by a side door and mount a stairway to the quarters built especially to lodge the abbey's more distinguished guests. The two women sank down with sighs of relief on the first seats that offered, thankful for rest after the long hours of walking and standing. Eleanor was happy to think, as they drank the refreshing wine provided by the thoughtful Suger, that they were leaving with the little abbot a valued remembrance. Louis, she reflected, might at that very moment be presenting to Suger the gift they had agreed upon.

This was indeed the case; for Louis, after resting a while in the dormitory, had risen and, with Odo, himself a monk of St. Denis, and a few others, had entered the refectory. Louis, just as they were finishing the meal, beckoned to his chamberlain to approach and asked for the token with which he had been entrusted. The chamberlain brought forth from a soft leathern bag the goblet given by the unknown Mitadolus to Eleanor's troubadour grandfather, and by her to Louis. The king took the goblet in his hand and called Suger to him. "My dearly beloved Lord Abbot," said the king, "behold this crystal vase, precious because given to me by my queen. It is our wish that you should have by you, whilst carrying on the burden of government during our long absence, some token of our remembrance. Take then this cup as a reminder of our lasting gratitude and love." Suger, overcome by his sovereign's gracious act, fell on his knee. Just as his hand closed on the gift, a shaft of light from the declining sun fell upon the goblet's crystal cup, turning it blood red. This sign of heavenly favor clearly sanctified the chalice: Suger dedicated it to the Blessed St. Denis as a receptacle for his Saviour's blood.

After the king and queen had departed on the crusade, Abbot Suger had engraved on the goblet's base these words:

Hoc vasa sponsa dedit Aanor regi Ludovico,
Mitadolus avo,
Mihi rex,
Sanctisque Sugerus.

Eleanor, his wife, gave to King Louis this vase,
Mitadolus gave it to her grandfather,
The king gave it to me,
I, Suger, gave it to the Saints.

The Crusaders' Trials Begin 1147

ON THE DAY FOL-
LOWING LOUIS'S
CONSECRATION,
ELEANOR DEVOTED
herself to the packing of her
own belongings and those of
the young noble women who
were to be her companions.
She had hoped to take Pétronille with her but, since she
and Count Ralph still suffered
from the taint of excommunication, Eleanor had chosen
Louis's cousin Elaine instead.
A day or two later, the queen
and her maids settled themselves in chairlike saddles strapped side-
ways on their palfreys and followed after the king and his escort,
headed toward the rising sun.

Thronging thousands welcomed the royal couple as they approached Metz and wound their way between hundreds of tents
till they came to their quarters. Louis and his shadow, Chaplain
Odo, entered the king's tent where Louis's first thought was for
prayer at the portable altar which the chaplain had provided.

Eleanor's first thoughts were for the equipment of her tent. She found the ground covered with canvas, straw-filled sacks on pallet beds arranged around the tent's sides and a lantern hung on the center pole. Her inspection was interrupted by the entrance of her chamberlain followed by pages staggering under chests, boxes, and bundles containing toilette articles as well as fresh robes. Water was brought in to supply the wash basins; a piece of soap and some linen towels were also provided. After toilettes had been completed, Eleanor, escorted by her chamberlain, led the way toward the entrance of the dining tent, where she found her husband awaiting her.

Louis arose before dawn the next morning to join with Odo in the reading of prime. Then, after breakfasting on beer and bread, the king began dictating rules for the preservation of discipline. The plundering of villages was specially prohibited as was straying from the line of march for hunting and hawking. Later in the presence of the assembled barons, the king had Odo read from his scroll the regulations which all readily promised to obey. Then the bishops and abbots came forward, followed by Chancellor Bartholomew, Sir Everard Barres, Master of the Templars, and the other barons, to kneel beneath the scarlet and gold banner of St. Denis where each swore to keep his promise. Louis was pleased at the willingness shown in acceding to his wishes, but poor Odo later sadly wrote, "I shall not bother to put down these laws since the princes themselves gave so little heed to their keeping."

The king now instructed Bishop Alvise of Arras and Abbot Leo of St. Bertin to ride ahead to Worms and make arrangements for provisioning the host and for assembling boats to transport the army across the Rhine. When the army later began its march, the queen had an opportunity to observe the multitude of people who had undertaken to make the long pilgrimage on foot. Besides masses of soldiers there were throngs of unarmed pilgrims and camp followers, both men and women, whose numbers seemed countless to Eleanor as she rode by them. A quick sympathy drew her to these people who trudged along with scrips over their shoulders and staffs in their hands.

When, after a brief visit to Worms, the royal party approached the place of embarkation, they found the ferrying of the army going rapidly forward. The bishop and abbot had discharged their mission well. Through the medium of Latin, they had secured the aid of the German clergy as translators and had thus been enabled to make their wants known. Hundreds of boats, loaded to the gunwales, slowly made their way across the swiftly flowing Rhine, then came hurrying back to take on more loads. Eleanor led the way into one of these boats and her companions followed, stepping timorously aboard. The boatmen shoved off so smartly that their effort was greeted by feminine shrieks and elicited a sharp command from the queen to be more careful. After disembarking, the women rode, through crowds milling around the provision stalls, to the place of encampment.

The queen's party were in their quarters when they heard an uproar which increased in intensity. Eleanor hastily completed her toilette and hurried outside. Aided by pages and half-a-dozen men-at-arms, she threaded her way through carters struggling with their horses and warriors buckling on swords as they ran, until she attained a small rise. The queen viewed the confused scene and saw that the disturbance came from the market stalls. Realizing that serious trouble was brewing, Eleanor dispatched one page to inform Louis, who was still at his devotions, and another to discover the cause of the uproar. Just then Bishop Godfrey de la Roche and other barons drew rein at the foot of the hillock and were urged by the queen to hurry on. Eleanor watched their progress until they disappeared in the welter around the marketplace. The tumult there gradually lessened and a division appeared in the crowd as part of it withdrew toward the boats at the river bank. The boats were filled and headed back across the river until not one remained on the French side. The queen's scout reported just at this moment.

The trouble had begun at the landing place. Provisions had been hard to get, prices outrageous, the money-changers extortionate. The hungry crowd rushed a boat as it was landing and pitched the crew overboard. Friends of the crew ran to beat off the pillagers with oars and knives. One of the pilgrims was killed. A cry went up to burn the goods of the cursed merchants. At this point Bishop Godfrey and his companions began dispersing the fighters by driving their chargers into them and laying about with the flat of their swords. Louis had now joined Eleanor, and upon questioning the page he learned that the merchants had ordered the boatmen to cease the transportation of food.

Louis, at first more concerned over the death of a pilgrim than at the plight of the army deprived of provisions, paid scant heed to Eleanor's urging that instant action be taken to remedy

− 41

the situation. However, he soon recovered himself sufficiently to ask for advice from an ill-favored counselor, a beardless eunuch, Sir Thierry Gualeran, detested and often derided by the queen. The bulbous-nosed Thierry advised that Bishop Alvise be sent to straighten out matters. The king acted upon this advice, and the bishop was so successful in this mission that the ferrying of food was resumed in a few hours.

Chaplain Odo, in relating this episode, bitterly characterized it as the first illustration of the crusaders' folly which was to display itself time after time on the remainder of their journey. But the crowding at the market-places was natural enough considering the difficulties in supplying food for the thousands composing the army. Prices were inevitably high, and those with the fatter purses would always have the advantage. After the French reached the Danube it became even harder for them to satisfy their needs, since from that point on to Constantinople the German host had preceded them by only a few weeks, sweeping the country bare and antagonizing the inhabitants by foraging freely on either side of the line of march. As a result, when the French came along, the Greeks in many towns barred their gates and from the top of the walls let down by ropes whatever the crusaders had bargained for. The French found the method so exasperating that they often foraged in the surrounding country just as had the Germans.

Word now reached King Louis that deputies from the emperor at Constantinople were awaiting him at Ratisbon. This was welcome news especially to Eleanor and her companions who were early astir on the following day, ready to take their places in the line of march. The army stretched out into a narrow column which seemed endless to Eleanor as she looked back at the undulating stream extending as far as she could see. A week of pleasant travel through the south German country brought them to the Danube opposite Ratisbon. Here the queen's party rode at ease over a splendid stone bridge toward the town's red-tiled roofs gleaming in the July sun. Cheering crowds greeted the crusaders as they entered the city. The clergy and wealthy citizens gave King Louis and the leaders a formal welcome, then escorted them to the fields where tents were being erected. Eleanor and her attendants hurried to make themselves presentable for the hearing to be given the Greek envoys, who were eager to discharge their mission.

When the queen entered the audience tent she found the prelates and nobles gathered about the king, who was seated on a dais. Eleanor took her place beside Louis and gazed around for a sight of the strangers. She did not have long to wait, for the Greeks, escorted by Bishop Alvise, Chancellor Bartholomew and Archambaud de Bourbon soon entered the tent and made their way slowly toward the king. All eyes were upon the two ambassadors and their numerous suite as they made profound obeisances, and handed the king their beautifully written credentials. The party was equipped with folding chairs which, at the word of command, were opened with a snap and deftly placed for the more important members of the group. The attendants stood like statues, each with head bent forward and eyes fixed intently on the face of his own master. The effect of this scene was enhanced for the observers by the strangeness of the actors' costumes. The Greeks wore richly embroidered garments like mandarins' blouses. The long, tightly-fitting sleeves were fitted to the hand after the fashion of wrestlers or boxers.

The envoys addressed the king in such adulatory terms that Louis blushed. The repetition of this form of address with each successive embassy was so exasperating that finally the forthright Godfrey de la Roche took pity on the king's agony and brusquely interrupted: "My brothers please refrain from telling us so often of the glory, the majesty, the wisdom and piety of the king; both he and ourselves know it well. Tell him then quickly and without so many digressions what it is that you wish to say."

In this initial interview at Ratisbon, the demands of the two deputies, Demetrius and Maurus, caused no little debate. One of these was readily granted: the demand that the king should not take away from the emperor any city or castle. The French, however, thought the second demand unreasonable; namely, that the French should return to the emperor any possessions formerly belonging to him which they might take from the Turks. After several days of debate, a number of barons on the king's part swore to guarantee the safety of the emperor's empire. The final settlement of the second demand was deferred until the two sovereigns could confer about it personally. Demetrius and Maurus in behalf of the emperor swore to provide proper facilities for exchange and everything else that might be necessary. Demetrius then hurried off to report to Manuel the partial success of his mission, while Maurus followed soon after, accompanied by a mission from Louis to the emperor, consisting of Bishop Alvise, Chancellor Bartholomew, Archambaud de Bourbon and several others.

One evening King Louis's brother, Count Robert de Dreux, told the queen that an enormous quantity of boats had been assembled by which those travelling on foot were to be transported down the Danube to Belgrade, and suggested a stroll to watch the embarkation. Eleanor and her ladies, joined by others as they walked along, came to a halt on a slope overlooking the river. A busy scene revealed itself—streams of people, mules and carts, making their way toward the landing places. The drivers, shouting, cursing and cracking their whips, strove to guide their clumsy charges down the banks and up the gangplanks into the boats. The boats were cast off and drifted down the river, men and women leaning over the sides, shouting farewells to those still on the bank.

The main army resumed its march early the next morning. For the next few months the crusaders were to follow the course of the old Roman road to Constantinople. This led them beside the Danube to a point opposite Vienna where they took a short cut across lake-dotted marsh country to meet the Danube again at its junction with the Drave. The next stages took them to Belgrade and up the Morava, then southeastward over mountainous country to Sofia, along the Maritsa to Adrianople and finally to the capital of the Eastern Empire. On this long stretch the crossing of the Drave was one of the chief difficulties encountered. There was no bridge over the broad river whose farther bank was slippery and steep. Only a limited supply of small boats was available for transport. Drivers unloaded the pack animals, mounted them to swim them across and struggle up the muddy bank.

The rugged Bulgarian territory also tested the powers of man and beast. Mule and horse sweated to drag the clumsy carts up the steep inclines. Often a vehicle would break down, occasioning wearisome delays. When the impatient sought parallel paths to avoid these blocks and strayed too far, they were apt to be slaughtered by bands of barbarous natives.

The routine of the march, however, was sometimes enlivened by amusing or interesting incidents. One of these occurred on the night after the Drave crossing, when loud shouts awoke the queen. Eleanor leaped out of bed, hastily donned a robe and stumbled to the tent's entrance, her maids crowding around her. The flare of torches revealed a naked man shouting out expostulations in a barbaric tongue as he was hauled along by a group of men who passed on toward the king's tent. The mystery was not cleared up till the next morning.

44 -

The captive was a certain Boris, a rival claimant to the throne of Hungary, who had been marching incognito with the French forces. He had jumped out of bed to escape from the spies of the reigning king of Hungary and had leaped at a man on horseback, hoping to secure the horse. But the rider's shouts brought friends who dragged Boris to King Louis to be tried as a horsethief. Boris shouted his name repeatedly and finally succeeded in making his identity known to Louis. The French king gave orders to have the prince properly clothed, and promised to conduct him safely to the Greek emperor Manuel, whose niece was Boris' wife.

A pleasant incident occurred later as the crusaders approached Sofia, where the usual procession greeted them. The attention of the Latin Christians was first attracted by the Greek clergy, clothed in embroidered vestments and bearing aloft gorgeously embossed representations of martyrs and saints. All eyes, however, were soon centered on a splendidly apparelled horseman advancing toward the king. This princely person announced himself as the duke of Sofia, a cousin of the emperor, instructed to greet King Louis and assist him on his march. The duke discharged his task so well that he earned the only good words bestowed by Chaplain Odo on any official of the Eastern Empire. The upright duke maintained the peace, saw that food and other necessities were provided in satisfactory quantities, and looked out especially for the king and his household, retaining for himself scarcely anything at all and giving what remained both to the rich and poor. But the duke's influence extended only a few miles on each side of the king, who marched in the middle of the huge array.

A story both fantastic and tragic was related to the French when they encamped near Philippopolis, where they found that an extensive suburb had been burned to the ground. The fire was the result of a fracas at an inn, where some German soldiers had been drinking when a wandering entertainer, a Greek snake charmer, drew a snake from his bosom, placed it on a taboret in the middle of the crowd, and began making passes and uttering strange words. The terrified pilgrims, crying out that the magician was casting a spell over them, rushed upon him and trampled him to death. Confusion spread throughout the suburb and into the city; the Greek governor of the city rushed out with his soldiers. The result was a pitched battle in which many on both sides were killed and the suburb burned.

Toward the end of the journey, Emperor Manuel made an

effective diplomatic gesture. An embassy that reached Louis at Adrianople brought from the empress a letter of greeting addressed to the queen. Eleanor eagerly opened the impressive-looking missive and noted with pleasure that its beautifully engrossed contents were written in Latin rather than in Greek—a delicate attention from one Latin to another, for the Empress Irene was a Westerner, a daughter of Berenger, Count of Sulzbach. The letter was stiffly formal yet expressed joy at the prospect of seeing someone from the Latin West, from which the empress had been so long exiled. The note of homesickness touched Eleanor. She impulsively called for her chaplain-clerk to whom she dictated a reply, formal yet responsive to Irene's veiled appeal for companionship. The French queen's letter so pleased the empress that she replied immediately and the two women were already on friendly terms by the time Eleanor arrived at the capital.

From the imperial ambassadors who brought these letters, as from others who had come earlier, King Louis anxiously asked about Chancellor Bartholomew, Sir Archambaud de Bourbon and their companions who had been sent on from Ratisbon ahead of the expedition to bear greetings to the emperor. To Louis's repeated inquiries the reply always had been that the envoys were safe and would return in good time.

On the first day's march out of Adrianople, Eleanor became conscious of a peculiar odor. She had been used to vigorous smells in the village streets of her own country, but the stench which now assailed her was of a devastating intensity far beyond anything in her previous experience. The cause was not long in appearing: the roadside ahead was bordered with dead bodies, naked, swollen, and mortifying in the sun—acres of them, it seemed to Eleanor and her horrified friends. The women tried in vain to urge their mounts to a faster pace; the slow-moving column could not be hurried. The ghastly sight had to be endured until "the Greeks armed were less dangerous to us than the Germans dead." For the corpses were in fact those of Germans who had lingered too long in the taverns of Adrianople. As they had straggled along, falling farther and father behind the rearguard, they had fallen prey to bands of plundering natives.

Three days later, within one day's march of Constantinople, Eleanor heard shouting ahead and soon saw from the top of a low rise the cause of the jubilation—the waters of the Bosphorus gleaming in the distance. That night her tents were pitched by its side.

The City on the Bosphorus 1147

AFTER THE NEXT DAY'S MARCH, THE ARMY PITCHED ITS TENTS close to the imperial city. Here, on the following day, King Louis and his counselors joyfully welcomed the long-awaited envoys, Chancellor Bartholomew and his companions. The French listened intently to the tale of Manuel's tortuous dealings with Emperor Conrad and his Germans, of attacks on advance parties of the French crusaders, of the Lorrainers led by the bishops of Metz and Toul who, disgusted with the conduct of the Germans, had deserted Conrad and were waiting on the other side of the straits to join the French.

Emperor Conrad and his army had conducted themselves badly at Constantinople. The Germans had seen near the city a vast, park-like area, stocked with game, containing several palaces, the whole enclosed by a wall. They had forced their way into this attractive place, almost wrecked one of the palaces, killed the game, and done much general damage. Emperor Manuel, though angered at these outrages, courteously requested Conrad to enter the city for a conference. This invitation was bluntly refused by Conrad, who styled himself not only "King of the Germans" but also "Emperor of the Holy Roman Empire." He declared that Manuel who, although he called himself "Emperor of the Romans," was really only emperor of Constantinople, should come to see him. Neither ruler would yield, but Manuel was ultimately delighted to speed the departure of these unmannerly Christians by providing them with boats for crossing the straits. The Germans, ninety thousand of them, according to the Greeks' count, were safely transported, and Manuel furnished them guides whose treachery became a byword among all the Latins. The main body of the army had set forth by the most direct route across Asia Minor, while a small force led by the emperor's brother, Bishop Otto of Freising, had chosen the longer road by the coast.

The most disturbing news reported by the envoys was that Manuel, instead of joining in the war against the Turks, as he had promised, had just made a twelve-year truce with them. The announcement was greeted by angry denunciations, and the younger men cried out for an immediate attack on these foul heretics, who compelled Latin Christians to be rebaptised before marrying a Greek and who purified the altar after a Latin priest had celebrated mass in one of their churches. They were little better than the infidel Turks, and it would be no sin but a good deed to kill them. Bishop Godfrey de la Roche even suggested an alliance with King Roger of Sicily, already at war with the emperor on the Adriatic. Constantinople with all its riches might then fall into Western hands and the heretical Greeks might be forever removed from the path of all subjects of Peter the Apostle. These proposals found no favor with the majority of the bishops and barons. They realized that Manuel faced a difficult problem, that their own men had not been without fault, and that the emperor, having suffered so much at the hands of the Germans, was naturally fearful of what the French might attempt. Louis, for his part, was determined to push forward.

The army resumed its march on the following day. As the crusaders approached the noble city, there poured from its gates a welcoming throng surpassing in its splendor anything of the kind they had hitherto experienced. Many clerics came bearing aloft sacred banners and ikons, with crowds of courtiers and dignified nobles, many of them close relatives of the emperor. They conveyed to Louis, Manuel's earnest desire that the French king enter the city for a personal conference. Louis set forth at once, taking with him his brother and some of the more distinguished counselors. Eleanor remained behind, but was later given an account of this first meeting of the two sovereigns by Count Robert de Dreux and Bartholomew the Chancellor, who also brought greetings to her from Empress Irene.

Constantinople was marvellous, declared Count Robert; full of marble structures of great magnificence. But it was also a city which abounded in dirt and filth. Their way had led them through dark, covered passages and crooked, narrow streets into a vast open space, surrounded by dazzling white residences. The most magnificent of these proved to be the imperial palace under whose portico stood a brilliantly dressed group, composed of the emperor and his courtiers. Manuel, by this departure from his usual custom, marked his appreciation of the French king's courtesy in coming to see him. The emperor, Robert said, was a young man like King Louis, not yet thirty. They were just about the same height, too, affording a contrast only in bearing and vesture. The two embraced and kissed, and then proceeded to a grand reception hall where two chairs were placed side by side on the dais. Each ruler took his seat, surrounded by his courtiers, and began to converse with the aid of an interpreter. Manuel inquired after the king's health, prayed that God might grant Louis all his desires, and promised to do all in his power to aid him. The emperor was so kind and seemed really to cherish such warm feelings for the king that Robert confessed he was puzzled. It did not seem possible that the man was as bad as he had thought him. Perhaps it was just as well that they had not attacked the city. Robert resumed his narrative to say that after the interview the two rulers separated like brothers. Then some of the highest placed nobles of the empire escorted the king to the palace of Blachernae which had been assigned to him and his queen.

Eleanor and her companions mounted their palfreys early the next morning, eager to view their new quarters. They found to be true all that Count Robert had said about the great city. Never had they seen such contrasting extremes of wealth and poverty. Masses of wretched hovels crowded into dark noisome lanes that unexpectedly issued into sunlit squares upon which marble palaces faced. The royal palace of Blachernae outshone them all. Eleanor had never seen such a residence. She discovered that she was walking over a tessalated marble pavement laid with exquisite skill.

Her eyes were greeted on all sides by intricate mosaic work and mural paintings in scarlet and gold such as she had never even dreamed of. Her delight knew no bounds when she entered the quarters assigned to her and her suite. She exclaimed over the large windows, the coverings of the couches, the rugs and hangings. Chairs and cushions took the place of chests as seats. Elaine called to Eleanor from one of the windows to come and look. Kneeling in the cushioned window seat the queen saw the sea gleaming close by. From another window she could see stretching away a level plain dotted with green gardens through which wound canals bringing in the city's water supply. The window on the third side revealed the most interesting sight of all: the city itself, its buildings, tower upon tower, and far in the distance the golden domes of a great church named, as she later learned, Santa Sophia, the Church of the Holy Wisdom.

Her inspection of the apartments was interrupted by the arrival of a eunuch bearing an invitation to view the sights of the city with Empress Irene while the king was being shown around by Emperor Manuel. The queen and her companions began immediately to prepare for the visit. When all were properly dressed, the queen's party was escorted across the length of the city to the palace of the emperor and empress. The two young women met in Irene's apartments where they exchanged greetings. Though they were not able to dispense entirely with the aid of an interpreter, they nevertheless succeeded in establishing sympathetic relations before Irene rose to begin the sight-seeing.

The chief sights of the city were its churches, and above all, Santa Sophia. Eleanor was left speechless by its grandeur, the magnificence of its dome, the beauty of its mosaics, the splendor of its gold, blues, and scarlets. Louis, whose visit had preceded Eleanor's, had also been moved by these splendors. His deepest emotions, however, had been roused by the relics. The most awe-inspiring of all these was the wonder of wonders, the Crown of Thorns which had pressed upon the brow of his Saviour. He knelt so long before this, his eyes wet with tears, that Manuel found some difficulty in getting him to move on. Eleanor, also, knelt reverently before the Crown of Thorns, but she rose willingly enough to look at the next attraction—a delicately carved ivory reliquary, with an intricate design of crane-like birds standing one on top of the other, each seizing in his beak a leg or the curved neck of another.

The way back to the palace led through squares lined with bazaars. The silks and satins, the rugs, the bronze vases, the sparkle of jewels caught the queen's eye as she rode by, and she resolved to spend a morning or two in these shops if ever the opportunity offered.

Eleanor found on her return to the palace that their hosts had prepared a splendid feast. She was impressed by the luxury of this Eastern court: by the decorated hall, the tables covered with damask cloths, the perfection of arrangements such as she had never seen before. She was interested in the rare foods, amused by the feats of tumblers and jugglers, entertained with the music of novel instruments. She rode home that night revolving in her mind the improvements she would make in the rude castles of her homeland.

The next morning brought disturbing news of the rowdy conduct of pilgrims encamped outside the walls. Property over a wide area had been wantonly destroyed, houses had been burned, and olive trees cut down. A score of marauders were brought before the king, who condemned some to lose their ears, others their hands, still others their feet. But Louis was to discover that these punishments proved no deterrent to the rank and file who, like their superiors, regarded the Greeks as heretics whose property it was no sin to confiscate or to destroy. The chopping off of hands and feet continued daily until finally the king gave up in despair. He saw that nothing short of killing his whole army would put a stop to the brigandage. It was no wonder that Emperor Manuel, anxious to rid himself of such a mob, began restricting the markets. Yet at this very time he showed to Louis a signal instance of his many attentions.

The occasion was the feast day of France's patron saint, Louis's beloved St. Denis. Mass was about to be celebrated when a procession of fifty gorgeously-clad Greek clergy arrived, bearing aloft large candles painted in varied colors. All eyes were centered on the Greek clergy during the services. Eleanor noted their rhythmic movements, the slow waving of their arms, the graceful inflections of their bodies. She was charmed above all by the singing of these imperial choristers. Though they sang in unison as did the Franks, the blending of the clear, high voices of the eunuchs with the sonorous basses produced a novel and most pleasing effect. The completion of the service left the Franks in a kindly mood toward the emperor. But they suffered a revulsion of feeling when

- **51**

they saw the Greek priests begin as usual their rites of purifying the altar, profaned by the ceremonies just performed by their heretical Latin brothers. The fiery Godfrey de la Roche and many others left the church uttering curses upon the Greeks.

King Louis had been waiting for the arrival of his uncles, the count de Maurienne and the marquis de Montferrat, who had marched through Italy to Brundisi, crossed the Adriatic to Durazzo, and were on their way from there over mountainous roads to Constantinople. The emperor, fearing lest the unruly forces outside his gates be increased by these prospective arrivals, kept urging on Louis the advisability of going to the other side of the straits, where the army could spread itself out in greater ease.

When the king broached this matter to his counselors, the malcontents once more strongly advocated taking the city. Godfrey de la Roche made another angry speech. The elders spoke on the other side as before, saying that the sovereign pontiff had given them no such orders; on the contrary, under his command they had banded themselves together to visit the sepulchre of the Lord and to expiate their sins by the slaughter or conversion of the pagans. It might indeed be possible to take Constantinople and enrich themselves with untold wealth, but such an attempt would involve massacring and being massacred. If they thought massacring Christians would be reckoned as an expiation of their sins, by all means let them take arms at once. If not, let them cease this talk and push on to the accomplishment of their vows.

Nevertheless, Bishop Godfrey might have prevailed had not the crafty Manuel resorted to another device. He bethought himself of stirring up the humbler masses, already complaining about the delay, by spreading reports of German successes against the pagan Turks. Rumors were spread that a great battle had been fought, the Turks had been routed, thousands slain, and the Germans had enriched themselves with an unimaginable amount of spoil. Iconium had fallen and Emperor Conrad was asking the emperor of Constantinople to take it over. These false reports fired both the zeal and the cupidity of the Franks. When King Louis informed the emperor that he had decided to cross the straits, Manuel expressed regret that the French were leaving, and secretly gave orders to decrease market supplies and raise prices. The queen and her gay young ladies-in-waiting found the passage of the Bosphorus a holiday affair. They used a much-travelled ferry with convenient arrangements for embarking and landing. Manuel did everything in his power to speed their transportation. Across the straits he had the Franks directed to excellent camping grounds where ample markets were immediately provided, though at prices double what they had been at Constantinople. This Eleanor discovered when she sent her chamberlain to buy some silk chemises.

The queen's irritation at this experience was soon driven from her mind by the report of an incident that had taken place at the booths of the moneychangers. On their tables they had spread out a tempting array of gold and silver coins. The sight attracted a group of men-at-arms whose fingers began itching to plunge into this loot. Finally a greedy Fleming could stand the strain no longer. Shouting out to his friends to follow him, he dived for a pile of golden bezants. His companions followed suit. The infection spread through the crowd which charged en masse; the tables were upset, and showers of gold and silver were spilled. Each plunderer struggled to get a share. The dazed money changers rescued what they could, made for the boats, and pulled off for the other shore, as did the merchants. Many honest pilgrims, anxious to complete their purchases of food and clothes, followed after the merchants. The Greeks wreaked their vengeance on these innocent people, whom they held as hostages for reparations.

Eleanor was angered at the plunderers for smirching the good name of the Franks, while Louis was especially outraged that pilgrims, signed with the Cross, should have committed such vandalism. He had the ringleaders hanged, compelled the other culprits to give back what they had stolen, and repaid the moneychangers at their own estimate of what they had lost. Furthermore, he sent off Arnoul, Bishop of Lisieux, and Chancellor Bartholomew to placate the emperor, to free those who had been seized in the city, and to arrange to have the markets opened once more. The emperor refused to see the French envoys on the day of their arrival. They were compelled to wait in an antechamber, feasting their eyes on the paintings while their stomachs remained empty, and to sleep on the pavement. Manuel spoke to them harshly the next day when he did grant an audience. It was some time before the two elder statesmen were able to mollify him. At last he agreed to release the innocent Frenchmen and to restore market facilities. In return he demanded that King Louis come back to see him. A series of diplomatic exchanges then took place: Louis insisted that Manuel now fulfil his promise to furnish men of standing as guides; Manuel demanded a personal conference.

Time hung heavily upon the hands of all. The nobles occupied themselves with hunting. Eleanor and the other women
occasionally joined in the hunting and hawking. At other times the
younger people would gather near the queen's tent for chess,
checkers, or dice throwing. Sometimes at Eleanor's request a
jongleur would seize his guitar and start a carol. The music
brought them all instantly to their feet, dancing in a circle and
singing such songs as:

> Fair Yolanth in chamber hold
> Lets fabrics on her knees unfold,
> One spun of silk, one strung with gold.
> Her nagging mother comes to scold.
> "I chastise you, fair Yolanth.
>
> "To Count Mahee you speak each day,
> Let sorrow on your husband weigh.
> He is aggrieved, I pledge and say.
> Do this no more, I fondly pray.
> I chastise you, fair Yolanth."
>
> "E'en though my husband swear, my dear,
> Both he and all his kinsmen here,
> Howe'er he grieve in anguish drear,
> I'll not relinquish love this year."
> "Twere best you did, fair Yolanth."

Louis came one day while Eleanor and her companions were
absorbed in these recreations and stood, a sober onlooker in black,
listening. He had never particularly liked these southern frivolities
of his queen, and on a crusade he thought them out of place. Yet
he uttered no rebuke. He simply reminded Eleanor that it was
the hour for vespers and requested her to accompany him to the
chapel tent. Eleanor, though vexed at this interruption of their
gaieties, yielded with what grace she could. She took her husband's
proffered arm and, bidding the others follow, walked with him to
where Odo and his assistants waited.

Louis took Eleanor in to supper with him after the service and
told her during the meal that Manuel had not only renewed the
demand for homage from the king's followers, but had added a
new condition in return for the promised aid: he now demanded
a marriage alliance for his nephew. The girl he had selected was
Louis's cousin, Elaine, to whom Empress Irene had taken a
strong liking. Louis said that both demands had been discussed

in council. The majority, to secure the emperor's good will, favored rendering homage on condition that liege homage be reserved to their king. The question of the marriage alliance had been left entirely to Louis and Eleanor. He did not like the idea, but felt that he might have to call on Elaine to sacrifice herself for the safety of the crusade. He wished, however, for Eleanor's opinion, especially since she loved Elaine so fondly. Eleanor knew that the king had the power to, and would, force Elaine into this marriage if he thought the success of the crusade depended on it. She knew well, also, that girls were considered useful pawns to further political ends. Nevertheless, she was revolted at condemning Elaine, who was barely seventeen, to the rigid formalities of the Byzantine court. The girl would pine away and die in that alien atmosphere far from her home and friends. Eleanor resolved that in some way the marriage must be prevented.

On arriving at her quarters, the queen found that Elaine, already informed of the fate proposed for her, was in tears. The girl's wretchedness strengthened Eleanor's determination to save her. At this moment Robert de Dreux opportunely appeared, raging at the emperor's designs on Elaine. He threatened to refuse allegiance to the emperor and swore that many of his friends would join with him. A plan began to form in the queen's mind as he stormed on. She drew Count Robert aside for a whispered conversation at the end of which the young lord hurried away. Then Eleanor drew Elaine toward her and kissed the girl, at the same time whispering something to her. Elaine uttered a cry of joy, embraced her mistress, and darted off to pack her belongings in chests and saddlebags. The other girls were consumed with curiosity, but the queen gave them no satisfaction beyond smilingly putting a finger to her lips as she ordered them all to bed. Eleanor then summoned her old nurse, Thessalia, and bade her make ready for travel. About midnight some of Elaine's friends were sleepily aware of the neighing and stamping of horses outside their tents. They awoke the next morning to discover that Elaine and Thessalia had disappeared.

The king received word, just as he and Odo had finished celebrating prime, that Count Robert and a score of other nobles with their followers had struck camp and ridden off for Nicomedia to escape rendering homage to Manuel. Louis was irritated by this independent action, and when he learned at dinner time that Elaine too had disappeared, he grew pale with anger. He turned to Eleanor and bluntly asked what she knew of her cousin's flight. Eleanor deftly avoided Louis's question. She was all astonishment and alarm. But it was rather romantic: the young scapegrace's snatching Elaine away for himself. It was clever of him, too—cheating the emperor at one and the same time of homage and the marriage alliance. It would only be giving the heretical emperor his due if the whole army followed Robert's example and marched away. The emperor had made them waste a whole month enriching his merchants and wasting their own substance while Jerusalem was as far away as ever. The last point especially struck a responsive chord in Louis's breast, for he was burning to throw himself at the foot of the Holy Sepulchre. His anger subsided into pensiveness.

In the next morning's council, he was surprised to hear Godfrey de la Roche urge the very action which Eleanor had suggested. The bishop, backed by a large majority, argued that this course might bring Manuel quickly to terms. The king was finally won over, and gave word to stock up provisions in preparation for starting the next day toward Nicomedia.

The news that the Franks were preparing to leave did push Manuel into action. The army had scarcely gotten well under way when his envoys overtook the king. They prostrated themselves before Louis and begged him to return for a conference with the emperor, who had graciously crossed over to meet the king of the Franks halfway. This Louis agreed to do. He called to him Arnoul, Bartholomew, Everard de Barres and three hundred men-at-arms, and set out for the castle near the shore appointed as the rendezvous. He found the emperor attended by a numerous suite, a large force of archers, and a fleet conveniently in the offing. Manuel, well aware of Elaine's elopement, waived the marriage alliance, but urged the Franks to assist him in fighting King Roger of Sicily, and still insisted on homage. The request to join in a war against Roger was impatiently gestured aside. A number of barons, however, rendered the desired homage, reserving a superior allegiance to their own king. The nobles who were to have accompanied the Franks to see that the emperor's governors and castellans gave them proper treatment were, Manuel said, unfortunately detained in Constantinople, but in their place he could provide trusty guides at once. Louis had to content himself with these humble substitutes and, courteous as ever, he bid Manuel farewell and led his escort off at a brisk trot to overtake the army.

CHAPTER - - - - - - - - - *vi*

Christian Swords and Infidel Blood 1147-1148

WHEN THE ARMY REACHED NICAEA, ELAINE WAS THERE to throw herself into the arms of the queen. Elaine had begun the tale of her escape when the sound of trumpets was heard. They looked up to see at a distance a group of horsemen making their way toward the king's tent. As the knights dismounted a cry of astonishment went up from the crowd: "The Germans! The Germans!" What were these Germans doing at Nicaea when, according to Greek reports, they had beaten the Turks and taken Iconium? Louis came hurriedly from his tent and warmly greeted the red-bearded German leader, whose story brought shocked surprise to his listeners. The conversation had lasted only a few minutes when the king was seen issuing orders to squires and pages who darted off in various directions.

One of the squires hurried over to Eleanor's group. The

story he told was one of dreadful tragedy. The great German host, beaten by the Turks, was in full retreat. The bearer of the news to King Louis, none other than the emperor's nephew, Duke Frederick Barbarossa, brought an urgent request from Emperor Conrad that Louis ride at once to meet him. This the king was preparing to do. The queen and the rest of the army were to remain encamped until he should return. After this brief explanation the squire dashed off to join the forces about to march. He left his hearers thunderstruck at this calamity. The word ran rapidly throughout the army, spreading consternation everywhere. How had the disaster happened? Why had God permitted this splendid host of Christians to be defeated by these infidels? What were the French to do now? Should they follow the route on which the German pilgrims had come to grief, or should they follow another? All was doubt and gloom. In the queen's quarters that night there was no singing.

Louis and his men returned the next day about sunset. The king ate supper with his counselors but sent his brother to report to Eleanor. The young count soberly related his experiences to the silent group.

No sooner had they reached the highroad, Count Robert said, than they saw an endless stream of people plodding dispiritedly along. Some carried bundles on their shoulders, all were ragged, many shoeless. Here and there a gaunt mule or horse could be seen. It was several miles before they saw any mounted men, and these, too, presented a wretched sight. Men-at-arms, knights, and barons all showed what an ordeal they had passed through. Duke Frederick threw some light on what had happened.

Provisions began to grow scarce not long after the German army had passed Dorylaeum, Frederick declared. The country was more barren, grass for the horses grew scantier, bands of Turkish horsemen began to harry the flanks. The Germans accused the Greek guides of purposely misleading them; and the Greeks, fearing for their lives, deserted. The Turks attacked more boldly. They would ride up close to the Christians, discharge flights of arrows, then dash off so fast that the Germans on their weakened horses were unable to catch them. It was decided finally, since Iconium was still far off, that, shameful or not, they must turn back.

Duke Frederick had interrupted his narrative at this point, said Robert, to indicate ahead a better-mounted group, in the midst of which rode Emperor Conrad. The duke had then ridden off to notify his uncle of the French king's approach, while King Louis and his immediate escort dismounted. Conrad and his men soon arrived, and the two sovereigns met. The once proud Conrad, when he saw the glistening ranks of the French knights, was overwhelmed by his own wretchedness. Tears sprang to his eyes as he received King Louis's embrace.

The French decided, as a result of the interview, not to follow the route taken by the Germans, but instead to pursue a more southerly road, farther away from the Turks, through territory where Greek influence was still relatively strong. It was agreed, therefore, that King Louis should lead his men along the coast road and should encamp near the castle of Lopadion. Conrad was to remain some days at Nicaea to salvage what he could of his broken forces and then to join the French at Lopadion.

The rising sun found all astir in Eleanor's quarters the following morning. She and her companions mounted their horses and started off at a trot to take their place in the long column as it headed west. The usual foraging and plundering took place on the journey to Lopadion, and the angered peasants took their revenge on the small German force journeying over the same road several days later. Louis sent off a rescue party which convoyed the Germans close to the French encampment, and Louis went the next day to greet Conrad and to learn more fully the causes of the Germans' defeat by the Turks. That night he gave Eleanor an account of the interview.

The king was impressed above all by the humility of the German ruler, who was still shaken by his experiences. For Conrad blamed no one but himself for the destruction of his hopes. He had relied solely on the arm of flesh, proud of his earthly greatness. The Almighty had laid him low because of his pride and his unregenerate life. His people had melted away, stricken by hunger, smitten by a continuous hail of arrows, by which he himself had been twice wounded. Thousands had died even after they had returned to Nicaea. Thousands more, forgetful of their vows, wanted only to return home. The emperor asked for himself and his men, barely a score of barons and a few hundred men-at-arms, permission to march with the French. He suggested that they be assigned a position in the middle of the line of march, since they were too feeble to be of much use either in the van or in the rear.

Conrad had, Louis remarked, high respect for the Turks as fighters. He had been especially impressed by the carrying power of their bows and arrows. The masses of defenseless pilgrims had suffered most. He lamented that the foot soldiers, who were armed with swords and had few bows and arrows, died by the score. Eleanor could not refrain at this point from expressing the wish that Pope Eugenius, instead of prescribing the shape of the garments to be worn and prohibiting the carrying along of dogs and falcons, had ordered all the foot soldiers to carry good bows and arrows and had forbidden the weak and defenseless, who were a constant source of trouble, from coming at all.

The French had intended to follow an inland road to Philadelphia. But Conrad's nervous dread that they might lack for provisions induced them to make for the seacoast. The women were introduced to the real rigors of campaigning on this stage of the journey. Eleanor soon decided that she had had enough of the side-saddle, after guiding her struggling animal up one mountain that seemed to reach to heaven and trying to maintain her seat while the poor beast slithered down the side of a gorge that seemed to reach to hell. It was agreed that night, after some debate, that the women would have to ride astride. Eleanor's chamberlain was commissioned to procure the necessary equipment. When it arrived the women tried on the men's breeches and burst into laughter at their appearance.

Eleanor and her companions set forth the next morning after some practice riding with saddles and stirrups. They had to endure the jibes of the young men for a while, but not for long, since the renewed difficulties of the road required each rider's undivided attention. Up mountain and down gorge went the trail. Sometimes the travellers had to pick their way across the rocky, dried-up beds of mountain streams, one of them so twisting that it crossed the road nine times in one day. Yet luck favored them, for no storm came; any heavy downpour of rain would have turned the trickling streams into raging torrents, "holding them prisoners," Odo remarks, "for the rest of their lives with nothing to do but repent of their sins." In some places the baggage animals would lose their footing and roll down the steep side of a canyon, carrying with them clothes, weapons, or money chests. The merchants of the coastal towns often loaded their supplies on vessels, from which they drove such hard bargains that some of the poorer pilgrims even gave themselves up as slaves to the Greeks.

The only bright spots for Eleanor were her conversations with young Frederick Barbarossa. He had composed several lyrics in the French tongue, which he delighted to sing for her whenever a few miles of level road gave him the opportunity. Both were loath to break their acquaintance when, at Ephesus, Emperor Conrad decided to take ship for Constantinople where Manuel had invited him to spend the winter.

The ship which had brought Manuel's letter of invitation to Conrad also brought a letter to King Louis. In it Manuel warned him that the Turks would attack beyond Ephesus, and urged him to halt for the winter near that town, where the emperor's castellans could provide him with shelter and his army with provisions. Nevertheless, Louis decided to continue as he had planned. But as Christmas was near, he proceeded only a short distance inland and camped in the fertile valley of Ephesus to celebrate the feast of the Lord's Nativity.

Manuel's warnings were not without foundation. On Christmas Eve, just as mass was about to begin, the Turks attacked. There was a tumult and a call to arms. The king and his men rushed out, mounted, and rode off. The queen and her ladies, left behind, heard the distant clamor gradually grow less. Then Louis and his men, in the glare of the torches, were sighted riding back down a long avenue between the tents. The engagement had amounted to little. Some revengeful Greeks had aided the Turks in an attempt to stampede the horses picketed outside the camp, but the guards had been too quick. A strong body of knights had gotten quickly to horse and charged the raiders, killing many and driving off the rest. The returning fighters dangled, before the eyes of the women, infidels' heads, still dripping blood.

Eleanor awoke the next morning to hear rain beating on the tent. She had to endure the dreary sound for the next three days. But the morning of the fourth day brought relief, with the early sun giving the distant snow-capped peaks an Alpine glow. The army proceeded with great caution when the march was resumed, because a large body of Turks was near. The Christian column was headed by a force of knights, numbers of whom were also distributed along its flanks, while its rear was guarded by another company. In the column itself, defenseless pilgrims trudged along, a stream of carts and animals loaded with equipment and provisions crept forward, and a multitude of foot soldiers marched. Eleanor and the noble women rode near the middle of the column, protected by a special escort. The army made its slow way eastward in this formation with the broad river Maeander on its right.

The column came to a halt about noon of the second day at a point where the ground sloped gradually to the river. Here the Turks had gathered on both sides to attack the crusaders as soon as they should become involved in fording the stream and struggling up the steeper incline of the opposite bank. The leaders of the vanguard were debating a plan of action when three Turkish horsemen on the opposite side dashed into the water, drove their mounts almost across the river, and began shooting arrows at the French. The Turkish forces raised a frightful din at the same moment, shouting like wild men. Three knights led by Thibaud of Champagne's son, Henry of Blois, infuriated by this action, dashed down the bank and made for the three Turks who, with equal speed, turned and headed back. Henry, with his two companions, Count Thierry of Flanders and William de Macon, crossed the river in pursuit, drove up the bank and charged full in the face of the astounded enemy. These incontinently fled when they saw their arrows fall harmlessly from the crusaders' helmets and mail shirts—they did not care to face lance and sword at close quarters. Louis and the others spurred to meet the yelling enemy as they began swarming down from the foothills into the plain, turned them back, and drove the infidels far into the mountains.

The Turks paid dearly for their rashness in wounded, slain, and captured. One captain, an emir, was quickly dispatched by the sword because he could give little information and no promise of ransom. His executioner, Odo says, rejoiced that he had acquired merit in the eyes of the Heavenly Father by wetting his blade in pagan blood. The army, encouraged by this success, effected the crossing with the loss of a single man, a knight, swept to his death when his horse fell. Not a man had been lost in battle. Clearly the hand of God had been with them. Many, indeed, swore that they had seen a knight, clad in white, leading the crusaders to the attack, and that after the battle he had faded away into the sky like a cloud.

The march toward Laodicea was resumed on the morrow. The Turks had disappeared, but so had the Greek natives. The French found the city deserted and denuded of everything useful: all foodstuffs carried off, concealed, or burned; all animals driven away to the hills. The Greek governor had fled. The crusaders lost a day in fruitless discussion and search for provisions, then prepared to push on toward the difficulties of the great Cadmos Mountain pass which lay not far ahead.

King Louis arranged the order of march with especial care, anticipating renewed attacks. Geoffrey de Rancon and the count de Maurienne led the vanguard formed by the main body of knights. Next to them were placed the queen and the other noble women, escorted by Count Robert and his men. Behind them followed the baggage train and the mass of pilgrims on foot. Louis himself took charge of the rear, assisted by forty knights, the flower of the army.

Not long after the crusaders left Laodicea, the wind bore to Eleanor and her friends a well-remembered stench, the sickening odor of decaying human flesh. The women urged their horses as fast as they could past dead bodies—mute witnesses to the toll inflicted by the Turks on Bishop Otto's Germans who had passed this same way not long before. The whole column, in fact, moved by a common impulse, was making unusually good time. Eleanor realized suddenly that they were beginning to climb upward and were entering the pass of Cadmos Mountain. There foamed on the left below them a stream that had cut a gorge through the flank of the mountain which rose steeply on their right. The queen saw ahead of her the slender column winding its way along the shelving mountainside. She hurriedly summoned Count Robert to her side and reminded him that the king had given strict orders to the leaders not to cross the pass that day but to pitch camp at the foot of the mountain and take the whole of the next day for the crossing. The young count could give no explanation for the leaders' failure to obey marching orders. He felt, however, that the only thing to be done under the circumstances was to follow on: to halt where they were would cause inextricable confusion.

The queen and her party found themselves about two o'clock riding downward toward a spot where they saw those preceding them preparing to encamp. Eleanor immediately dispatched Count Robert to summon to her presence the two leaders of the vanguard. These great barons promptly obeyed the summons, though somewhat astonished at being called to account for military conduct by their young queen. They had yet to learn that Eleanor, while she was very much a woman, was also very much a queen, prompt to assert her authority whenever circumstances demanded. Geoffrey and De Maurienne urged, in extenuation of their breach of the king's orders, their unexpectedly early arrival at the mountain's foot, the absence of the enemy, the ease with which the journey over the pass had been made, and the advantages for camping afforded by their present location. It was still only a little after three o'clock and it seemed as though no serious consequences were to result from the breach of orders, since the head of the baggage train was beginning to draw into sight. So the queen dismissed the two nobles with a warning against repetition of such conduct. But they were not to escape so easily. Disaster was impending.

Anxiety was first aroused by the cessation of arrivals at the camp. No movement could be discerned on the road descending from the mountain. Finally Eleanor, unable to endure the tension longer, summoned once more Geoffrey and the Count de Maurienne. After a brief consultation, the queen ordered them to send back a party to investigate. A cry went up from those watching the road while the leaders were preparing to carry out this order. Eleanor turned and saw in the distance a mounted figure making its way down to the plain. Soon a shout went up: it was Odo, the king's chaplain. But where was the king, where his bodyguard, where the pilgrim host? Odo was at first too faint to reply to their questions when at last, his cowl blown back on his shoulders, the skirts of his gown torn to shreds, he was helped from his drooping donkey. But be began eagerly to pour out his tale after he had been refreshed with a cup of wine brought at Eleanor's command.

The king was badly in need of aid, trying with his few companions to rescue the disordered host from the Turks and Greeks. A cursed cart had broken down and blocked the road near the top of the pass. But the stream of men and animals behind kept pressing forward, making a confused jam around which the column sprayed out over the mountainside. Animals often lost their footing on the steep declivity and rolled over and over to the bottom of the gorge. They carried destruction to all in their way. Dislodged boulders added to the carnage. A confused mass of men, animals, and equipment of all sorts piled up at the bottom of the canyon. At this sight, the Turks and Greeks darted out from their ambush on the other side of the gorge. They shot at the fallen men and at those making their way along the steep incline, dodging the flying animals and boulders as best they could. The uproar arising from all this had finally reached the king who led his men forward as rapidly as the rough ground would permit. When he came within sight of the turmoil, he saw that the Turks had crossed the stream at the bottom of the gorge and were attacking the mass of defenseless pilgrims. The king ordered a charge to drive off the enemy, and had commanded Odo, "who could not fight but only pray," to hurry and bid the vanguard come to the rescue.

The courageous monk had guided his sure-footed little beast up the steep mountainside, skirted the seething crowd, and finally reached the unimpeded downward path to gain the camp in safety. His last view of the king, Odo said, showed that his onset had turned the enemy's attention away from the unarmed pilgrims. But the king's company was fighting under difficulties. The roughness of the ground prevented them from charging with any force, and the numbers of the enemy were so great that the French were being engulfed and separated from each other. Eleanor scarcely heard the chaplain's last words; she had turned to speed the rescuers on their way. Yet, though Geoffrey and his fellows spurred their horses forward, they found the pace agonizingly slow, doubly retarded by the trail's upward slope and by the crowd which they soon began to encounter. It seemed as though they would never reach the king.

Louis and his companions had been fighting desperately all this while. After their horses were shot down they fought on foot, plying their swords with deadly effect. Each formed a ring of slaughtered foes around him, only to see other yelling infidels take their places. One by one the king's men fell, mortally wounded. The count de Varenne and his brother, Everard de Breteuil, both went down to glorious martyrdom; down too went Manassé de Beuil, Gaucher de Montjoy, and a score of other nobles. The king himself would have fallen, save for a fortunate happening.

Louis, fighting fiercely but slowly yielding ground, found himself, by the providence of God, close to a projecting mass of rock, covered with interlacing tree roots. Hope renewed his strength. He charged his enemies and drove them back with a shower of blows. Then he turned and ran for the rock, summoned all his strength, gave a leap, and clutched the roots with both hands. He succeeded in scrambling up while arrows rained upon him but fell harmlessly from his mail. Safe upon the top, Louis planted his feet securely on the rock and faced his foes. These vainly resumed the attack. Those at a distance shot incessantly at the king, but their arrows found no crevice in the steel links of his armor. Others rushed the rock, but the king's sword flashed on this side and on that, lopping off hands and cleaving heads.

The deepening twilight finally came to his rescue. The discouraged Turks gave up the attack and began to withdraw to the other side of the gorge. The king's heart was flooded with gratitude to St. Denis whose relics, encased in his sword-hilt, had saved him from the Infidel. He pressed the blood-stained handle to his lips.

Heartened by this act, he turned to overtake the army and began stumbling along through the darkness over the mountainside. Soon his eyes were gladdened by the sight of dim figures ahead of him. The men, delighted to discover their king, hurried to secure a horse for him.

It was then that Geoffrey and his companions came upon him. They were overjoyed at the sight of their lord and king, but dismayed to see that not a single knight rode with him. Every one of the escort had perished, the king said, but not without dyeing their swords in pagan blood. They had won the martyr's crown. Angels had carried their souls to heaven, and it rejoiced him to think that even at that moment they were singing praises around the throne of God. This reflection brought little consolation to his listeners, least of all to Geoffrey de Rancon who, with head bowed upon his breast, turned his horse to retrace the road to the camp.

Count Robert posted off to tell the queen of the king's safety. Louis's own first inquiry had been about his wife. The royal couple embraced each other with unrestrained joy when at last Louis reached the camp. Eleanor's first thought was of Louis's comfort. She gave him wine, saw that he was quickly relieved of his heavy suit of mail and sweaty leather shirt. Then with her own hands she bathed and massaged him. Louis gratefully arose to be clothed with clean underwear, tunic, and cloak. He gave Eleanor a warm embrace which she returned in kind: her heart was all Louis's when he was the warrior. But she sighed when he turned monk and, after a hasty farewell, walked away with Odo to the chaplain's tent, there to kneel before the altar saved from the wreck of that dreadful day.

Confusion and sorrow reigned throughout the camp. Individuals rushed distractedly hither and thither, searching for their friends. Women mourned for their lost husbands or rejoiced hysterically when some straggler, given up for dead, appeared unexpectedly. Yet one emotion gradually mastered all others—anger at the leaders responsible for this needless death and destruction. Desire for revenge mounted among the men gathered around the camp fires, where demands for the death of Geoffrey de Rancon began to be heard. Bishop Godfrey de la Roche and many of like temperament felt that death alone could atone for this disastrous breach of the king's explicit command. Yet the less impetuous pointed out that Louis's uncle, the count de Maurienne, was equally to blame: they should think well before condemning him to death. Consequently, opinion was by no means unanimous when the king, after a sleepless night, summoned his counselors.

Louis was in a difficult position. Both he and Eleanor were warmly attached to Geoffrey de Rancon. Furthermore, he was highly regarded by the barons of Aquitaine, whom the king wished to attach more closely to the crown. Again, there was his mother's half-brother, the count de Maurienne; whatever penalty was to be meted out to Geoffrey must be meted out to him as well. The condemnation of de Maurienne might stir the anger of unruly elements in southeastern France, where Abbot Suger was having none too easy a time enforcing obedience to the crown, as appeared from letters received at Constantinople. Yet Louis worshipped justice, and he would not have hesitated to condemn his two companions to death, if he were convinced that it was his duty. He perceived to his great relief that, while violent denunciations were made during the debate, no one advocated the death penalty. Finally all approved Chancellor Bartholomew's opinion that henceforth the two leaders should be excluded from council and from any position of responsibility in the army. Geoffrey and de Maurienne thus found themselves condemned to an almost complete ostracism, only gradually relaxed as the common danger and suffering drew all men together during the days that followed.

The discussion of Geoffrey's case had brought out the necessity for the introduction of stricter discipline. Arnoul, Bishop of Lisieux, called attention to the order and discipline practiced by the Knights Templar. Not one of them broke ranks to try his strength in single combat, but, divided into groups under leaders, they waited for the word of command and charged together. Nor did they continue in pursuit when the enemy had been put to flight, but at the trumpet's sound they returned to their place in the column. "Let us follow where the hand of God points," continued Arnoul, "and imitate the example of Sir Everard and his knights."

The bishop had scarcely finished before the impetuous Godfrey de la Roche leaped to his feet to second the suggestion, promising to obey the master of the Temple, should he be willing to command the host. This sentiment was instantly welcomed by the whole council, including the king, who said that as an example to all he would gladly submit to the authority of Sir Everard if he would accept the responsibility.

Sir Everard's first care was to arrange for the solemn administration of oaths binding all to obey his commands and those of the leaders under him. He next reorganized the army by dividing the knights into companies of fifty and placing a captain over each company. He assigned to each group a special position in the line of march and instructed it to return after a sally whether stationed in the vanguard, rearguard, or on either flank. Since many of the knights as well as great numbers of the lesser folk had lost their equipment and supplies, the king attempted to supply their wants from his own resources. Those knights who still lacked both horses and arms were given bows and joined to the soldiers stationed at the rear of all those on foot. King Louis wished likewise to be placed in some company under the command of a leader. Since, however, no one could be found who was willing to give orders to his sovereign, Louis was given a force of knights to act as a flying squadron and to be led wherever they should be most needed.

All were delighted at last to leave the cursed mountains and move out once more on level ground. Eleanor's spirits rose as she saw stretching before her the broad valley through which their road ran. Even the renewed attacks of the Turks did not oppress her when she saw how perfectly the new discipline and formation worked. For now no high-spirited knight dashed out singly to take vengeance on the taunting enemy when the infidels dashed in, showering arrows on the column. Instead, each company under the command of an experienced Templar awaited the word of command. Then, at the signal, out would charge the squadrons. It was a novel sight to the Christian onlookers. The crusaders began scattering over the field in pursuit when the enemy fled. Then occurred the greatest marvel of all, for when the charge had accomplished its purpose, the trumpets sounded along the line, and the excited pursuers, obediently checking their horses, headed for the pennons of their commanders, who caused them to re-form and led them at a trot back to their appointed positions. The orderliness and the rhythm of the squadrons greatly impressed the queen.

The route to the seacoast, the immediate goal which the crusaders were seeking, now branched from the main road which ran eastward, and turned sharply to the south and southwest. The pinch of hunger began to make itself felt during the succeeding days. Though the country was becoming more fertile, the Greek natives continued to be hostile and to coöperate with the Turks. In consequence, the crusaders found the country swept bare before them. The weakened horses began dying. The losses became so serious that the loads which the horses had been transporting could no longer be carried by the footmen who were themselves becoming progressively weaker. As a result, the leaders resolved to burn everything that was not absolutely essential. So tent-poles were piled together and gear of every description was thrown on top, including chests with all spare clothes. Eleanor and the other women forlornly watched the destruction of their remaining finery. Doubtless they would have taken the loss more to heart, had not the insistent pangs of hunger driven from their minds every thought but an overmastering desire for food.

They were not alone in this condition. Everyone in the host was urged on by the same desire. The solution of the problem was suggested when hungry eyes surveyed the vast number of horses lying around on every side, useless for transportation, but serviceable for another purpose. The humbler folk led the way in seizing on this convenient food supply. One and all capitulated as the savory odors of broiling steak floated through the camp. The queen hesitated only a moment before sending an order to the kitchen tent to prepare the roast meat as quickly as possible.

The cook already had a dozen roasts turning on spits before the fire, in anticipation of the order. The hungry women, drawn by the odors, cast dignity aside and gradually moved over toward the fire. They watched every motion of the cook as with deft hands he patted into shape chunks of dough, made from flour and water, and placed them on the hot stones close to the glowing embers. Eleanor and her maids seated themselves when the meal was ready, and placed on their knees flat pieces of wood provided by the pages who then ran to cut off slabs of the roast. They poised these on the points of their daggers until they could deposit them on the improvised trenchers. Eleanor drew a small dagger from her belt and with it pinned the meat to her trencher while a page cut her portion into smaller pieces. The queen took one of these in her fingers and gingerly essayed the first bite. She found the morsel delicious, if not tender. All the others had the same experience. Each ate her portion quickly and called for more. The cakes, brought crisp and hot from the fire, won unstinted praise.

It was with strength renewed and spirits refreshed that the crusaders resumed on the following day their march toward the seaport of Adalia. Here they arrived after four days' march without further mishap and encamped outside the city walls.

Eleanor had looked forward to the arrival at Adalia in the hope that the privations of the preceding weeks would be ended. With this hope she had kept up the flagging spirits of her companions. But in this expectation she was disappointed. The crusaders were to experience during the following weeks discomforts more trying in some respects than any they had suffered so far.

The greatest of these was the incessant rain which soaked the tents and made the pallets on which the women tried to sleep cold and damp. Tempers were sorely tried. It required all the young queen's tact and wit to keep up even a semblance of good nature in her entourage. Food, to be sure, they had, since Landulph, the Greek governor, opened up the markets to them after he had first compelled the hungry barons to swear once more to keep peace with the emperor. But the prices were inordinate and became higher as the halt lengthened into weeks. For one egg they were ultimately compelled to pay twice as much as at first they had paid for a dozen, and so with onions and other articles of food. At these prices only the king and the wealthier barons could buy food. The others sustained life on horse meat or sold their possessions to keep body and soul together. There was no grain for the horses and mules, since supplies were held up by the Turks at the river fords several miles away. The rocky pastures stretching from the city to the river supplied only a scanty growth, so the animals continued to die.

Louis had been absorbed as usual in his private devotions during these miserable days, and on February 2, the Purification of the Blessed Virgin was celebrated with what ceremony was possible. Louis was moved to action at last, and at a council exhorted the barons in terms that did more credit to his piety than to his good sense. Since the horses were dying, he said, it was shameful to delay there longer. It was their duty, even though they were sick and fatigued, to march on without relaxation toward the accomplishment of their vows, in order to secure the crown of martyrdom which God accorded to those who lost their lives in such enterprises. In reply, the barons respectfully pointed out that all the king's paid men-at-arms had lost their horses and arms, that they had no money to buy horses, and that it was impossible to procure food for the beasts if they had them. Then they emphasized the advantages of going by sea. "Yet as for us," they concluded, "we wish to live and die with you and are only anxious to learn your commands."

The king replied that as long as he was rich no man of honor should remain in want and that none would be a man of honor who did not know how to support misery with him. Then he promised to fit them out with horses and weapons, and to send the masses of defenseless pilgrims on by sea. "As for us, we will follow the road which our fathers have trod, by which their valor has acquired renown throughout the world and the glory of heaven." The barons rejoined that they wished to yield in nothing to the glory of their fathers, but pointed out that their fathers fought only the Turks and suffered no want, while they had to fight the Turks, the Greeks, and hunger. "Nevertheless," they said, "give us the horses and we will go." The search for horses proved futile, as the barons had forseen. So the king yielded at last to the inevitable and agreed to take the sea route to Antioch. Negotiations for transports were immediately begun.

The Greeks as usual promised great things. Landulph, the governor, and a special imperial representative who had arrived by sea, said they would soon gather vessels enough to transport the whole host. But the ships, when after some weeks they arrived, proved to be so small and so few that they could carry only a small portion of the army.

During this period the Greeks continued their policy of weakening the crusaders in every way possible. They refused to admit even the sick inside the city walls. The half-starved people continued to die in increasing numbers. The living, crowded closely together, buried their dead comrades as best they could. Conditions became daily more unsanitary and intolerable, what with the stench arising from the corpses, the accumulating excretions of the multitude, the filth and the mud. Landulph encouraged the Turks to attack the Franks in order to kill them off more quickly. The war horses of the Christians, he said, were so few in number and so weakened by lack of fodder that the knights would be able to make only a feeble resistance. Yet when scouts reported an impending Turkish attack, enough good destriers were assembled to enable the Frankish knights, led by King Louis, Sir Everard and the Templars, to drive back the overconfident infidels in confusion, killing many and driving others to death in the river.

The day after this event, a delegation from the foot soldiers and knights who had lost their horses presented themselves before King Louis. They were covered with confusion, they said, because they had previously refused to accompany him on land. Now they perceived that owing to the deceit of the Greeks, it would not be possible for them to travel by sea. They wished, therefore, to depart by land, preferring to expose themselves to the sword of the Turk rather than to endure longer the treacherous cruelty of the Greeks. Louis lavished money upon them in such profusion that he seemed to have no thought at all for the needs of his household. He turned over to the knights all the horses that were left. He obtained from Landulph, in return for a large payment, a solemn agreement to receive the sick inside the city, and to provide the remainder with a strong escort till they had crossed the rivers and were well on their way to Tarsus. Furthermore, he instructed Count Thierry of Flanders and Archambaud de Bourbon to remain in Adalia after his own departure to make sure that Landulph would carry out the agreement.

King Louis's suspicions were amply justified, as appeared some weeks later from Thierry and Archambaud's report when they had rejoined him at Antioch. Landulph refused to supply the pilgrims with any escort. The bowmen of the Turks amused themselves by shooting at the unprotected wretches huddled at the base of the city's walls. Some six thousand of the strongest, mounted and on foot, made a valiant effort to march on toward Tarsus. They succeeded in crossing one river, but were almost completely wiped out in attempting to cross a second. Only a few ever returned to the camp. Many of those who had not taken part in this venture were driven by want and hunger to give themselves up by hundreds as slaves to the Greek citizens. Strange to say, the Turks, who had been allowed by the Greeks to pass freely in and out of the city, took pity on the starving pilgrims, exchanged their own money for Greek coins and gave these to the astonished but grateful Christians. More than three thousand benefited by this calculated generosity, and, though they became slaves, were not compelled to change their faith. The last traces of the vast host that had set out so eagerly from France disappeared as an organized force with the departure of this body.

Eleanor had fortunately been spared experiencing these last agonizing events. She had continued through the preceding weeks her attempts to keep up the spirits of her companions, depressed by the sickening smells and sights all around them and terrified by frightful outbursts of thunder and lightning. The strain had taken a severe toll of her strength. Hence it was with unrestrained joy that she had set foot on the gangplank of the ship that was to bear her away to Antioch.

Scandal at Antioch
1148

THE VOYAGE FROM ADALIA TO ANTIOCH CONSUMED THREE storm-tossed weeks. Eleanor and her companions were wretched. They were forced to stay below deck in stuffy little cabins, and their cockleshell of a craft flung them about at times so violently that they clung together in fear. The storm slackened toward the end of the third week. The disheveled women straggled out on deck and looked with lack-lustre eyes upon the subsiding waves. A cry soon went up that land had been sighted. The women crowded forward around Eleanor as she pointed out the faint blue of a headland on the horizon. Gradually as they drew nearer, the harbormouth of the river Orontes opened up, and soon the little port of St. Simeon became visible, with figures moving about on its docks. The women hurried below deck to make themselves presentable for the landing.

None of the watchers on the dock awaited the fleet's arrival with greater eagerness than Eleanor's uncle, Prince Raymond of Antioch. He was her father's younger brother who, as a mere stripling, had been attached to the court of the English king, Henry I. Raymond had scarcely reached his twentieth year when he was chosen prince of Antioch. His journey to the principality took him through Italy where he assumed a disguise to avoid being captured by King Roger of Sicily, who cherished a claim on Antioch. During the early years of his rule, he had to struggle against plots fomented by the Dowager Princess, Alice, whom he had offended by marrying her daughter, Constance, instead of herself. The patriarch of Antioch sided with the Dowager Alice.

The fall of Edessa made his territory the northern-most of the Christian states, and exposed it to Muslim attacks. Prince Raymond, the ablest of the Frankish leaders, found the rulers of the other crusading states, Tripolis and Jerusalem, uncoöperative. Wrapped up in their own narrow interests, they failed to see how the fall of Edessa and the rise to power of the fanatical saracen Prince Nurreddin at Aleppo threatened the safety of the whole Christian East. When Raymond learned that the French were coming to the Holy Land, he determined to secure their aid in carrying out his designs on Aleppo. Even before the start of the expedition he had sent presents to Louis; nor did he neglect Eleanor. He had heard of the influence she exerted over her husband. It was therefore with the greatest eagerness that he looked forward to the meeting about to take place.

Eleanor, once more on deck, sought to single out her uncle from the crowd of brilliantly dressed knights gathered on the dock. She was not left long in doubt, for Louis had just landed, and a man of commanding presence stepped forward to welcome him. This person she felt sure could be none other than her uncle, Prince Raymond. Louis came quickly to meet her when she stepped on the dock, embraced her warmly, then turned to present the prince to his queen.

Eleanor saw before her a handsome man, scarcely a dozen years older than herself. She sensed his magnetism even in this first brief interview. Raymond, for his part, was struck by Eleanor's beauty. She had been only a child of five or six when he had left Poitiers for the English court and had hardly given promise of developing at twenty-six into the woman he saw before him, charming yet with a touch of decisiveness that he liked. He discovered later that she, like himself, had in her much of his father, the Troubadour Count. Raymond's eyes expressed a flattering approval of his niece's beauty, but his thoughts were for the moment concentrated on King Louis. He paused only long enough to exchange greetings and give orders that the queen and her suite be properly mounted for the march up the valley of the Orontes to Antioch. He then gave all his attention to the king.

Prince Raymond saw the hand of God in the safe arrival of Louis, still accompanied by many bishops, abbots, barons, and knights. He prepared to make the most of the opportunity, and rode by Louis's side on the march to Antioch. Near the city's gates they were greeted as usual by crowds of cheering citizens led by gorgeously robed clergy. The entrance to the city was through an imposing gateway in its massive walls. These, Eleanor saw, rivalled in height those of Constantinople. In other regards the city appeared nearly as magnificent as Manuel's. The queen noted the arcaded squares, the marble palaces. Each of these, she learned later, was provided with beautiful gardens and fountains. Before the most impressive of the palaces the cavalcade halted. The queen and her companions were guided by attendants to a series of chambers provided for them. At the sight of the beautifully furnished apartments, Eleanor almost wept. It was such a relief to have quarters like these after the hardships so recently experienced. While Eleanor and her maids were eagerly exploring the rooms, her chamberlain entered, followed by swarthy eunuchs bearing armfuls of clothes and toilette articles. These elicited cries of joy. Everything a feminine heart could wish was there: soft undershirts, silken tunics and dresses, embroidered robes, beautiful cloaks and capes. Among the toilette articles there were mirrors set in carved ivory, rouge of various shades, beautifully embossed bronze basins. The discovery of some soap reminded Eleanor that she had not had a real bath since leaving Constantinople, where she had revelled in the hot and cold water, hot rooms, and refreshing massages. The queen found on inquiry that Raymond's palace was provided with these same luxurious arrangements, and she and the others instantly prepared to enjoy them.

Prince Raymond at once began showering his attentions on the king and the other notables. He provided all with suitable quarters, though only Louis, with Odo, Thierry Gualeran, and one or two other intimate associates, had been housed in Raymond's own palace. A small oratory adjoined the king's chamber, where he could conveniently continue his daily orisons. Raymond was as anxious to win the favor of Louis's followers as he was to win that of the king himself. Each according to his station was supplied, in the days that followed, with food, clothes, weapons, and horses.

Raymond took occasion, as he moved about among the leaders, to make his ideas clear as to the strategy of the military situation. He tried to show them how the capture of Aleppo would extend control up the Orontes valley along the road between the Lebanons, the best route to Damascus and Jerusalem. Such a conquest would not only protect the Principality of Antioch, but greatly strengthen the position of the other two crusading states. He developed these same ideas in even greater detail in his frequent conversations with the king. Louis expressed interest in everything Raymond had to say, but was noncommittal about his own plans. He agreed, however, to the summoning of a great council at which the prince could set forth his arguments for a joint attack on Aleppo. Raymond was content with this arrangement, for in spite of Louis's unwillingness to commit himself, the prince felt certain that the king would finally consent to his desire; many of the French leaders had already expressed their compliance. Gratitude alone should impell the French king to help him. For had not Raymond out of his own purse reëquipped the crusaders? Without his generosity they would have been helpless to fight the infidels anywhere. Persuaded by his wishes, Prince Raymond confidently looked forward to the council.

On the appointed day, Prince Raymond, King Louis, and as many others as possible assembled in the beautiful church of St. Peter to hear mass. It was an impressive performance, for Raymond was devoted to magnificent services. The singing rivalled that of the Greek monks heard at Constantinople. Raymond led the way, after the service, to an amphitheater, centuries old and somewhat damaged by the earthquakes which Antioch had suffered from time to time, but still sufficiently intact to seat comfortably a large gathering. When quiet at last reigned, Prince Raymond rose for his supreme effort. He reiterated the arguments used in his private conversations and pointed out that now was the time to strike, since the Muslims were terrified at the news of the arrival of the great Frankish army. He then made a direct appeal to Louis for aid, saying that God had brought him to Antioch rather than elsewhere, thereby manifesting His will that the French should join in an attack on Aleppo.

All now centered their gaze on King Louis as he rose to reply, none more eagerly than Prince Raymond, who had the highest hopes that he had won over the king to his way of thinking. Louis began by saying that he had indeed come to fight for the Cross in the Holy Land. Yet even before Edessa had fallen, he had taken a solemn vow to expiate his sins against God and the Church by performing a pilgrimage to the sepulchre of the Lord. He would be ready to fight against the cursed infidels wherever and whenever it should seem best to the patriarch of Jerusalem and the other leaders after he had won forgiveness by kneeling at the tomb of the blessed Saviour. But there he must first go.

Raymond could scarcely believe his ears. Were all his scheming and dreams of aggrandizement to be brought to nothing? He was furious to find himself thwarted by this royal fanatic. He thrust himself past the king and hurried from the assembly, bent on making one last effort to bend this cursed zealot to his will. He would seek out his niece. She was intelligent, and could certainly be made to grasp the reasonableness of his plans. If she would try her powers of persuasion on her husband, he might yet change his mind and decide to fight here before going to Jerusalem. Once there, Louis would never come back; Raymond was sure of that.

Prince Raymond had been too closely engaged, since the arrival of the French army, to give any personal attention to his niece. He had, however, instructed his wife, Constance, to extend all possible courtesies to the French queen. On the morning of the assembly Constance had taken the queen and her companions off for a tour of the palace and its gardens, where they were delighted with everything. But when Constance, who was only twenty-three, exhibited her four children, Eleanor felt a touch of envy as she thought of Marie, her lone child. Constance ended the tour by bringing the party to a lovely garden surrounded by an arcade and shaded by palm trees. In the center played a cooling fountain, encircled by beds of gay flowers. Cushions and rugs spread over the tessalated pavement provided comfortable resting places. Bowls of yellow fruit cooled in snow stood on low taborets placed near each guest. Eleanor found this strange fruit, which Constance called "apricots," deliciously refreshing. While the queen was enjoying the pleasures of the garden, Raymond entered.

The passage from the assembly to the palace had given the prince time to collect his thoughts and control himself. He made his entrance quietly and greeted his niece, her companions, and his wife with all his accustomed grace of manner. He sat down beside Eleanor and engaged her in conversation. He was able, before long, to detach the queen, on the plea that he wished to show her a strange plant, and lead her into a far corner of the garden. He concluded his outline of the military situation by taking out his dagger and drawing on the ground a map showing the relation of Aleppo to the road leading northeastward toward the Euphrates and Edessa, and that leading south up the Orontes toward Damascus. Wrathfully he told how Louis had just refused to aid him. Eleanor exclaimed over her husband's fanaticism, his stupidity at not seeing the advantages to be gained for the Christian cause by immediately assisting Raymond. The prince urged his niece to try to persuade the king to change his mind. Confident of success, Eleanor consented.

But Eleanor failed utterly. Only when he had been purged of his sin and had become a consecrated instrument of God's will, Louis said, could he hope to fight successfully against the enemies of the Cross. Eleanor was baffled by this impregnability. She was accustomed to a Louis indecisive when confronted with a choice between two courses of action. He was apt to let his mind be made up by anyone who strongly urged one definite course. But in this instance, Louis had not the slightest doubt about his duty. His soul was stained by the sacrilege of Vitry-the-burned. To his Saviour's tomb he would go first.

This was to Eleanor a new Louis. She was used to his religiosity. It had been a jarring note in their relationship from the earliest days of their marriage; and the emotional climax reached in the consecration ceremonies at St. Denis seemed to have altered Louis so that at times he moved in a world where it was difficult for her to follow. Nevertheless, she was utterly unprepared to find him so rock-like, so inaccessible. She was not only baffled, she was chagrined. Eleanor was not accustomed to being refused. She was mortified at her failure, and her mortification was increased by the thought that she must relate it to Prince Raymond.

Eleanor sought the seclusion of the arcaded garden after her interview with the king. Here she was found by her uncle who seated himself beside her and inquired about the results of her mission. She was obliged to confess complete failure. Raymond sprang to his feet and began pacing furiously back and forth. He cursed Louis for an ungrateful fool and vowed he would frustrate his plans. He would not let him leave Antioch. He would find some way to keep him there until he agreed to join with him in an attack on Aleppo. At all events, he would be revenged on him in some way for his ingratitude. Suddenly he stopped short, checked by the thought that after all Eleanor might provide the way. Could he perhaps take advantage of her anger at her husband? In her expression of it was there not a hint of something more profound than annoyance at the present rebuff? He instantly resolved to delve into the matter. The thought enabled him to regain his poise. He seated himself once more by his niece, determined to discover just how she felt toward her husband.

The astute prince led the conversation around to his and her old home in Poitou, in the hope of drawing her out. He found no difficulty in getting her to talk freely on this subject. She was delighted to find someone interested in Poitiers. They passed easily from the topic of her early associations to that of her marriage and impressions of life at the French court. Paris itself was pleasant enough, she said, but the royal castle was not as comfortable as their own, and the court life was far less entertaining than at Poitiers. There was little of the gaiety which the troubadour tradition fostered at home. The courtiers were Northerners, to begin with, and the ecclesiastical atmosphere weighed upon everyone. She had tried to liven things, and in the beginning Louis had tried to help her, though without much success. He was too serious to care for light-hearted fun, song, and dance. He was a religious at heart, devoted to ecclesiastical observances, and ridiculously obsequious to churchmen. The duties of the kingship had still further sobered him. Then came that cursed burning of the church and the people at Vitry, followed by the La Chatre affair, with Louis's complete surrender to the pope and the pilgrimage vow. She had seen little of her husband since they had been on the crusade. All the time he could spare from business and fighting was given to praying. "I thought I had married a king," concluded Eleanor bitterly, "but I find I have married a monk."

Raymond was astonished at the intensity of Eleanor's feeling. Her dissatisfaction was more deeply rooted than he had dared hope. A hot-blooded Southerner wed to a cold Northerner, a pagan to an ascetic! By the bones of St. Simeon, he would profit by this situation. He would entice his niece to linger on at Antioch, then let Louis go if he could. He rose to his feet and said they would have a banquet in the great hall that night. He wished her to sit at his side.

Raymond appeared at the banquet dressed in a flowing robe after the Saracen fashion. He placed the French queen on his right, the king on his left. Eleanor was entranced by the sight of the banqueting hall, brilliant with the light of hundreds of perfumed candles which filled the air with a delicate fragrance. A fountain played in the center of the space about which the tables were arranged in a parallelogram. The tables, covered with white linen, were decorated with pink oleanders and mallows set in graceful porcelain vases such as she had not seen even at Constantinople. Swarthy, white-turbaned attendants pressed on the guests a succession of delicious dishes including a highly seasoned concoction of rice and goats' meat. Pork was not served, however, in order that no offense be given to the two or three captive Saracen emirs who were present. Raymond called the queen's attention to a neat device, a silver standard equipped with a revolving disk perforated with holes in which were set silver cups containing salt, pepper, cinnamon, cloves, and other spices. This "castor" intrigued Eleanor, who resolved to acquire one at the earliest possible moment. Persian wine was served along with fruits of many descriptions: figs, oranges, bananas, and once more the delicious apricots.

The prince pointedly turned his shoulder on Louis all through the banquet and payed marked attention to his niece, laughing and talking with her incessantly. Toward the end of the feast, Raymond gave a signal, and a bevy of Arabian dancing girls came tripping in. One glance at the sinuous movements of their half-naked bodies was enough for Louis. He retired hastily, saying that it was time for compline and that Odo was awaiting him in the oratory. The Prince scornfully remarked to his companion, as the king disappeared, "Good riddance to your monk!" Raymond arranged to spend the whole of the following day in the queen's company. He wished her to see his horses, falcons, and above all a cheetah trained for hunting, a present from one of his Mohammedan friends. Then they might go for a ride along the river, to the charming suburb of Daphne with its lovely gardens.

The next morning, after Raymond had taken Eleanor on the promised tour of the stables and mews, they rode out of the city and cantered their horses beside the river. When the pace slowed to a walk, Raymond entertained his companion with tales of his life in England and told her of the embassy that came there to offer him the Principality of Antioch. When they reached the grove of Daphne, the prince halted and ordered his attendants to lay down rugs and cushions. After his niece was comfortably settled, Raymond asked if she would not like to remain at Antioch till she could fully recover from the hardships experienced in the recent weeks. She replied emphatically in the affirmative, saying it was both restful and interesting at Antioch and that she had no desire to resume tent life yet awhile.

"But if the king should decide to leave within a few days, what then?" queried Raymond.

"Do not speak of it! How could he think of making me leave in so short a time!"

On the way home, Eleanor spoke of having enjoyed the music at the banquet and expressed interest in the skilful manner with which the minstrels used the bow. Raymond said they would have some more music that night in his private quarters where he kept a variety of instruments. He could play on the rebec himself, and would show her how to use the bow.

Day after day the prince continued his assiduous attentions to the queen, often on one pretext or another engaging her in long conversations with him alone in his private suite. One morning the king and Odo were overtaken, just as they were leaving the palace courtyard on the way to hear mass in one of Antioch's numerous churches, by a gay cavalcade led by Raymond and Eleanor. The couple halted only long enough for Eleanor to explain to Louis that her uncle was going to show her how to hunt with the cheetah, and dashed away again.

This incident increased the king's uneasiness. Raymond's marked attentions to the queen on the night of the banquet had, as he intended, caught public attention. The court had begun to whisper. The gossiping increased when the prince took the queen away for one all-day jaunt after another, followed by prolonged tête-à-têtes at night. Now they were going off for another long day together. Furthermore, Louis was convinced, from what he knew of Raymond's career, that the Prince was capable of the most shameless trickery when pursuing his own interests. The king decided that it would at least be advisable to speed up preparations for departure. He resolved to leave Antioch within the next few days, and to communicate his decision to the queen.

It was not till the following morning that Louis was able to talk with his wife alone. And then it was only to receive a disconcerting surprise. Eleanor said she was not ready to leave. She had been so exhausted by the last trying stages in Asia Minor and so tossed about on the sea trip that she and her companions needed more time for recuperation. Besides, she had not seen her uncle since she had grown up, and they had many things to talk over together. Who knew when they would ever see each other again? If Louis were so anxious to reach Jerusalem, let him go at once in God's name. She would follow later and discharge her vows all in good time. Louis replied with unwonted decision and some asperity that this could not be. It was her duty and his wish that she accompany him. She could have a few more days for rest, but then she must be ready to depart. He abruptly quitted the apartment, leaving Eleanor vowing that she, a ruler in her own right of half of France, would not endure being treated in such fashion. Louis was unbearable. She would stay if she liked.

The news spread rapidly through the court that the French king had decided to leave Antioch. Raymond, disturbed by the report, determined at once to secure an interview with his niece. He had one more card to play and now, if ever, was the time to play it. He hoped so to work upon her dissatisfaction with her husband that she would welcome a suggestion that he had been holding in reserve. If she could be persuaded to act on it, he would wreck her relations with Louis forever and revenge himself on the man who had ruined his own plans. He hurried off a request to the queen that she join him as quickly as possible. Eleanor responded immediately, glad of the opportunity to unburden herself.

The instant they were alone, Raymond asked if she had heard the news. The question released Eleanor's pent-up wrath. She sketched briefly the interview with her husband and ended with a reiteration of her determination to stay in Antioch. If the king still insisted on her leaving with him, he would have to take her by force.

"You need never go, if you do not wish to," interjected Raymond. "Merely inform your husband that you can no longer live with him."

"Such a thing would be impossible," exclaimed Eleanor.

"Impossible? Have you not heard that you and Louis have married within the degrees of kinship forbidden by the Church?"

"Why yes," Eleanor replied hesitatingly, "Abbot Bernard and others have made such a claim, but there was so much uncertainty that no one has ever taken the matter seriously."

"But it could be taken seriously if *you* wished. It should not be difficult to secure bishops to swear to the fact, if they were properly approached."

"Yes, easy enough," assented Eleanor, "if Louis would consent; but how is one to persuade him?"

"Can you ask that when you know so well his deep-seated reverence for the laws of the Church? The matter has never been presented to him strongly enough. He is bound to be impressed, once convinced that *you* take it seriously."

While Eleanor was considering this proposal, Raymond enlarged on the possibilities opened up by an annulment of her marriage. She could free herself at one blow from all the irritating restrictions which now bound her: free herself from daily association with this ascetic monk. She would really be duchess of Aquitaine for the first time in her life, free to manage her own court as she pleased. If she desired to marry again, there would be no dearth of opportunities. There was her neighbor in France, young Henry of Anjou, vigorous, able, and no saint, if all reports were true. His prospects were brilliant. He would certainly inherit the counties of Anjou and Touraine, almost as certainly the Duchy of Normandy, already practically conquered by his father, Geoffrey. These three made a pretty handful, but that was not all. Henry, through his mother, was in line for an even greater prize—nothing less than the crown of England. She would be doing well to exchange the king of France for the king of England. As for Antioch, she could linger there as long as she pleased.

Eleanor's expressive features reflected varying emotions as she envisioned this alluring picture of freedom. The prospect of marriage with the vigorous Henry of Anjou appealed to the queen's imagination. Such a possibility offered a brilliant way out in case of a complete breach with Louis. In her first marriage she had been merely a pawn: in this case she might move where she chose like a queen. Yet Raymond was not sure, when they parted, what Eleanor would do, though he counted on her impulsiveness. He hoped his niece might, in a burst of recklessness, play the trump card he had placed in her hand, if the king once more stirred her smouldering resentment. He was not to be disappointed.

The queen's chamberlain announced the king on the following morning before Elaine had finished dressing Eleanor's hair. Louis's arrival at this inopportune moment augured ill for the success of his mission. His preparations for departure, he said, had proceeded more rapidly than he had expected, so she must be ready to leave early the next morning. Eleanor irritably exclaimed at the shortness of the time allowed her and refused to leave in the morning, saying that she could not possibly be ready by then. Louis, angered in his turn, said he wished to reach Jerusalem before Easter, and commanded her both as king and her wedded husband to obey him. Eleanor, provoked by Louis's tone and words, burst out: "My lord, you are indeed my king, but you are not my husband, for we have never been lawfully married." Louis gasped, his eyes wide with surprise. "Why do you feign astonishment, my lord? You know well enough that Bishop Bartholomew of Laon has shown we are related in at least the fifth degree. Is it not clear that we have incurred God's anger by our marriage? Our first child was still-born; for five years after, no child blessed our union; and when at last the holy Bernard interceded for us, the best his prayers could procure was a girl. No heir to the crown of France will ever be born to us. Our marriage is accursed. Think on that!"

Louis sank down upon a chest, his head in his hands, his mind confused. He knew that what his wife said was true. Could it be that the long unbroken succession to the French crown was now imperilled through his sin? The thought was terrible. Terrible, too, was the thought that he might have to give up his wife whom he loved so passionately. Why had she done this thing? Did she no longer love him? Had she given her love to Raymond? Eleanor saw the pain she was causing her husband, but if she had any misgivings, she showed no sign of them. Louis rose at last. He could give her no answer for the moment. The matter was too grave. He must first reflect and seek counsel. He walked blindly away.

The king at once summoned Odo. In relating the interview, Louis showed how fearful he was that he had brought God's curse on the kingdom by breaking the law of the Church. The devoted monk was distressed by his sovereign's suffering and disturbed at the success of Raymond's machinations. His designs were now revealed. He aimed to hold Louis at Antioch through Eleanor or else to disgrace him forever. Clear now was the meaning of all this ardent wooing in public, of those long colloquies in private. He would have the court and the world believe that the queen, impassioned of his person, had become unfaithful to her husband. How could they help believing it if she remained at Antioch? The artful prince had bewitched her; she must at all costs be removed from his influence. True or not, this was no time or place to decide the claim of unlawful marriage. But how to make the king see that? Odo, however, felt sure that Louis, following his usual custom, would consult his council. Its members must be prepared for the issue. The anxious chaplain determined to seek out at once Louis's trusted counselor, Thierry Gualeran.

The council was summoned to meet that afternoon in the palace where Bishop Arnoul was quartered. Bishops and barons, as they gathered in the hall, awaited with grave anxiety their sovereign's address. They were moved to astonishment, sorrow, and anger by his words. The fiery Godfrey de la Roche could scarcely wait before he burst out in a fierce denunciation of the queen's reckless folly and of the malicious deviltry of the half-infidel prince, who consorted freely with the enemies of God, filling his palace with Syrian eunuchs and Saracen dancing girls. Arnoul of Lisieux denounced the insane madness of the queen, but said that her charge, if pressed, would have to be considered, since there was indeed some weighty evidence in its favor. Others followed in similar vein, but no course of action was resolved upon until the king called on the ill-favored Thierry Gualeran. The bulbous-nosed eunuch, butt of many a jest on the part of the queen, treasured no love for her. Here at last was a chance to take full revenge: he made the most of it.

The venemous counselor bitterly condemned the queen for her conduct. She had, he said, made her name a byword throughout the whole court and brought shame on the king and all the French host. Her claim was but a ruse to cover her guilty relations with the prince—at least that was what all the world would think. It would be a blot upon the name of France if it could be said, in addition to all the misfortunes of the expedition, that the king had been robbed of his wife or abandoned by her. They must leave that very night, and with the greatest secrecy, lest Prince Raymond seek to restrain them by force or trickery. Above all, the queen must be compelled to go with them. Thierry's vehemence finally decided the wavering king, who at first had been more than half inclined to quit Antioch without the queen. It was agreed, therefore, that they should depart, but that no move be made until darkness had settled down and the army could march out of the city unobserved. The heart-sick king, unequal to undertaking it in his own person, delegated the task of abducting Eleanor to Thierry—a most unfortunate choice.

Meanwhile, for Eleanor, the day had dragged along wearily. It had taken her some time to regain her composure after Louis's departure and to rally her spirits sufficiently to allow her toilette to be completed. When she met Raymond that afternoon she revived somewhat in relating the results of the crucial interview. Raymond could scarcely contain his exultation when Eleanor concluded her story. His plot had worked. Louis was completely unmanned, to judge from Eleanor's account. He was wounded in a vital spot and would put up no fight. Eleanor, however, did not share in Raymond's exhilaration. The difficulties in her way, the gravity of her situation, had begun to come home to her. She took leave of the prince after a short while, pleading weariness. The exultant Raymond little thought that he was looking upon his niece for the last time.

When she returned to her apartments, Eleanor found Thierry Gualeran confronting her. Startled at the sight of the detested eunuch, she angrily demanded the meaning of his intrusion. Thierry replied that he bore an order from the king bidding her have her things packed at once in preparation for departure that night. "What outrageous insolence is this!" exclaimed Eleanor. "Am I, the queen of France, to be dragged from my chambers by force and by the hand of such a one as you? Never in this world, as long as I have a friend at hand to save me." With that she called upon a page to summon Raymond to her aid. But it was in vain. Guards stationed at every exit effectively prevented communication with other parts of the palace. The queen paced up and down like a caged tigress, furious above all that her husband should have entrusted this mission to that one of his counselors whom he well knew she so thoroughly detested. Elaine, frightened at the violence of her mistress' passion, begged the queen to calm herself. Eleanor, yielding at last to the entreaties of her maids, allowed herself to be led away to recline on a couch in another room. She thought over every possibility of escape as she rested there. Finally, convinced that she had no recourse but to yield, she accepted the situation, and gave orders to pack.

Hours later, in the dead of night, a group of heavily cloaked women issued from a small doorway at the rear of the palace, escorted by Thierry and his men. Thence the queen was conducted toward one of the city's gateways, through which a stream of men-at-arms was already passing. There Thierry delivered Eleanor into Louis's keeping. The royal couple rode out of the city side by side, the violence of their resentments concealed by an outward calm.

Counsel of the Holy Father 1148-1149

FOR THE FIRST DAY OR TWO AFTER HER DEPARTURE FROM ANTIOCH, ELEANOR WAS still too absorbed to pay heed to anything except her own confused thoughts. Her anger at Louis would rise up and almost stifle her. Yet a secret admiration would mingle with her wrath: Louis had at least acted like a man. She had provoked him. She had wounded him too; she had rashly challenged their marriage. Should she really attempt its annulment?

At Tripolis she was forced to rouse herself to greet Fulcher, the Patriarch of Jerusalem. He had been sent by the queen dowager, Melisend, potent in the affairs of the Latin Kingdom, to urge the French king not to delay but to make all speed to the Holy City lest others exploit Louis's aid for their own ends. Fulcher was delighted to discover that the king needed no persuasion. On the contrary, Louis's intention was to reach the scene of the Resurrection before the end of Passion Week if possible.

Eleanor's interest in her surroundings began to revive during the succeeding days. The queen had to look sharply to the footing of her beast at the Dog River, where a protruding spur of the Lebanons forced the traveller to choose between a road cut by the Romans through the rock and a narrow strip of beach washed by the waters of the Mediterranean. Eleanor's eye was attracted by inscriptions on the face of the towering cliff, incised there by conquerors of old: Egyptian, Persian, Greek, and Roman. They turned from the coast, after Sidon, Tyre, and St. Jean d'Acre had been left behind, and entered on the broad plain of Esdraelon. Here they encountered for the first time caravans hailing from Damascus and headed for the seaports. Eleanor was intrigued by the camels with their long necks, spongy feet, and humped backs loaded with enormous burdens. After marching for some time inland, the column of crusaders turned southward. As they followed the ascending road, they scanned the horizon for the first glimpse of the Holy City. Cries of thanksgiving arose when at last they caught sight of Jerusalem on its rocky height. Even Eleanor's thoughts were diverted from herself when she beheld the goal for which they had suffered so much.

Eleanor saw the boy king, Baldwin III, at the head of the welcoming procession, and beside him his mother, Melisend, splendidly robed. Eleanor viewed with interest this French woman born and bred in the midst of Palestine's varied social mixture. Melisend, for her part, looked with curiosity at the French queen. Rumors of her conduct at Antioch had already reached the gossips at Jerusalem. The dowager queen, however, was not forgetful of her duties as hostess. After they had entered one of the great gates she told Eleanor that the great dome rising above the other buildings, though built by the Muslims, was the holiest place in the city because it covered the altar of Solomon's temple. Eleanor noted that Jerusalem could not compare for magnificence with either Constantinople or Antioch. Nevertheless, she discovered that in the royal palace itself she was surrounded with many of those conveniences she had so enjoyed in both those cities, especially the bathing arrangements. It was fortunate that she liked her quarters; she was to occupy them for a year.

Eleanor had the bitter satisfaction of seeing her husband experience during this period the crowning humiliation of the whole dismal expedition. He and Emperor Conrad, who had now arrived, had been persuaded to join forces with the leaders of the Latin Kingdom in an attempt to capture Damascus. Both rulers had fought well, but had been forced to rely on the advice of the resident Christian leaders, particularly the Templars. There had been mismanagement, if not actual treachery. The Templars seemed none too anxious to press the campaign, since they enjoyed much income from their trading privileges.

On his return from this expedition, Count Robert de Dreux declared to Eleanor that he was sick of the bickerings and jealousies among these Christians who had lived so long in the Holy Land. They were all too friendly by far with infidel Saracens: they exchanged visits with them and shared their hunting grounds, and sometimes even their cultivated fields. They had adopted Saracen dress and were becoming more like them every day. Count Robert said he had done his duty by slaughtering the infidel dogs, had sought forgiveness for his sins by kneeling at the tomb of his Blessed Lord, and was bent on returning home, as were most of the other barons and knights. If Louis wished to stay on, let him do so; that was his affair. As for himself, the count concluded, he must return to look after the welfare of his possessions, heavily mortgaged as they were. How he was to secure money enough to live on he scarcely knew. He must now wish her well and say good-bye.

The departure of Count Robert and his friends left the queen and her companions, especially Elaine, lonely and depressed. The prospect of an indefinite stay in Palestine had very little appeal for Eleanor. She had been calmed by praying at her Saviour's tomb and had been enabled to live on more cordial terms with her husband, though the possibility of someday winning her freedom increasingly occupied her mind. But there could be no thought of any such attempt until the return to France. Meanwhile she feared that time would hang heavily on her hands.

Yet the pageant of the East presented her daily with some piquant novelty. The bazaars were a never-ending source of delight, with their silks and embroidered stuffs of every description, porcelain vases from Persia, brooches, jewelled rings and bracelets. The highly polished copper utensils also took her fancy, especially the braziers which, because of their removable tops, might also be used as taborets.

Melisend was as devoted to the hunt as Eleanor herself, and many mornings saw them riding out from the city, hawks on their wrists. Nor was their sport tame. On one of the hunting expeditions, Eleanor nearly lost her life when a lion leaped out at her horse. The fierce beast, foiled by the queen's adroitness, succeeded only in gashing her mount's flank. One of the attendants pierced him through with a lance before he could strike again. Melisend had the great beast skinned and gave its hide as a trophy to her guest. Eleanor kept it ever after as one of her most treasured possessions.

Once Melisend took her companion along a rough trail leading from Jerusalem's height precipitously down nearly two thousand feet to the level of the Dead Sea. Eleanor was astonished at the sudden change in temperature. It was a freezing cold day in January when they left Jerusalem. They felt uncomfortably hot a few hours later when they arrived at the shores of the Dead Sea where even the foliage was tropical. Melisend, however, did not rest until she brought exclamations from Eleanor's lips at the sight of several pillars of salt. The most twisted and deformed, Melisend said, was the very one into which Lot's wife had been turned when she disobeyed the Lord and looked back at Sodom.

Eleanor passed the time pleasantly enough, entertained by such diversions, until the revolving months brought springtide once more to carpet the hills and valleys with such a wealth of color as Eleanor had never before seen. Nevertheless, she was delighted to hear Louis announce early in March that he would leave for France shortly after Easter. It was hard to leave these sacred places so dear to his heart, so gravely threatened by the growing power of the Infidel. But Abbot Suger had again written begging him to hasten back to his kingdom, whose peace was threatened by his brother and other barons disposed to take advantage of his absence.

Louis kept silent about another item in Suger's letter, though it had quieted his thoughts. Louis had written to the abbot while his feelings were still in a state of turmoil over the queen's conduct at Antioch. In the letter the king had revealed his violent resentment at Eleanor's relations with Prince Raymond and had shown deep concern over her claim that God was punishing him for their unlawful marriage by denying a male heir to the crown. In his reply the abbot had soothed the king's spirit by advising him to act as though nothing had happened until he returned home, when they could consult about the matter. This advice fell in with Louis's feelings which had long since begun to moderate.

Many factors had contributed to this attitude during the months which had elapsed between the writing of his own letter and the receipt of Suger's reply. Constant formal association with his wife at Melisend's court, during which Eleanor had discretely refrained from any reference to the unlawfulness of their marriage, her otherwise exemplary conduct, and his own fondness for her had all tended to restore at least friendly relations between them. So it was with somewhat kindlier feelings on both sides that the king and queen of France began their preparations to leave for home. These were soon completed. The royal couple bade farewell to their hosts and headed for the valley of Esdraelon and the port of St. Jean d'Acre with a much reduced following.

Two vessels sufficed for the party, one for the king and his attendants, another for the queen and her companions. The Island of Rhodes was disappearing astern, several weeks later, when the lookout reported a ship just coming into sight far ahead on the horizon. Soon others appeared and the whole fleet made straight for the royal vessels. The anxiety of the French was heightened as the approaching ships, now identified as belonging to the Greek Emperor's navy, manoeuvered to encircle them and finally compelled them to stop. The Greek commander sent a crew and some soldiers to take charge of the queen's ship, while he himself boarded Louis's vessel. Emperor Manuel, it appeared, was desirous of seeing once more his good friend and brother, the king of France, and had dispatched this fleet to guide him safely to the city on the Bosphorus. The silken words of the invitation did not prevent Louis from suspecting that Manuel's real purpose was to keep him away from the emperor's mortal enemy, Roger the Norman, King of Sicily. The Greek admiral said he would take personal charge of the queen, while the king might follow in his own vessel. Perhaps King Louis would not object to signing, purely as a matter of form, a written promise that he would follow on to Constantinople in case he became separated from the admiral's protection. Louis was caught. Even the clever Thierry Gualeran could suggest no way of escape from these Greek wiles. Consequently, Louis accepted the situation with what grace he could. The scroll was drawn up and Louis was about to sign when his hand was stayed by the sounds of shouts and trampling about on the deck above.

The Greek admiral rushed up the companionway and saw to his consternation that an enemy fleet twice the size of his own was approaching. Eleanor and her companions saw the attackers' powerful galleys, driven by double banks of oars, ram and sink two of the imperial ships. The attackers bound themselves to other imperial ships with grappling irons, then fought the Greeks on the decks. The struggle was sharp but short. The outnumbered Greeks were soon forced to give up. The rescuers had been sent out by King Roger, who was determined that Manuel should not snatch the French king away from him a second time.

When Roger's Admiral Gregory boarded the king's ship, Louis complimented him on his victory, then begged that he show mercy to the captured Greeks. The Emperor of Constantinople was a Christian ruler, and though he had permitted the Turks to harass the French in Asia Minor, he had entertained the crusaders and given them some assistance. Admiral Gregory finally yielded to the French king's insistence and released the Greeks. After disposing his fleet to protect his royal guests' vessels, he headed for Crete and Sicily.

That very night a fierce storm scattered Gregory's ships far and wide. Louis scanned the horizon next morning for a sight of Eleanor's ship but could find no trace of it. For weeks, his anxiety mounting every day, he paced the deck until the southern shores of Italy were sighted. He stepped ashore only to meet with disappointment: Eleanor was not there. After three weeks, a rumor that her ship had been sighted off the shore of Africa determined Louis to seek her there. But before he took ship, word came from Eleanor herself that she was safe. After having been driven far out of its course, her ship had finally rounded the western end of Sicily and reached Palermo. Eleanor had been most warmly received at the royal palace, where she would halt only long enough to recruit her strength. The queen followed her letter within a few days.

Louis was now ready to accept King Roger's invitation to visit him at Potenza. Here Roger received them both with unaffected pleasure and a magnificence that rivaled anything they had experienced either at Constantinople or at Antioch. He reëquipped Louis and his entire company with horses, garments, and weapons. He added to Eleanor's purchases from the bazaars of Jerusalem other products of the Orient. Two gifts in particular, quite diverse in character, endeared King Roger to Eleanor. When he discovered that she had acquired in the East a taste for sugar, he insisted that she carry back with her a twenty-pound chest of it; when he found out her delight in literature, he presented her with a beautifully illuminated copy of Boethius' *De consolatione philosophiae.*

The royal party, after three days, set out on its journey northward up the peninsula, guided by King Roger's men until, beyond Naples, the limits of Roger's kingdom were reached. At this point the royal party was met by an escort sent by the Pope, Eugenius III, to guide them through his dominions. They turned aside at the foot of Monte Cassino and climbed up the height, to be welcomed by the abbot of that famous monastery. Here they were detained by an illness that seized the queen. The tedium of convalescence was relieved by the librarian, who brought in for her inspection from time to time some of his choicest treasures. One of these especially attracted Eleanor, not so much by its beauty as by its contents. It was a small volume by the Latin poet, Ovid, entitled *Ars amatoria.* The queen begged the monk to have a copy of it made and sent to her.

Shortly after the journey was resumed they came in sight of the towers of the papal residence at Tusculum, where Eugenius received them as an old friend, resolved to remove all causes of ill-feeling between them. The pope had not only heard the rumors of their quarrel at Antioch, he had been more explicitly informed about the matter by Suger. The abbot had emphasized the supreme importance of one thing: the necessity of removing the haunting fear rooted in the king's mind that his marriage was accursed and that therefore he would never have a male heir. The king's fear was groundless. A year had elapsed since the affair at Antioch, and Louis's ardent devotion to his wife seemed to be completely restored. Now the couple must be induced to resume normal marital relations as quickly as possible. Let his Holiness look especially to that. Once a male heir was born, the question of annulment would be forgotten forever. Internal peace and the possession of Aquitaine would be assured. In the name of the Blessed Denis, let the pope by prayers and deeds secure this boon for France.

Pope Eugenius was devoted to France and scarcely needed the abbot's exhortations to use every means in his power to bring about a reconciliation between the royal couple. Moreover, he loved the devout young king and his vivid queen. So the elderly pope greeted the returning pilgrims with unwonted warmth.

After his guests had had opportunity to rest and refresh themselves, Eugenius withdrew them to a small, comfortably furnished room. He wasted no time in coming directly to the point.

He abruptly asked Eleanor why she had raised the question of blood relationship and what proof she had that she and Louis were related within the seventh degree. Eleanor, startled by the question, replied that her Uncle Raymond, who claimed to know the family history, had insisted that she and her husband were related within the prohibited degrees; also that Abbot Bernard of Clairvaux and others had made mention of the matter. Pressed for details, she became badly entangled in the branches of her family tree, to say nothing of Louis's. She insisted, however, that their common ancestor was a certain William the Tow-head, Duke of Aquitaine, whose daughter was said to have married Hugh Capet from whom the kings of France had descended straight down to her husband.

Eugenius pointed out the guesswork and doubtful inferences which made this story of the remote relationship utterly unreliable, and then asked Louis if he had any proof that they were too nearly related. The king declared that he had none. He only knew that there had been talk of it by the learned bishop of Laon, the holy Bernard, and others. But the fact which troubled him most was that no son had yet been born to him. This made him fear that God held his marriage accursed.

A faint smile played about the lips of the pope as he gently reminded Louis that he was still a mere youth of thirty, and that his wife would be capable of bearing children for nearly a score of years to come. In that space of time, more than one boy might easily be born to them. It was far too early to give up hope, at all events; far too early to think of any curse resting on his marriage. The very next child might be a boy. He would himself besiege the throne of God with daily petitions to that end. There must never again be any mention of this baseless claim between him and his wife. It must be completely forgotten. He would solemnly confirm their marriage both by word and by writing, and would prohibit under threat of anathema anyone from impugning it. Eleanor's heart sank when she heard these words, but all Louis's doubts were set at rest. With tears in his eyes, he reverently kneeled before the pope, thanking him for the great boon conferred upon him. Then he rose and turned with outstretched arms to his wife. But Eleanor, though she felt constrained to accept her husband's embrace, was not happy. She yielded to the situation since she saw for the moment no other way out. Nor did she realize, for that matter, along what path she was being led.

Eugenius was determined to make sure that the marriage should be reconsummated that very night.

For the moment he turned the conversation to other topics and began by drawing his guests out on the subject of their recent experiences. He listened with intentness to the recital of Manuel's attempt to make them return through Constantinople and of the dramatic way in which King Roger had thwarted this move, since the relations of these rival powers bore directly on his own political interest. He was equally interested in the royal couple's impressions of the ambitious king of Sicily. When the queen expressed her delight in the gardens at Palermo, Eugenius suggested a stroll in his own. He led them from the gardens, talking familiarly the while, back to the chapel for vespers. The short service over, he had them partake of the evening meal with him in private. Then after compline, Eugenius prepared for his great stroke. He suggested that they must now wish to retire, and led the way to a chamber richly furnished, but provided with but one bed. When Eleanor grasped the pope's intention, she hesitated at the entrance. But the beneficent Eugenius took her gently by the hand and said: "My children, I wish you to sleep together in this bed. I shall most earnestly beseech the Holy Mother of God for a child to be conceived tonight who shall bring happiness to you both and security for the future of France." The stately old man added his blessing to these words of adjuration and walked slowly from the room.

The Queen Discards Her Crown 1149-1152

THE FOLLOWING DAY WAS SPENT IN FURTHER IN-TIMATE CONVERSE, varied by the presentation of gifts. The pope gave to Louis an illuminated breviary and one of the most beautiful diamonds the world has ever seen; to Eleanor, a magnificently embroidered robe of state and an illuminated hymnal. This volume, Eugenius said, was peculiarly precious to him because of its contents: melodious sequences composed by the gifted Adam of St. Victor's. The tunes to which they were to be sung were represented in such a way that they could be accurately reproduced. The system of notation, an advance over older methods, had been worked out some years ago, he explained, by an Italian monk, Guido of Arezzo. Eleanor was immediately interested, for she admired Adam's work and had heard something about that of the Italian monk. She saw at once that the symbols showed how long to dwell on a note and that their position on the four-lined staff indicated with precision their relative pitch. Since she expressed a wish to see if she could reproduce the tunes, Eugenius sent for the precentor of the papal choir with instructions to bring a psaltery. This wire-stringed instrument was laid flat on a stand before her, and Eleanor tapped out the tunes with two small round-headed rods. The precentor complimented her on the correctness of the rendition, but said she should hear the hymns played on an organ and led her off to the chapel.

On the next day they took their departure. Eugenius made no effort to detain them longer. His own task had been accomplished with the Lord's aid. The stern old man could scarcely restrain his tears when they knelt before him for his parting blessing.

Early on the day after the departure from Tusculum, the royal party ascended a hill from whose crest, they were told, the city of Rome could be seen. At their first sight of the Eternal City there rose in the minds of all the familiar opening lines of the pilgrim hymn: *O Roma nobilis, orbis et domina,* O Rome the noble, ruler of the world. As they drew nearer the city, Eleanor saw the usual procession coming to meet them, headed this time by Roman senators and nobles. The more closely they approached the city the denser became the crowd of those welcoming them. The royal couple, once inside the city, began making the circuit of its innumerable holy places where monks, nuns and novices came forth to greet them, singing: *Benedictus qui venit in nomine Domini,* Blessed be he who cometh in the name of the Lord. Louis was determined to make the most of his one day in Rome, so he passed with tireless zeal from one shrine to another. Eleanor's interest flagged long before the day was over and she was relieved to sink down at last on a couch at the palace where they were to spend the night.

From Rome, the way led up the peninsula and over the Alps to the abbey of Cluny. Here Louis found Abbot Suger who had come to inform him of conditions in the realm.

Abbot Peter the Venerable took it upon himself to entertain the queen while the king and his minister were closeted together. Abbot Peter directed her steps toward the vast church then in process of building. As they picked their way through the work yards, Eleanor stopped before one of the sculptured capitals lying on the ground. Peter told her that it belonged to a series illustrating the seven liberal arts so necessary in the work of salvation. This particular one showed one of the musical tones. Later he pointed to carvings in the nave, showing men playing on musical instruments: harp, fiddle, lute, and dulcimer. Eleanor admired the play of fancy shown in other scenes, as well as the grandeur of the whole structure.

Before they returned to the refectory, Peter entered the cemetery. Here he showed Eleanor the spot where the remains of Peter Abelard had first been laid. The abbot said that he had later sent the body to the Paraclete at the request of its learned abbess, Héloise. The mention of these lovers, happy at least in their mutual passion, sharply reminded Eleanor that she was still yoked to one whose love she could never return.

From Cluny the royal couple proceeded to make their way toward Paris. During the journey, Eleanor's mind began to be increasingly disturbed by the suspicion that she had become pregnant. The suspicion had become a certainty by the time they arrived in Paris. Horrified by this turn of fortune's wheel, she nevertheless immediately conveyed the news to her husband, who rejoiced to hear it. All would now be well, Louis rashly concluded; for this time God would surely reward his hopes. Eleanor fluctuated between fear and hope. If she should give birth to a boy, her fate would be sealed: all Louis's doubts would be wiped away and she would have to resign herself to remaining his wife until her dying day. But if she should give birth to a girl, perhaps Louis's doubts could be revived. In that case she might still wrench herself free. She would pray for a girl.

July arrived at last and with it the day long awaited anxiously by the whole court. There gathered around Eleanor's bed shortly before the expected birth of the child not only physicians and the king, but also Count Ralph of Vermandois, Abbot Suger, and many other notable witnesses to the authenticity of the event. The whole audience waited with strained eagerness when at last the child arrived to learn the sex of the newborn infant. A sigh of regret swept through the hall as word went around that the baby was a girl. Louis bore the disappointment with what fortitude he might, supported by Suger's whispered encouragement. A close observer could have detected a faint smile on the queen's face.

Eleanor's first interest was to discover how Louis felt. He was disappointed that the Lord had not blessed their union with a boy, but said they must not give up hope. They were both young, and among the offspring to follow surely one would be a son. Though her husband spoke bravely, Eleanor thought she noticed a trace of irresolution. She felt sure that doubt about the lawfulness of their marriage had again begun to stir in his mind. She determined to strengthen this doubt in every possible way.

As month after month went by, the queen continually reminded the king that no sign of pregnancy had occurred. She spoke of her doubts to others and attempted to stimulate anxiety about the succession among the king's counselors. The continued failure of a male heir had before this time engaged the attention of the royal counselors. Some of them, indeed, had already suggested annulment of the king's marriage. The Antioch episode had increased the number favoring such a step. Nevertheless, Abbot Suger's influence with Louis remained dominant. He kept his statesman's eye fixed on the retention of Aquitaine and steadily encouraged the king in the hope of ultimately securing a male heir.

Yet Suger was not immortal. This ardent lover of the Saints, this able servant of France, passed to a well-earned rest in January of 1151. Suger's death opened the way for a realignment of forces at the French court, strengthening the party who favored divorce. Eleanor's path was being made easier. Her design was facilitated, also, by a series of political events which brought her, for the first time, face-to-face with young Henry Plantagenet, son of Geoffrey the Fair, Count of Anjou.

Count Goeffrey the Fair had succeeded in recent years in making good the claim of his wife, Matilda, daughter of Henry I, to the Duchy of Normandy and the County of Maine, which lay directly north of Anjou. Having secured these lands, he turned southward to attack a troublesome noble, Gerald of Montreuil-Bellay, who held a fief in the borderlands between Anjou and Poitou. Gerald had erected a castle at Montreuil, from which center he harassed the surrounding country. Count Geoffrey had taken and dismantled this stronghold after a year's siege and made captives of Gerald and his family. King Louis, on his return from the crusade, took up arms in behalf of Gerald, who represented the royal interests in Poitou. But the king was taken sick on the expedition and forced to resort to negotiations. In the course of these, Geoffrey agreed to come to Paris for a conference; and on the journey he brought with him his nineteen-year-old son, Henry, in order that the latter might render homage and receive investiture with Normandy which had been given to him by his father.

Queen Eleanor met Henry for the first time at this conference held in August, 1151.

Eleanor looked forward to this meeting with the utmost eagerness. The thought of Henry Plantagenet had been frequently on her mind ever since her uncle had spoken of him. Prince Raymond had expatiated on the vigor of Henry's character and on the brilliance of his prospects, but what was he like? She felt secure on one point at least, for Raymond had assured her that the young man was no saint.

Eleanor began her preparations for the crucial meeting determined to look her best. She summoned her tire-maidens and set about to make an elaborate toilette. Water was heated, a commodious tub brought in and filled. Eleanor felt much refreshed after her bath, though she had sighed for the refinements to which she had become accustomed in the East. Melisend had given her a silk chemise. This she put on first, and over it a long slip. Then she sat as patiently as she could while Elaine's practiced fingers plaited her hair in two braids which were brought forward over her shoulders and reached nearly to her knees. Next she bade Elaine fetch a richly embroidered dress, a closely fitted garment with long, tight sleeves. With the help of her tire-maidens, Eleanor put on the dress. She shook out the long pendants attached to the wrists, gave a few vigorous kicks to free her feet from the enveloping folds which swept the floor, and declared herself reasonably satisfied. The delicate task of applying rouge she entrusted to no one but herself, acutely conscious of the fact that she was dangerously near thirty, while the young man whom she wished to impress was not yet twenty. Next came red slippers of Cordovan leather, and around her slender waist she placed a girdle from which hung a beaded pouch containing keys and a handkerchief which exhaled a delicate perfume bought in the bazaars of Jerusalem. A sheath of embossed leather containing a small dagger-like knife also hung from the girdle. Her toilette was completed by the addition of a silken wimple which, bound over the head and under the chin and held tightly with jewelled pins, effectively framed her face. Elaine placed a wreath of daisies on her mistress' head as a final touch.

Eleanor was resplendent when she stood with Louis in the great hall to receive the nobles. She looked with eagerness on the group of men approaching. At their head were two figures, one of whom, from his more mature appearance, blond hair, and beard, the queen surmised to be Geoffrey the Fair. The broad-chested young man by his side, wearing his reddish hair closely cropped, could be none other than the duke of Normandy.

Eleanor's first impression of Henry of Anjou was of a figure undistinguished either for height or for grace: the cropped head, bull neck and slightly protuberant eyes were not calculated to attract a feminine observer. The young fellow's cape was askew, and in general he had the appearance of one who cared little about dress. Yet there was something about Henry's whole bearing that made an observer look twice. He was clearly no weakling. Eleanor felt even more convinced of this at the first glance of his penetrating grey eyes. Henry's first thought, as he gazed at the most talked-of woman of the day, was that she might well be expected to do the unusual. He did not dream how quickly he was to find his guess true; for Eleanor soon made up her mind. She felt convinced that, young as Henry was, he was already a man, and one who would have the daring to undertake the risks involved in her plans and the skill to carry them out. But the time of his visit was short; so if she wished to win him as an accomplice, she had no time to lose. The task was difficult but worth trying.

Her first opportunity came when the court gathered for a feast in the hall. The king and queen sat together at the center of a long table with Count Geoffrey on Louis's right and Duke Henry on Eleanor's left. During the course of the meal, the queen led the young duke on to talk of himself, his past life, his interests, and his prospects. She showed a deep interest in everything he told her and succeeded in getting on quite a friendly basis before the end of the meal. The conversation turned to hunting, and Eleanor mentioned that she possessed a white gerfalcon. Henry expressed such keen interest in this bird that Eleanor invited him to try it out with her the following day after mass.

Duke Henry could scarcely keep still at mass the next morning. He squirmed around, nudged his companions, and whispered to them. He directed their attention to a scene sculptured on one of the capitals, representing the bad children mocking Elisha, and laughed out loud at another which showed Jonah leaping from the whale's mouth. All at once, the queen noticed, he fished out a piece of charcoal from the miscellaneous contents of his pouch. With this he sketched on the shaft of a nearby pillar the rude outline of a bird. Eleanor, covertly watching, could hardly refrain from laughing. Nor could she help contrasting Louis's devout absorption in the service with Henry's utter lack of reverence. "Certainly Raymond was right," she thought; "the duke is no saint." Yet though no saint, Henry worshipped at the shrine of St. Hubert, patron of the hunt, as he proceeded to demonstrate when mass was over. Eleanor showed herself both a skilful and a tactful companion, and at the end of the day's sport, filled Henry's cup of bliss full by making him a present of the magnificent falcon in whose prowess he had taken unalloyed delight.

Duke Henry was detained a long while at a great council summoned the next day to debate the issues which had arisen between the king and Henry's father. It was not till late in the afternoon that Eleanor succeeded in securing a much desired tête-à-tête with Henry. It was high time, she felt, to disclose to him something of the plan which she was revolving anxiously in her mind. She had discovered that the duke shared her passion for chess and had challenged him to a game. Henry sought out the queen as soon as the adjournment of the council set him free. He found Eleanor superintending the watering of her flowers, sadly parched by the August drought, and demanded that she make good her challenge. She ordered a page to set out the board and chessmen on a bench in a retired corner of the garden. The couple seated themselves and began the game. Eleanor rejoiced to find in Henry an expert opponent, and became so intent on the play that she almost forgot herself. Rather than beat Henry at this game, it was her purpose to secure his coöperation in winning another. She suspected that he might prove to be a bad loser. She recollected herself just in time to move a knight in such a way that Henry was ultimately enabled to take her queen and at the same time triumphantly proclaim checkmate. In a flash, Eleanor saw the opening provided by this chance dénouement and boldly resolved to make the most of it. She remarked laughingly: "My lord Duke, you have taken a queen at chess. Could you, I wonder, capture one in the game of life?"

"Possibly, but I should have to see her first," Henry carelessly replied, his gaze still fixed on the board.

"My lord, you have but to raise your eyes."

Henry's head shot up. He stared at her in astonishment.

"What do you think of her?" continued Eleanor, with a coquettish turn of her head. "Is she not fair? Is she not worth a struggle?"

"By the eyes of God, yes!" exclaimed Henry, jumping to his feet and scattering the chessmen on the ground. "But you speak in riddles, my lady. One must have the skill of Merlin e'er he could read them."

"Have you not," rejoined Eleanor, "heard the rumors circulating about the court that my lord the king, gravely disturbed over the blood-relationship existing between us, thinks daily more seriously of annulling our marriage? Our wedded life has extended for nearly fifteen years and still there has been born to us no son, no heir to ensure a peaceful continuance of the monarchy. God denies this boon, my lord Louis thinks, because he is angered at our unholy wedlock. Therefore, he and many others feel that our marriage should be dissolved, if God is to bless him with a son."

In reply to Henry's query as to how she felt about the matter, Eleanor very frankly exposed her mind. She knew not whether God was angered at their union, but she herself was much irked by it. Louis was devoted to her, but he was too pious, too absorbed in monkish ritual. She would be glad to be freed from the restraints of this marriage, free to return to the South, to her own Aquitaine.

But would she be free, would she be permitted to resume control of her duchy? Henry inquired. Would the French monarchy allow this vast territory to slip from its grasp without a struggle after having held it for fifteen years? Would not Louis and his counselors force her to renounce her rights and enter a nunnery rather than lose such a prize? "Let them try," flared Eleanor. "They'll find me hard to hold." Yet it would be a difficult situation, she admitted; it would not be easy for her, unaided, to defend her independence. "Had I a man by my side, I would fear nothing." She reminded him that his ancestors, the counts of Anjou, had been anxious to extend their control southward over Poitou for generations. She allowed her hand to rest seductively on the board and said: "If you accept this hand, you will win at a blow more than your ancestors ever dreamed of. You will control more of France than Louis himself."

Henry, fired by this appeal to his ambition and daring, seized Eleanor's proffered hand and kissed it. Then as Eleanor rose and moved closer to him, he embraced her passionately. Pushing Henry gently from her, Eleanor said: "Softly, softly, my lord—the dissolution is yet to be procured."

Before the week was over, King Louis and Count Geoffrey reached an amicable agreement. Gerald and his family were to be set at liberty, but were to be bound by oath never to rebuild the castle of Montreuil. Geoffrey gave up all claim to a portion of the Vexin, the small but strategic piece of territory between Normandy and the royal domain. In return for this concession, Louis confirmed Geoffrey's cession of Normandy to Henry, received the latter's homage, and gave him investiture with the duchy.

On the following day, Geoffrey, Henry, and their retinue set out for home. Count Geoffrey noticed the splendid bird which Henry was carrying on his wrist as they rode along, and asked him how it came into his possession. When he learned that the falcon was a gift from the queen, Geoffrey remarked on the rapidity with which Henry had won his way into Eleanor's good graces and on the frequency with which he had been seen in her company. "Have a care, my son, have a care," he said, thinking it time for some fatherly admonition. "The less you have to do with that woman the better. She is an imprudent person, dangerous as she is beautiful, if all that is said of her be true. Never forget, too, that she is the consort of your liege lord and suzerain, whose man you have just become and whose honor you have sworn to uphold in every way." Henry was silent for a moment, pondering his father's words. Finally he decided to tell him the daring proposal which the queen had made, without going into the details of their interview.

Geoffrey's face reflected astonishment and concern as his son sketched out the plan. He could scarcely wait for Henry to finish before bursting out with maledictions on the queen and fierce commands to his son to have nothing to do with such a scheme. Any attempt to carry it out, he said, would be bound to end in failure. The king, with all the barons of France at his back, would rush to the attack. Henry would be much more likely to lose Normandy than to acquire Aquitaine. Never as long as he lived, said the father, would he permit a son of his to engage in any such foolhardy venture. "Gently, gently, father," Henry rejoined, "the annulment is not yet procurred and may never be. But if it is, there will be many a baron who will try to seize both the Lady Eleanor and her lands. By the eyes of God, I'll not stand idly by, twiddling my thumbs, while another man seizes such a prize."

Eleanor's plans might have received a rude check, had Count Geoffrey lived. But farther on the journey, the sight of the river Loir's cool waters tempted Geoffrey to take a plunge at the end of a hot day's ride. The shock proved fatal: he received a chill from the effects of which he died a few days later, on the seventh of September. His death made Henry the head of the Angevin house and master of his own fate. One of his first acts was to hurry off a messenger to Paris with the news.

When Eleanor learned how fortune had played into her hands, she became all the more determined to prepare the way for divorce. She worked upon her husband's sensitive conscience by commenting daily on her barrenness since the birth of little Adele nearly a year and a half ago. She made herself increasingly unpleasant to the venemous Thierry Gualeran in the hope that this mortal enemy might more strongly urge on Louis the advisability of ridding himself of such a consort. She flirted outrageously with every gallant at court in order to stimulate among the clergy the feeling that it was high time for the king to separate himself from a woman who showed such scant respect for the royal dignity. She counted above all on the abbot of Clairvaux. Bernard's influence was supreme, now that Suger was no longer there to oppose him. He was a fanatical advocate of the canonical laws regulating the sacrament of marriage. His views on the unlawfulness of the king's marriage were well known. The abbot might move her husband to take decisive action, if she could but work Louis up to the point of consulting him formally on this subject.

Bernard attended court at Christmastide of that year, 1151. Louis was persuaded to consult him. The abbot's reply was so blunt that the king was crushed. For Louis it was as though he had heard the voice of God. He had contravened the laws of the Church, Bernard said, by marrying a woman related to him within the forbidden degrees. He had angered God by this act, endangered his own soul and the safety of the monarchy. There was no escape for him; the marriage must be annulled.

The report of this verdict brought a surge of joy to Eleanor. She concealed her happiness, however, as she had no wish to hurt her husband. He had been consistently considerate throughout their married life. She respected his deep feeling for her, though she had never been able to return it. Nevertheless, she bent every energy to hasten the annulment. One necessary preliminary was to have the king's men withdrawn from the key castles in Aquitaine, if she was to secure her independent action after divorce. She was relieved to find that Louis offered no objection to this proposal. He was apparently too much depressed at losing her to give thought to the retention of her lands. In January the royal couple set out on a journey which carried them through the circuit of Eleanor's possessions. They returned to Paris early in March and learned that arrangements for the annulment proceedings had been completed.

The council was held in the royal castle of Beaugency on the Loire, fifteen miles southwest of Orleans. A great assemblage gathered for this important procedure: high dignitaries of the Church, relatives of the king, and the great barons of the realm. The ecclesiastics acting as judges took their places at one end of the hall. The king was seated at their right hand; at their left, the queen. The first witness, a relative of the king, was called, came forward, and stood ready to swear the necessary oath. It was a tense moment for the queen. What if someone should protest? Eleanor gripped the arms of her chair and leaned forward, scarcely able to bear the suspense. But the first witness, and each of his successors, swore without the least hesitation that their royal sovereign, King Louis, was related by blood to the most noble Lady Eleanor within the seventh degree. No protesting voice was raised, and the annulment of the marriage was formally pronounced. Eleanor did not relax until the last word was said; then she went suddenly limp, unable to move. But she was herself again in a moment. She rose from her chair, addressed the court, accepted the judgment as just, bade them all a formal farewell, and swept grandly down the hall. Louis kept his eyes intently fixed upon her, as one in a dream, till she passed from his sight, out of the gloomy hall and into the sunlight.

Freedom and a New Alliance 1152

ELEANOR QUICK-ENED HER PACE AFTER SHE HAD LEFT THE HALL. SHE was free, free at last; but she was not safe. She knew, as Henry had warned her, that once the news of the dissolution of her marriage spread abroad, her person and lands would be considered fair game. She must make all speed back to her own country where she would be among friends. Consequently, she hurried to her quarters, where attendants stood waiting with horses saddled and mules loaded with chests and bundles. She pulled on her gloves, mounted her palfrey, and started off.

Beaugency luckily was near the southern boundary of the royal domain, well on the road toward Blois and the southwest. Eleanor planned to stop for the night at Blois. Its young lord, Count Thibaud, she knew well, and felt sure of a courteous welcome from him.

Thibaud did indeed readily open the gates of his castle, but when he learned that his guest was no longer the queen of France but the unwed, unprotected duchess of Aquitaine, his ambition was aroused. Why should he not keep for himself this royal bird that had flown into his cage? He could offer her both protection and an illustrious name. Was he not the descendant of that great William who had made himself king of England, and was not his Uncle Stephen king of England at this very moment? His generous brother, Henri, now become, since their father's death, count of Champagne, would support him. His own good looks, his courtly training, should certainly recommend his person to the duchess.

Count Thibaud did his utmost to make a favorable impression upon his guest. He urged her, after she had had refreshment, to prolong her stay, and invited her to go hunting with him in the morning. Eleanor begged to be excused, on the plea that she must quickly seek the protection of her vassals. Thibaud gallantly offered himself as her vassal for life. He protested that he had always admired her from afar, and urged her to accept his hand. The duchess, amused at the suddenness of this proposal, politely but firmly declined his offer. Thibaud was not, however, to be put off so easily. He went tiresomely over the advantages of the match until Eleanor lost patience and sharply repeated her refusal. She rose and bade the count a curt good night, requesting to be shown to her apartment. Thibaud, his pride wounded, determined to show her that he was not to be so lightly turned aside. He changed his tone and brusquely said: "Very well, my lady, retire if you wish. I trust you will find your quarters comfortable; for I propose to keep you here a while as my guest. Perhaps a few days' reflection may induce you to look with less scorn upon the idea of becoming the countess of Blois."

Eleanor replied, with a bow of mock humility, "As you wish, my lord," turned, and quickly left the hall.

When Eleanor reached her room, she sent one of her pages to explore the possibilities of quitting the castle that night without raising an alarm. The lad darted away, to return in a short while with the report that, with good luck, an escape might be managed. They would be able to pass into the outer bailey, if the drawbridge were not raised. There was an unguarded postern gate in the wall of the bailey near the quarters where their men-at-arms were lodged with the horses and baggage. He was not sure what was on the other side. Eleanor decided to make the attempt.

The little procession started in the dead of night. They tip-toed down the narrow winding staircase, and past men-at-arms sleeping in the great hall. The page carefully slid back the bolts of the huge doors and opened one of them noiselessly. They found to their relief that the drawbridge had not been raised. These were times of peace and the guarded main gateway in the outer wall was considered sufficient for protection. The party moved on quickly to reach the attendants who had the horses ready, saddled and loaded. The page led on to the postern door, peered out, and gave a smothered exclamation of dismay: the moat had no foot-bridge. But a scout reported that the moat was almost dry, so they began the descent and after much scrambling and muttered curs-ing, found themselves on the other side. Eleanor murmured a prayer of gratitude to the Virgin, seated herself in the saddle, and urged the party forward on the road to Tours.

At dawn they left Thibaud's dominions and entered Tou-raine. This territory was under Henry Plantagenet's control, so Eleanor felt somewhat safer. Nevertheless, after her experience at Blois she decided to avoid castles, and chose as her next stop the great monastery of St. Martin at Tours. The guardian of its gate no sooner learned the identity of the visitors than he opened wide the doors and led them to the guest quarters attached to the abbot's residence. Abbot Michel, informed of their arrival, came quickly to greet them and had brought for their immediate re-freshment glasses of the sparkling Vouvrais for which the abbey was famous. Then Eleanor spoke briefly to the abbot of the events which had brought her to his door and asked if she might remain at the abbey for the night.

Shortly after Eleanor had withdrawn to prepare herself for supper, a clatter of hoofs announced the arrival of another party at the abbey's gate. The leader of the small group of horsemen, an athletic youth of eighteen, leaped from his horse, threw the bridle to his squire, walked to the entrance, and announced himself as Geoffrey, son of the late Lord Geoffrey the Fair, Count of Anjou. He had come on a pious errand for his brother, Henry, now the reigning count of Anjou and duke of Normandy, who wished to endow a chapel in the abbey church where masses might be said perpetually for the rest of his father's soul. Abbot Michel went to greet Geoffrey and had just had time to tell him that the divorced duchess was in the abbey, and to relate her troubles with Count Thibaud, when Eleanor herself appeared.

Geoffrey was a rash young man, a younger son who envied his brother Henry's great estates and his chance to gain the crown of England. He was not at all inclined to censure Thibaud's ambitious plan: he merely despised him for his lack of success. Now looking upon the beauty of Eleanor, Geoffrey himself was moved with desire and ambition. He set out to make himself agreeable. Eleanor conversed with him eagerly, anxious to learn of his elder brother. Henry, Geoffrey reported, had been busy since his father's death. He had travelled this way and that to receive homage from his vassals and to put down the lawless who sought to profit by his youth. He had recently gone northward to deal with some recalcitrant barons in Normandy.

Their talk was interrupted by Abbot Michel who led the way to the refectory. While they were at table, the talk flowed on. There was gossip of one thing and another. When Abbot Michel asked her what route she would take to Poitiers, Eleanor answered carelessly that she would go to her mother's old home, Châtellerault, by the ferry across the river Creuse at the Port de Piles. To this information Geoffrey listened intently.

The next morning Eleanor awoke late, much refreshed. She was to remain a whole day at St. Martin's, to allow the horses to recuperate. The next stage was to be a long one, for she intended to make no other halt till safe in her uncle's castle of Châtellerault. She spent a lazy day, and after compline that night Abbot Michel was showing her a beautifully illuminated manuscript of the renowned Bishop Gregory's *History of the Franks* when a visitor arrived. He proved to be a former member of the monastery, now chaplain at the nearby castle. He was at first hesitant about broaching the subject of his visit in the presence of the duchess. He made bold to begin, however, since what he had to say concerned her so nearly.

The chaplain was disturbed by a venture in which his young master, Lord Geoffrey, seemed about to engage. He was not certain of its exact nature, but was afraid it concerned the Lady Eleanor. He had been reared near the Port de Piles, and Lord Geoffrey had called him aside that morning after mass to question him about the crossing there. Later in the day the chaplain had heard Lord Geoffrey mention the Lady Eleanor's name to his companions, and the word "ambush" had reached his ears. Furthermore, his lord, with three companions and a dozen men-at-arms, had mounted their chargers only a short time before, and ridden off southward. The chaplain felt that her Ladyship should be warned that something was afoot.

There was no doubt at all in the minds of the duchess and the abbot as to the nature of Geoffrey's plans. They were certain that he was bent on attempting to succeed where Thibaud had failed. Both of them thanked the chaplain for his warning and Eleanor pressed on him a purse of coins as he was departing. In the counsel that followed, it was agreed that the crossing at the Port de Piles must be avoided. Fortunately, the abbey owned a manor on the river Creuse about five miles upstream from the Port de Piles. Abbot Michel assured Eleanor that even if the river proved unfordable there, the men of the manor would certainly be able to get the party across in boats.

Early the next morning the duchess' party was again on the move. Eleanor was in high spirits, keyed up by the thought of possible danger, though she hoped they would frustrate Geoffrey's plans. They followed the main road till well into the afternoon, then went off onto a less-travelled path branching to the left. A couple of hours' ride along this detour brought them to the manor house. Amidst the barking of dogs they were admitted to the courtyard where they were glad to dismount. There in the rude hall of the dwelling, Eleanor and her companions devoured the coarse bread and cheese, and drank the wine set before them by the bailiff. Explaining that the water was too high for fording, the bailiff offered them two scows for the crossing. Two trips, and the whole party was on the far side. They continued their way slowly over the rough trail till they entered the main road again at the village of Dange. The party quickened pace, and it was not long before the keep of her uncle's castle at Châtellerault gladdened Eleanor's eyes. She rode into the friendly courtyard just as the long twilight deepened into gloom. Vicomte Hugh, though surprised, welcomed his niece warmly. At supper, Eleanor briefly explained her situation, then excused herself and retired to rest.

The following morning Eleanor regaled her uncle with details of her escape from her would-be suitors. They laughed heartily together at the picture of Geoffrey waiting futilely at the Port de Piles. Eleanor kept a discreet silence about her plans for the future. Eager to reach Poitiers and send a messenger to Duke Henry, she soon bade the vicomte farewell and she and her party set off for home. The familiar road followed up the valley of the quietly flowing Clain. A day's ride brought them at last around the shoulder of a steep cliff, where they caught their first sight of Poitiers. Eleanor reined in her horse and sat for a moment gazing happily at the familiar walls. She was home at last.

After a night's rest, Eleanor's first care was to inform Henry that she was free. It must be done in utmost secrecy so that Louis should not be forewarned of her intended marriage. She decided not to trust the message orally to any messenger, nor even to dictate it to her old friend, Pierre the chaplain. No, she must write it herself, and she was thankful that Pierre had taught her the art. Accordingly, she made her way up the winding stairway in Maubergeonne's Tower to her grandfather's old writing nook. Fortunately, the chaplain had taken over this spot as his study, so she found ready to her hand a writing desk, pens, ink, ruler, and some blank parchment leaves. Eleanor sat down resolutely to work.

It was no easy task to write fairly on parchment. Eleanor's fingers grew stiff and her back ached before she finished. But at last the important missive was completed. Eleanor gazed at it with satisfaction. It was no work of art but it was legible. Fortunately, she reflected, Henry could read Latin, for he had been tutored by William of Conches, a great scholar. Her secret would be revealed to no prying eye, but to Henry's alone. She hoped the letter would find him still anxious to have her, as well as her lands. She told him that she was free and fully mistress of Poitou and Aquitaine. All the royal castellans, prevosts, and bailiffs had been withdrawn, and their places filled with vassals and servants loyal to herself. All was in readiness: he had but to come and claim her. Had he the courage to dare the venture? There were some who had already tried to seize her, among them his brother Geoffrey. There might be others; he had best hurry.

After she had dispatched the letter, Eleanor found plenty to keep her busy for the first week or two. House-cleaning was the first task to which she devoted herself. The castle was in a frightful state, particularly the old main hall; the Tower hall and the apartments above were in better condition. The hard-packed earthen floor of the main hall was covered with old rushes, bones, and other refuse. This litter was all taken out and burned in the courtyard. The floor was then swept clean with twig brooms and covered with clean hay. The table-boards and the wooden horses on which they rested were scrubbed and replaced in orderly fashion, inclined against the walls, ready for the next meal. The stone floor of the Tower hall was more easily cleaned.

The rooms on the second floor Eleanor decided to use as her own. The task of furnishing these was one of pure delight. The chests containing her belongings were brought up, their contents hastily examined and laid aside ready for use. Memories of the bazaars at Jerusalem flooded her mind. The room soon began to bear no small resemblance to one of these, with rugs, hangings, cushions, bronze and ivory caskets, ebony taborets, and a copper brazier or two scattered around helter-skelter. Eleanor rose after a while to survey the confusion she had wrought and began to plan how she would arrange the things in the larger room and the smaller one adjoining it. For her old couch she would have a new mattress made, stuffed with hair instead of straw and covered with a silk coverlet. She would place some of the smaller rugs on the window seats, refinements introduced by the Troubadour when he had built the Tower. She would have cushions everywhere. She wished she had a chair or two with backs, such as she had been used to in Antioch and Jerusalem. The thought of Jerusalem brought to mind Melisend and the lion skin. The huge trophy was pulled out from a chest and stretched in tawny magnificence on the floor before the fireplace.

Eleanor looked ruefully at the window openings. She wished they could be made wider and fitted with glass. Perhaps some day she could manage it, though the walls, even at this height, were still five or six feet thick. The glass she might obtain from Chartres where glaziers were still working. From alterations in the Tower, her thoughts turned to improvements in the great hall. It would be wonderful to renovate the whole castle, making it more livable, more like the palaces she had so admired in the East.

As often as she could snatch time from her labors indoors, Eleanor would betake herself to the plaisance. Here the flowers would soon be coming to life. Buds had already started on the half-dozen linden trees, and the old pine tree was as vigorous as ever. The plaisance was rather formless compared to the palm-shaded courts of Syria and Palestine, yet the spot had a charm of its own. Eleanor, trowel in hand, kept the attendants busy planting and transplanting, fetching pail after pail of water.

Eleanor scarcely expected to hear from Henry before the end of the third week, but her anxiety mounted as the fourth week passed without a word. She was about to dispatch another messenger when her first one returned. In her eagerness, she almost snatched from his hand the packet held out to her. But she suddenly hesitated, struck by the fear that Duke Henry might have refused. Then with a quick gesture she tore the parchment from its pouch. "My Lady Eleanor," she read, "I dare the venture. I will be with you soon. My heart is yours." Eleanor almost wept with relief and happiness. She had won Henry. She had outwitted the court of France. Aquitaine was safe.

The messenger told her, in explanation of his delay, that he had tracked the duke from Rouen to Jumièges and Caen, and had finally caught up with him near the boundaries of Brittany. Duke Henry had received him courteously, read the letter with deep interest, and sent him off to be hospitably treated. Early the next morning, the duke had delivered his reply with orders to make all speed back to the duchess.

Eleanor wished that Henry had been more explicit as to the date of his arrival, though she realized that he must leave no centers of disturbance behind him. He would have plenty of trouble on his hands the moment the news of their marriage became public—the king of France would see to that. For her part, she must make certain that her Aquitainian subjects would support her. To this end she had already caused notifications to be sent out stating that she was now countess of Poitou and duchess of Aquitaine in her own right, owing to the dissolution of her marriage. In consequence, every vassal must render homage and swear fealty anew if he wished to hold his lands in peace. Chaplain Pierre, aided by skilled clerks from the nearby abbey of St. Hilaire, had busied himself in writing out these documents while Eleanor had had the die for a proper seal designed and cut.

For this delicate task she had secured from the abbey of Montierneuf a monk skilled in the engraver's art. After several attempts, he made a sketch which was reasonably satisfactory to the duchess. It represented her standing, full-face, bare-headed, holding in her right hand a flower stem with three blossoms, in her left a falcon. The exaggerated slimness of the figure made her look, Eleanor said, like a nun after a thirty days' fast. Nevertheless, it would have to do: it carried her name, her style as duchess of the Aquitainians, countess of the Poitevins, and the traditional symbols of her house. So she ordered the artist-craftsman to cut the die at once, since the notifications would soon be ready. When the documents were completed, the round waxen seal stamped with the new die was attached. They were then entrusted to horsemen who carried them to their widely scattered points of destination.

By these measures, Eleanor counted on bringing together at Poitiers about the time of the marriage a goodly number of the more important barons who would lend dignity to the ceremony. Her vassals, each attended by a group of his own knights and men-at-arms, began to arrive shortly after she had received Henry's reply.

First to ride up was a former counselor of her father's, Saldebreuil, whom she immediately appointed her seneschal. Then followed Hugh, Vicomte de Châtellerault, accompanied by another of her mother's brothers, Raoul de Faye, shifty and shrewd. Next came Eleanor's neighbor, Hugh de Lusignan, trouble-maker par excellence. His entrance was followed by that of the bishop of Saintonge, shepherding Eleanor's Aunt Agnes, Abbess of Saintes, eager to have all her convent's grants of lands and privileges renewed and to secure new ones if possible. She brought along with her two young cousins to add to the group of tire-maidens which the duchess was forming about herself. Eleanor's warmest welcome was reserved for her former guardian, Geoffrey du Lauroux, Archbishop of Bordeaux, along with whom came the Gascon barons. The rooms of the castle were soon filled and the duchess was obliged to lodge her guests in the nearby monasteries and the homes of wealthy citizens.

Another problem began to be somewhat embarrassing, that of detaining these people, summoned, as they thought, merely to offer homage and fealty and to receive reinvestiture of their fiefs. The first to arrive had now been at Poitiers nearly two weeks and were anxious to return home. Eleanor strove to distract them with hunting and jousting by day, with the songs and recitals of jongleurs by night, but she grew more and more anxious. What possessed the duke that he waited so long! It was near the middle of May, and still he had not come.

Her anxiety often drove her to ascend the winding stairway of Maubergeonne's Tower. From the roof she could see for many miles the road by which Henry would come. Eleanor's vigil was at last rewarded. One evening she saw rising against the golden sky a cloud of dust. There gradually emerged from this a small group of horsemen riding at a furious gallop. Could it really be Henry? Convinced at last that it was, she rapidly descended the dark stairway. She passed by a passageway from the hall of the Tower to the main hall where she found a large number of guests had already assembled, preparatory to sitting down for the evening meal. The duchess made her way through the crowd to the dais where she tried to conceal her excitement by conversing gaily with those around her. She watched the entrance covertly while the moments seemed to drag themselves out into hours. Would he never come?

Before long there was an unusual stir at the entrance. The assembled guests, drawing aside to let the strangers pass, wondered who they might be. They were not kept in ignorance long; for, as the young noble knelt to kiss her hand, Eleanor raised him up, made him stand beside her, and said: "My lords of Poitou and Aquitaine, I have an announcement of great moment. My Lord Henry here, Duke of Normandy and Count of Anjou, has done me the honor to ask my hand in marriage. I have accepted him as a man of high birth, capable of giving me and my possessions protection against all dangers, from whatever source they may threaten. We have neither sought for nor received the consent of the king of France. As duke of Normandy and duchess of Aquitaine we rule more than half of his kingdom. What boots his wrath to us? Should he, in the name of my daughters by him, attempt to wrench from us this land of ours, I count on you, descendants of vassals long faithful to the house of Poitou, to hurl him back. What say you, my lords, do you accept Lord Henry as your future duke, and will you stand by him and me in the protection of our lawful possessions?" The astonished nobles held silence for a moment, then roared their assent. Upon this, Henry instantly stepped forward to thank them for their acceptance of him and to promise that they would ever find in him one who would protect their rights. Eleanor then motioned for silence and invited them to attend mass the following morning in the cathedral where, with the consent of the Lord Bishop, the marriage would be solemnized.

The War of Eleanor's Husbands 1152-1153

ELEANOR'S SEC-
OND HONEY-
MOON WAS
BRIEF. BOTH SHE AND
Henry realized that theirs
was a precarious position.
They had flouted King
Louis's authority and must
be prepared for attack. This
would fall on Normandy,
Henry felt certain, so to
Normandy he was anxious
to return. Eleanor did not
seek to detain him. The two weeks of his stay at Poitiers had been
long enough to assure them that there was no immediate danger
to be feared in Aquitaine. The critical situation in England increased Henry's anxiety to return to the north.

Henry's mother, the Empress Matilda, had tried unsuccess-
fully for years to compel all England to recognize her as its rightful sovereign. But the English barons, seeking only their own
profit, had kept alive the civil war, siding sometimes with Matilda's
cousin, Stephen, sometimes with her. The empress, worn out by

the struggle, had at last quitted the Island, returned to Rouen, and left Henry to carry on the fight and win the crown for himself if he could. Preparations for an expedition across the Channel were already under way when he had left to come south. So Eleanor, as eager to be queen of England as Henry was to be king, willingly bade him Godspeed when he rode north early in June.

Eleanor waited in vain for news from her young husband for several weeks. Then late in July she learned that he had found at Barfleur a considerable force of knights and foot soldiers ready for the expedition to England. But all thought of a crossing had been immediately driven from his mind when he learned that King Louis had issued a summons for him to appear before the royal court within forty days to answer for his conduct. Certain that the duke would defy the summons, the king had begun gathering forces with which to enforce the expected sentence of confiscation of both Normandy and Aquitaine.

At the end of the forty days, King Louis had assembled several hundred paid men-at-arms, a host of lesser vassals, and many of the greater barons. King Stephen's son, Eustace, was there, eager to meet Duke Henry in battle and to eliminate this rival for the inheritance of the English crown. Conspicuous among Louis's confederates was Henry's disgruntled brother, Geoffrey, who once more thought he saw the duchy of Aquitaine within his grasp.

The main host, led by Louis, had proceeded from Paris westward along the Seine, crossed the Epte into Normandy, and laid siege to Neuf Marché. By this move they hoped to draw Henry northward, leaving Geoffrey free to ravage in the south. This strategy proved to be well calculated, since Henry had decided to disregard Geoffrey's movements for the time being, to strike directly at the main body of the enemy, and to relieve Neuf Marché if possible. The duke had set off on the sixteenth of July toward the besieged city after urging his wife to be on guard against Geoffrey.

Eleanor could not repress a smile at the mention of Geoffrey's name, although she realized how dangerous a foe he might prove to be. He possessed by his father's will three great castles, Chinon, Loudun, and Mirebeau. Loudun and Mirebeau, the latter less than twenty miles north of Poitiers, both commanded the road south from Anjou. It certainly behooved her to have her own castle well manned and stocked with provisions.

During the succeeding weeks, Eleanor's scouts brought reports of Geoffrey's activities. These at first gave her no anxiety, since they were directed westward toward Anjou. Here Geoffrey was able, by a show of force, to induce a number of barons to desert to his banner. These men allowed him to garrison their castles, and then they joined him in burning the villages and crops of those who continued loyal to Henry. Eleanor, angered at this ravaging, was on the point of taking the field herself when she was halted by good news: Henry himself was rushing to punish Geoffrey.

In the north things had not gone so well at first. Before Henry could reach Neuf Marché, it had been treacherously handed over to King Louis. News of its fall had caused the Norman barons to hesitate to support Henry. But when he arrived on the scene, they soon changed their minds. He had attacked, captured, and burnt to the ground castle after castle; then turned southward to protect Verneuil, toward which King Louis seemed to be moving. But when Henry had proceeded more than a day's march in this direction, he learned that the French king had cut in behind him to attack Sir William de Pacy's castle, twenty-five miles back on the Eure. William himself had sent an urgent request for aid. At this call for help, the impetuous Henry turned and led his companions back at such speed that before they could reach Pacy many of their horses died on the road. King Louis, when he heard of Henry's arrival, cautiously withdrew across the Norman border into France.

By these rapid and successful actions, Henry had made the Norman barons realize that, young as he was, he was their master. After seeing the duke destroy five or six castles in as many weeks, and the king of France refuse battle, they had concluded that, of the two, the duke was the more to be feared. Consequently, on Henry's demand for hostages, the barons had quickly sent their sons, brothers, or other relatives over to his camp. Henry then had left a portion of his followers to defend these border lands, and hurried southward to attend to his brother.

Geoffrey and many of his followers had withdrawn into the strong castle of Montsoreau on the Loire. Its conquest proved difficult: it was not until mid-October that the half-starved defenders yielded to a direct attack. Even then Geoffrey eluded his brother's grasp by escaping from the castle and making off with some companions by boat. But Geoffrey's other friends, discouraged by the fall of Montsoreau, quickly yielded their castles to

Henry. Geoffrey soon gave up the struggle and threw himself on his brother's mercy. Henry exacted an oath of fealty and took away from Geoffrey the three castles bequeathed to him by his father. Then he journeyed to each of these in turn, to replace Geoffrey's men with his own. It was from Mirebeau, early in November, that he set out to cover the scant score of miles to Poitiers.

When Henry reached the castle, Eleanor warmly congratulated him on his successes and expressed the hope that Louis would now accept the results of their marriage and allow them to enjoy their possessions in peace. That was more than could be hoped for, Henry replied; but he felt sure that Louis would not trouble them again for some time. Later on at supper, when Eleanor was plying Henry for details of his exploits, she got little satisfaction until she asked whether he had ever met Louis face to face in the field. At this question Henry burst out laughing and answered that her former husband always withdrew so courteously before him that he had never had a chance to see even his back. Finally Henry cut her inquiries short by saying that he was starved for the chase and eager to bring down the boar that had escaped him on his previous visit. Eleanor promised him his opportunity in an all-day hunt set for the morrow.

After a few days, however, sport had to give way to business. Henry had to learn more about his duchess' lands; he should, in particular, visit Limoges, where traditionally the dukes of Aquitaine were wont to be invested with the ducal crown. Accordingly, just as dawn was breaking the next day, Henry and Eleanor led a small cavalcade through narrow streets, down the long sloping hill to the Clain. After crossing the river, they filed through a break in the sharp cliff opposite the city and came out on a level plateau to face the eastern sky crimsoned by the rising sun. They set out at a brisk trot southeastward in the direction of the Limousin.

The visit to the ancient city of Limoges was marked on Henry's part by an abrupt assertion of his authority as duke; and Eleanor, to her chagrin, found herself relegated to second place in the management of her ancestral possessions. The duke and duchess had been enthusiastically welcomed by the populace and by Jean, abbot of St. Martial's, who had marched out to meet them at the head of the abbey's monks. The tents for the ducal party had scarcely been pitched outside the monastery walls before the butler reported that no provisions of any kind had been sent to the kitchen tents. Henry at once sent a demand for the dues of entertainment owed him by the monastery. Some of Henry's followers began going into town to help themselves. Their free-handed attempts aroused the ire of the shop-keepers, who caught up their weapons and beat off the raiders. Just as these men came streaming back to camp, Abbot Jean's reply was delivered. He absolutely refused to comply with Henry's demand, saying that the abbot of St. Martial's was obliged to supply victuals to the duke only when he was lodged *within* the walls of the town. As Henry read the words, the veins on his forehead bulged and his cheeks flushed. He cursed the abbot for a niggardly knave, and in a burst of rage, ordered the town's walls torn down, so that henceforth no abbot of St. Martial's could use them as an excuse to rob his duke of just and reasonable dues. Eleanor was startled at her husband's ferocity, but she acquiesced in his orders since she knew that to yield to vassals in such matters was fatal. With a new sense of her husband's masterful nature, she accompanied him a few days later as they continued their southwestward journey.

The remainder of their trip carried them without incident to Bordeaux and back to Poitiers. The news that awaited them here caused Henry to set out the very next day for the north.

What made Henry take horse so quickly was not so much word that King Louis and his brother Count Robert had been ravaging again, but rather, an urgent call for aid from his supporters in England. Consequently, after a hurried survey of the Norman border, where he discovered that no castles had been yielded and that King Louis had withdrawn to Paris, apparently for the winter, he headed for Barfleur. Here he learned that his supporters had been steadily losing ground to King Stephen. Castle after castle had yielded to the king, who was even now besieging Wallingford. Henry began rushing his preparations for the crossing. Some thirty or more vessels were already in the harbor. In less than two weeks he succeeded in gathering around him a well-equipped force of nearly one hundred and fifty knights with their mounts, and three thousand on foot. Yet it was not until 1152 had passed into 1153 that a favorable wind enabled him to set sail, on the fifth of January, for the southern shore of England.

Meanwhile Eleanor, left alone in charge of Aquitaine, was preparing herself for a period of dreary waiting when she was cheered by the discovery that she was going to bear Henry a child. She hurried to the nearby church of Notre Dame la Grande, to humbly beg the Virgin for the boon of a male child.

Eleanor soon found that time would not hang heavily on her hands. Visitors of all sorts thronged the court. Monks and townsmen, barons and knights came seeking favors, confirmations of privileges, or the settlement of claims. Some came to place their sons or daughters in their duchess' charge to receive social training or to win a husband. Rumors that the traditions of Duke William the Troubadour were being revived by his open-handed granddaughter drew to Eleanor's court poets and singers. One outshone all the rest. His youth, his great gifts as poet and composer of haunting melodies, the subtle appeal both of voice and of person, won for Bernard de Ventadour the instant acclaim of all. Eleanor, too, though more critical than the others, was soon compelled to admit the supreme artistry of the man.

Bernard's fame was not unknown to Eleanor. Jongleur and troubadour, travelling from court to court, entertained his hosts not only with song and story, but also with news and gossip. So it was that the duchess knew something both of Bernard's songs and of his tragic love affair with the beautiful Margarida, Vicomtesse de Ventadour.

When Ebles III, Vicomte de Ventadour, brought home his young bride, she found Bernard living at the castle. The boy, though of humble birth (his mother's husband had tended the great oven on the manor), had been given every advantage by Count Ebles II, who treated him as his own son—as perhaps he was. Ebles II, bosom friend of Eleanor's grandfather, and, like him, a skilful poet, had detected Bernard's genius and devoted himself to its training. When the elder Ebles was succeeded by the younger, Bernard remained at court, for Ebles III regarded him almost as a younger brother. Bernard was fired by Margarida's charm and beauty. He called her his *Bel Vezer,* his "Fair to See," and poured out his devotion in lyrics. Margarida merely tolerated his attentions at first. Gradually, however, his tactful persistence began to have its effect. She fell passionately in love; yet, fearful of the consequences, she begged Bernard to leave the castle. But Bernard lingered till her husband's suspicions were aroused. Ebles shut Margarida in a room of the tower and compelled her to send a message to Bernard commanding him to depart. Bernard perforce obeyed and despondently vowed he would forswear love:

> Henceforth all ladies I will flee,—
> No more in hope or trust I'll sigh;
> Oft have I been their guarantee,

But now for champion let them hie
Where'er they will; for one could bless
My life, yet binds me to the stake;
They're all alike, and I profess
That all alike I now forsake.

Bernard wandered over the countryside a good two years without finding any new comforter at whose shrine he might worship. Eleanor's reception of him, however, revived his spirits, and in her congenial presence he soon began once more to pour out his soul in song:

It is no marvel if I sing better than any other singer, for my heart draws me more toward love, and I am more obedient to its command. I have given up heart and body and wisdom and wits and strength and power to love, the bridle draws me so towards it that I care not a whit for any other thing.

Again he writes:

Alas, unhappy wretch, what shall I do and what counsel shall I take? For she does not know the grief that I endure, nor do I dare to beg for mercy from her. Poor fool, indeed you have little sense, for she would noways love you in word or deed, but would see you dead first.

Since I will not send her a messenger and it is not fitting that I should speak to her, I know of no counsel to take, but I am greatly comforted by one thing; she knows and understands how to read, and it pleases me that I should write the words, and if it pleased her, she could read them for my salvation.

Once more he sings:

I am servant and friend and slave to my lady, and I ask no other kindness from her but that she should secretly turn her lovely eyes towards me, for her look does me much good when I am sorrowful, and I will give her praise and a thousand thanks for it, for I have no friend in the world who is worth so much to me.

It is a happy day for me when I behold her, her mouth and eyes and forehead and hands and arms, and her whole person in which there is nothing that is not beautifully fashioned. Beauty could make no one fairer than she is, although I have great grief and trouble from her.

* * *

124 ~

Within my heart I am grieved and angry because I follow my wishes so much, but no man ought to say such a thing, for he does not know how fortunate he is. What then shall I do about the fair secret glances? Give them up? I would rather give up the whole world.

Nevertheless, Bernard was compelled to give up for a while "the fair, secret glances" and withdraw to other courts; for Eleanor's interest was becoming more and more centered on Henry's child to which she soon expected to give birth. The gracious Queen of Heaven heard Eleanor's continued prayers. Two days after the Feast of the Assumption, on the seventeenth of August, 1153, Eleanor gave birth to a son. While her first thought was to send the good news to Henry, she yet had a malicious wish also to inform Louis, who still, after eighteen months, had not recovered sufficiently from the divorce to marry again.

During the nearly nine months since his departure, Henry had been busy. He and his men had landed on the Hampshire coast on January 6, and had at once directed their steps to a nearby church to give thanks for their safe crossing. It was the Feast of the Epiphany. Just as they entered the holy place, the officiating priest was pronouncing the opening words of the Introit for the day: "Behold the Lord, the ruler cometh, and the kingdom is in his hand." The duke and his companions heard these words with joy, for they gave assurance of divine favor and of Henry's success. So it was that, after the end of the short service, they all started off with increased confidence to win the "kingdom." Their confidence grew when they heard that King Stephen's eldest son, Eustace, had died, struck down, not by the sword, but by the manifest hand of God. Eustace had become angered at the abbot of St. Edmunds for having refused him money, and in revenge had ordered the monastery's crops burned. The Saint's vengeance for this act followed swiftly. For that very day, when Eustace sat down to dine at the refectory table, he choked on the first morsel of food and died in convulsions. King Stephen was crushed by the loss of his son and heir and dismayed by the successes won by the energetic Henry. So when the clergy, weary of the prolonged civil war, urged Stephen to compromise, he consented to meet Henry in conference at Wallingford. There, early in November, the king recognized Henry as heir to the kingdom, and Henry agreed not to contest the kingship during the lifetime of Stephen. Later in the month a full assembly of bishops, earls, and barons held at Winchester ratified the treaty. From Winchester, Stephen and Henry journeyed together to London, where the citizens gave them a jubilant reception.

Shortly after Christmas Eleanor's messenger returned with news from the triumphant Henry in London. She was impressed with his victories, but she wanted most to hear how he had reacted to news of his son's birth. "Ah, my lady," was the reply, "you should have seen him. He could scarcely contain himself for joy. Just before I left London he entrusted me with this gift for you." Eleanor eagerly undid the wrappings of the small packet handed to her, and exclaimed with delight when she saw a necklace made of delicate gold links with a pendant ruby. On a piece of parchment attached to the chain, she read: "For my lady. Praise God! Henry."

Rouen: Days of Anxiety
1154

THE YEAR 1154 HAD BEEN USHERED IN AUSPICIOUSLY FOR ELEANOR BY THE good news from Henry. The expectation of his return served to make the wintry days of January and February less dreary, while the first hints of spring brought back Bernard and his harp to cheer the gatherings in the hall. But Eleanor's interest was centered in her baby boy. He had been christened "William," the traditional name of the counts of Poitou and one made famous in Henry's own family by William, Duke of Normandy, the Conqueror of England.

The baby was eight months old when Henry, one day in April, dashed into the courtyard. First greetings over, the duchess eagerly led her husband through the great hall to the hall of Maubergeonne's Tower. From there the two proceeded by the winding staircase to her apartment, now kept relatively draft-free by window openings tightly fitted with tiny bits of leaded glass. On the floor, before the hearth-fire, baby William was disporting himself on a mattress. Henry gazed with delight at his first-born; then, kneeling, he placed his great hands gently about the little body, lifted the child up, and embraced him.

The days that followed were spent in making a tour of western Poitou, to increase the duke's acquaintance with the lords and castles of that country. The couple were cordially received wherever they went, even at the castle of the stormy De Lusignans. As they rode toward home, Eleanor entertained her husband with the tale of Mélusine, the fairy ancestress of the De Lusignans, who had built the castle in a single night. At Poitiers, news from the north started them again on their travels. King Louis, they learned, was preparing for another sally into Normandy. So the ducal couple, with baby William, soon departed northward.

Eleanor enjoyed the tour. Henry was in good spirits and took pleasure in showing her his own country, especially the ancestral castle at Angers on its black rock, and Le Mans, where he had been born. As they left Lisieux, and headed for Rouen, Eleanor became conscious of her increasing nervousness. In this ancient capital of the dukes of Normandy she was to meet for the first time her mother-in-law, the former empress, Matilda.

Matilda's reputation for affability was not high. Her experiences in life had not tended to develop sweetness of character. Married off at the age of eight to the Holy Roman Emperor, Henry V, who was twenty years her senior, she had been left a childless widow before she was thirty. She had come to love her husband's Germany, but her father, Henry I of England, had wrenched her away, into marriage with the fifteen-year-old Geoffrey of Anjou. The ill-mated couple were never happy until mutual interest in the future of their son, Henry, finally brought them into relative harmony. Matilda's experiences might well have soured a temperament far more angelic than her own.

It was the thought of being inspected by this grim-mouthed female that caused Eleanor's nervousness. The young duchess' hope was centered in her baby. The old empress would surely soften at the sight of her first grandchild. Eleanor braced herself for the ordeal.

When they reached Rouen, she was guided by Henry, closely followed by the nurse with the baby, into the great hall of the ducal castle. Henry's mother, with her ladies-in-waiting, stood upon the dais at one end of the hall. Matilda's was an impressive figure, but it was at her face, masklike and marked with lines of suffering, that Eleanor gazed. The sadness mirrored in that impassive countenance touched her heart. Matilda, for her part, after receiving her son's obeisance, gazed intently on his beautiful young wife as she sank in a graceful curtsey before her. When Eleanor arose, something constrained the stern empress to take her daughter-in-law's hand, draw Eleanor to her, and kiss her gravely on both cheeks. Eleanor, pleased at this unexpected graciousness, turned to take little William from the nurse when she was anticipated by her husband. Henry, darting forward, seized the little fellow and placed him in Matilda's arms. The empress, taken by surprise but utterly pleased, responded to her grandson's charms, while her ladies crowded around with exclamations of delight. When Matilda declared that the boy looked exactly like his father, Eleanor knew that the homecoming was a success.

Eleanor and the baby were first installed by the solicitous grandmother in a small chamber next her own, then all descended to enter the hall once more. Here they found Duke Henry surrounded by a group of ecclesiastics and nobles. At the duke's right hand stood Hugh, Archbishop of Rouen. He had just presented to Henry a scholarly-looking monk, one Robert of Torigny, formerly prior of Bec, but recently chosen to preside as abbot over Blessed Michel "in peril of the sea." The archbishop said that Robert's unanimous election promised to bring peace to that disturbed monastery, and he begged the young duke to give his assent. This Henry cordially did, thereby winning the devotion of a man who was to prove an admiring chronicler of his long reign. The various members of the group were then presented to their new duchess, who welcomed the opportunity to extend her acquaintance among the Norman leaders.

Eleanor greeted Abbot Robert with especial cordiality, adding her congratulations on his newly acquired honor. She encouraged Robert to talk of himself, of the chronicle which he had already begun, of his love for history, of literary matters in general. The duchess remarked that she ought to know more about the history of the English, whose queen she hoped some day to be. Robert strongly recommended a book which had come into his possession a few years earlier. It was by a certain Geoffrey of Monmouth, a dweller in the western parts of England bordering on the Welsh. Geoffrey had discovered by chance, Robert said, an old book written in the Welsh tongue telling about the ancient kings of Britain. This he had rewritten in Latin, adding some things of his own. He told much of a great king, Arthur by name, who had once ruled over Britain, and of a mighty magician named Merlin. When the duchess, attracted by the mention of Arthur's name, expressed a desire to have the book, Robert eagerly promised to have a copy made and sent to her at the earliest possible moment.

Before dawn the next morning, Eleanor was awakened by the stamping and neighing of horses in the courtyard. Hastily rising, she called on her sleepy maids to help her dress. Then she made her way down to the hall and found all in confusion, with Henry in the midst of it, munching bread and washing it down with wine, while a squire buckled on his sword. Henry, looking up, cried out to his wife that King Louis was making trouble again, threatening Normandy's eastern border. Eleanor, secretly wishing she could share the excitement of the field, could only utter wifely admonitions. Henry, from among the crowd of knights, horses, and dogs, shouted back to her: "Do you talk of danger when I ride against the royal Louis?"; and with a laugh he disappeared through the doorway. Henry's jest held more than a germ of truth: the fighting was over by the end of August. King Louis finally recognized Henry as duke of Aquitaine, and in return Henry did homage for the duchy and paid a large sum as relief.

During her husband's absence, Eleanor had made it her main interest to grow in the good graces of Matilda. Much of the time was spent in the shady castle garden, where they enjoyed the warm August days. Here the empress and her daughter-in-law sat, surrounded by their women and maids, busily sewing and embroidering, while little William, now just a year old, babbled and squirmed about on a pallet placed in the middle of the circle. Matilda talked while the needles flew. Eleanor concentrated on being a good listener and a skilful questioner. As she encouraged the older woman to talk of her past life, particularly of her experiences in England, Eleanor found herself both entertained and instructed; for the empress spoke out of a full knowledge of conditions in England and of its leading men.

Tales of daring and escape Matilda had to tell, stories of danger she had seen with her half-brother, Earl Robert of Gloucester. Robert had aided her with his diplomatic and military skill, from which Henry had also profited during the boyhood years spent at his uncle's court. Once when she and Robert, years before, had been besieging Lord Henry, Bishop of Winchester, heavy relieving forces had compelled them to flee. Earl Robert was captured in attempting to hold back the pursuers. She herself dashed to freedom escorted by a half-score of knights led by the faithful Sir Brian Fitz-Count. Their goal was Gloucester, seventy miles away. Seated in her sidesaddle, she slowed up the pace of the others who were in constant fear of being overtaken. Brian endured this situation for fifteen miles to Ludgershall Castle. Then, calling a halt, he begged the empress to abandon her sidesaddle and ride astride so that they could make better time. Matilda yielded to necessity. She dismounted, shortened her long skirt by pulling it up through her girdle, was helped up on another horse, thrust her feet into the stirrups, and set off with the others at a gallop. Another fifteen miles brought the party to Devizes. There the galled and exhausted woman, though refreshed by some bread and ale, declared that she could sit her horse no longer. The resourceful Brian solved this difficulty by procuring a bier. Matilda, half-dead with fatigue, allowed herself to be bound on this with ropes, as though she were wholly dead. The poor empress, jolted along for another forty miles, was borne at last into Gloucester Castle.

Eleanor was reminded of her own condition after the first day of bestriding a palfrey on the march through Asia Minor. There was nothing in her experience, however, to match Matilda's escape from Oxford Castle. This took place in the middle of winter, with the ground buried deep in snow and the Thames frozen hard. The garrison was on the verge of starvation after a three-month's siege. Matilda and three companions, draped in sheets, were dropped down at night by a rope onto the river. They crossed on the ice, made their way unseen through the enemies' lines, then went on foot for five miles till they reached Abingdon. There they procured horses and made their way to the castle at Wallingford where its constable, Sir Brian Fitz-Count, gave them a hearty welcome.

With Henry's return, the leisurely days of tale-telling were over; for Henry came back a sick man. Matilda summoned her physician, a thin, dark monk named Zumbro who smelled of drugs. Eleanor, whose future as queen of England hung in the balance, watched him intently while he made an unhurried examination of his patient. He laid his hand on Henry's forehead; he felt his pulse. Then he drew back and gravely began to speak: "He must be bled at once. Bleeding is the beginning of health. It makes the mind sincere, it aids the memory, it purges the brain, it reforms the bladder, it warms the marrow, it opens the hearing, it checks tears, it removes nausea, it invites digestion, it evokes the voice, it moves the bowels, it removes anxiety, it. . ."

"On with it, man!" Eleanor burst out. "The duke is dying. If he needs bleeding, bleed him!"

Zumbro, though flustered by the interruption, recovered himself, and immediately relieved Henry of a half-pint of blood. He next prepared to give Henry a purge composed, he said, of powdered helenium and purple betony plucked at the proper season of the moon, boiled in ale, and seasoned with honey and salt. As he stood with a cupful of this mixture held lovingly in his hand, he was on the point of giving examples of its effectiveness when Eleanor's obvious impatience determined him to administer the draft at once. After he had succeeded in getting the half-unconscious duke to swallow a goodly portion of this concoction, the learned physician took his departure.

Anxious days followed for Matilda and Eleanor who, aided by Eleanor's old nurse, Thessalia, kept constant watch at Henry's bedside. Henry's condition grew steadily worse in spite of repeated bleedings and purgings administered by the sallow Zumbro. Her husband's wasted form and delirious ravings drove Eleanor to the point of distraction. Yet wise old Thessalia bade her be of good cheer, declaring that she had seen many a man in the duke's condition live to recover his full strength. They would break the fever soon with the aid of God and a remedy of which she knew.

Without more ado, Thessalia sought out Zumbro in his laboratory to get the necessary ingredients. She crumbled the dried leaves of febrifuge and verbena into a mortar, added the dried root of sassafras, and with a pestle brayed them together. Next she emptied the powdered material into a small iron pot, filled it with water, and brought the whole mixture to a boil over the fire. She sprinkled some salt into the mixture and, last of all, threw in a dried bat's wing. Then while stirring the boiling mixture, Thessalia began muttering *Pater nosters*. When the prayer had been repeated seven times, she removed the pot and set it on the stone floor to cool. The cooled mixture was strained off into a cup carved from an elephant's tusk. With this in hand, Thessalia returned to the duke's chamber where she repeated the sevenfold Lord's Prayer and gave the sick man the potion. For a while Henry continued to toss about uneasily. Gradually, however, he became quieter and at last dropped off to sleep. The anxious watchers relaxed at this favorable sign and eventually they, too, fell asleep.

Hours later, Eleanor awoke with a start to find the sun shining through the narrow window openings. She arose and went to Henry's bedside. Placing her hand on his forehead, she found it cool and damp. As she bent over him, her husband opened his eyes. After gazing at her intently for a long moment, he feebly uttered her name. Eleanor's exclamation of relief brought Matilda to the bedside. When the patient later asked for something to eat, the two women knew that he must be recovering.

As Henry's strength began coming back, the problem of entertaining him strained Eleanor's resourcefulness. Fortunately, Henry liked music, so Eleanor would play short melodies on a rebec, or pick them out on a psaltery. But Henry liked it best of all when she took her guitar and sang songs of the crusades or troubadour lyrics. Henry's favorite was her grandfather's *Enigma* which began:

> A song of nothing I will write;
> Not of myself nor any wight.
> And not of youth or love's delight,
>   No, nor of aught.
> On horseback fast asleep one night
>   Of it I thought.

When Henry was strong enough to sit up he demanded the chess-board. After this had been placed upon the bed, with the stout ivory chessmen set in order, the duke and the duchess would match their wits for an hour or two nearly every day. Occasionally when Henry saw that he was about to be beaten, a violent upheaval of the bedclothes would send the chessmen tumbling in disorder; and would provoke Eleanor, irritated yet amused, to exclaim at his childishness.

But one of their greatest resources proved to be Geoffrey of Monmouth's *Historia regum Britanniae,* or *History of the Kings of Britain.* Abbot Robert of Mont St. Michel had been true to his promise. Rather than rely upon one of his monks, he decided to send for a professional lay scribe. On the scribe's arrival, Abbot Robert took him at once to his own quarters where, from a good-sized niche in the wall, he took out the precious volume and asked how long it would take to copy it. After examining the handwriting and noting the number of pages, the man replied that he might be able to do it in five or six weeks, provided he could have a proper desk and good light. Robert assured him that he would have the best desk in the scriptorium and everything else he might need—well-pumiced parchment, ruler, knife, and pens. The scribe soon commenced his exacting work. Tilting his desk to a convenient angle and affixing a sheet of parchment securely to it, he selected a quill pen, tested its nib, dipped it in the ink, and began with careful pressure the work of copying.

Day after day the experienced scribe kept steadily at his backbreaking task till he had the satisfaction of finishing the work—three hundred quarto sheets, six hundred pages—at the end of five weeks. The spaces left for capitals at the beginning of each book had been filled in with gilt and red ink by a monk of the abbey, a gifted illuminator. The whole would have done credit to any scriptorium, so Robert felt certain that his duchess would be delighted with the handsome volume. Upon receiving the book, she expressed her pleasure by rewarding the messenger and sending him back with her warmest thanks to the abbot, together with a gift of several pounds toward defraying the expenses which he had incurred.

Eleanor did not delay in putting the *History* to good use. The day after she received it, one of those moments came when Henry, the usual methods of entertainment having been exhausted, was becoming peevish. Bethinking herself of the recently acquired treasure, she had it brought in and began reading aloud. Henry liked the work so well that the reading was continued on succeeding days. Occasionally Henry would interrupt the cadenced Latin to ask Eleanor for a translation into French. This finally suggested to Eleanor the plan of having these stories put into French, written in verse like a *chanson de geste*. So she summoned a reading clerk at the cathedral of Caen, a poet named Wace who had already written a *Life of St. Nicholas* and other popular narratives in verse. When she made her proposal, Eleanor was delighted to find that Wace not only knew Geoffrey's book, but had already begun a rhymed translation into French. With a well-filled purse and a promise of more gifts, Eleanor sent him back to his task.

One day after nearly seven weeks of illness, Henry for the first time took a few steps about the chamber. To his astonishment, his legs would scarcely support him, and Eleanor had to lead him tottering back to bed. Some days later he called for his sword, but his inability to swing it freely convinced him that he was not yet ready to resume his active life. From that time on, however, his strength rapidly returned; so that when King Louis sent to ask his aid in punishing a rebellious vassal, Henry felt well enough to respond to his overlord's summons.

The campaign proved to be another short one. King Louis soon concluded a truce: he was anxious to be on his way to Spain, to prostrate himself at the shrine of St. James of Compostella, and then to get a wife. After resisting for nearly two years his council's plea that he remarry, Louis had finally consented to do so. His fiancée was Constance, daughter of the king of Castile.

News that King Stephen had died sent Henry hurrying back to Rouen. The English magnates desired that he, as acknowledged heir, should come to England at once. At long last he could cross the Channel in peace and claim his maternal inheritance.

Eleanor Assumes a New Crown 1154-1167

HENRY AND EL-EANOR WERE CROWNED AT WESTMINSTER, SUNDAY, December 19, 1154. Early that morning Eleanor was summoned from her apartment by Sir Ralph de Hastings, appointed to act as her chamberlain. With silver wand in hand, he conducted the queen forward, while two pages carried the heavy folds of her train. Her maids, augmented by four young English noblewomen, fell in behind while the chamberlain led the little procession down a short flight of stairs to the courtyard. From this point they made their way, preceded by a column of knights walking in twos, through the crowd to the west entrance of the abbey. Then they paced slowly up the center aisle to the seats reserved for them facing the altar. Scarcely had they settled themselves when another procession entered, led by the Archbishop of Canterbury, Theobald, clad in a richly embroidered chasuble, wearing his mitre, and bearing in his hands a gold crozier sparkling with jewels. Behind him followed a dozen bishops and a score of abbots, their crimson, gold, and blue robes illumined by the light of hundreds of candles. Eleanor then caught sight of Henry walking beneath a purple canopy of silk which was sustained on the points of gilded lances borne by four distinguished barons of the realm whose hereditary right it was to perform this service. At the chancel Henry was led to his appointed place and the solemn service began.

When it came time for the anointing of the candidate with the holy oil, a screen was raised to conceal Henry from the view of the audience. As soon as the king's clothes had been removed, Archbishop Theobald, dipping the fingers of his right hand in a crystal bowl filled with the consecrated chrism, offered by the bishop of London, crossed Henry on the forehead, chest, back, and feet. After the king had been clothed with fresh linen, a silken tunic, an embroidered robe, red leather half-boots without heels, and a scarlet cloak edged with ermine, he was led to the throne. Then followed the administering of the coronation oath and the formal crowning. Now at a sign from Lord John the Marshal, Eleanor rose, moved toward the throne, and took her place beside Henry. The bishop of London approached and placed upon her head a golden crown, companion to that worn by Henry.

When Eleanor returned that night to her chamber after the coronation feast, she noticed that the silken coverlet had been removed from her bed, and that the two silver basins had also disappeared. She turned with astonishment to Sir Ralph for an explanation. He replied that, by old usage, all the bed furnishings as well as the basins used by both king and queen on the night before their coronation were the perquisites of their respective chamberlains. Eleanor was somewhat reconciled to this English custom when Sir Ralph pointed out, among the new bedthings, a handsome coverlet of martin skins.

A few days later, the court moved from the palace at Westminster down the Thames to Bermondsey where, during the Christmas festivities, the queen was introduced to the magnates of the realm. She noted how favorably Henry impressed all of them by his charm of manner, his intelligence, and his decisiveness. They seemed to recognize in him the man of forceful character whom England had so long needed at its head.

The ready acceptance of their twenty-one-year-old leader appeared at the first meeting of the great council, where Henry announced his intention of carrying out the provisions of the treaty in which King Stephen had recognized him as his heir. It was a drastic program, but one whose terms had been agreed to by most of the leading men whom the young king was addressing. He was determined, he said, to restore the government of the realm as it had existed under his grandfather, King Henry I. All castles built since that time must either be given up to the crown or razed to the ground; all grants of royal properties and revenues he would reseize into his own hand; he would rehabilitate the machinery for administering these and for enforcing justice. He would demand the coöperation of all present in carrying out this program. The response to this speech was all that Henry could have wished. Archbishop Theobald and the respected Earl Robert of Leicester quickly rose in turn to pledge their support, and were followed by the others, both clergy and barons.

Henry at once proceeded to make good his word. He restored to the Exchequer his grandfather's skilful administrator, Bishop Nigel of Ely. He relied chiefly upon Earl Robert of Leicester and Sir Richard de Lucy for the reorganization of the courts of justice and the royal household. He was in constant consultation, also, with Archbishop Theobald. But the elderly counselor, when Henry asked him to act as his chancellor, pleaded age and his already heavy responsibilities as head of the ecclesiastical system of England. He called to Henry's attention, however, a member of his household, an archdeacon of Canterbury named Thomas Becket. Thomas was a young man of great promise and would make, thought Theobald, an efficient chancellor. The archdeacon's intelligence and wit had already appealed to the king, so Henry welcomed the recommendation and straightway appointed Thomas his chancellor.

After setting the wheels of government in motion at the center, Henry next prepared to make his authority respected in all outlying districts. A number of influential lords had not obeyed his summons to the council, but had remained defiantly at home strengthening and provisioning their castles. They must be brought to book quickly or he would be only half a king in England.

Before setting out, Henry instructed Eleanor to order everything she wished to make herself comfortable. She could secure all needful monies through the issuance of her own writs, since he had ordered that they be honored at the Exchequer. He would inform her of his movements. Shortly after the beginning of the year, Henry took leave of his queen to begin a career which was to make him one of the greatest of England's kings.

After her husband's departure for the north, Eleanor settled down to a life which, for the next dozen years or so, varied little in its main features. Largely engrossed with the care of her growing family, she yet played an active, if minor, role in government. She acted as one of Henry's representatives, especially when the royal couple were on opposite sides of the Channel, as they were several times during this period. The queen was in constant touch with the king, receiving and transmitting information and orders. In conjunction with the justiciars, De Lucy and Leicester, she issued writs and granted charters. But in the main, Eleanor's time was taken up with the bearing and rearing of children, and with unceasing efforts to improve living conditions everywhere. She devoted her leisure time to the cultivation of those social and cultural interests which had always had such a strong appeal for her. From her ordinarily quiet routine, the queen and her entourage would occasionally, especially at Christmas time, be snatched away by Henry and gathered into the swirl of his court.

Eleanor and Henry had seven children besides William. Four were born in England; three, on the Continent: Henry, 1155; Matilda, 1156; Richard, 1157; Geoffrey, 1158; Eleanor, 1161; Joan, 1165; John, 1166. The children's nurses and attendants added considerably to the size of the queen's household. This, though much smaller, was modeled on that of the king. Henry's was multitudinous, consisting in the first place of household officers who, in the course of long years, had been gradually transformed from the king's personal servants into great ministers of state: chancellor, chamberlain, steward, marshal, and constable, their personal services having become delegated, except on state occasions, to deputies. Besides these greater men and their staffs, there were hordes of lesser folk, grading down from ushers to larderers, cooks, and turnspits. Highly important, also, were the men who had charge of the king's hunting pack, and his hawkers and falconers.

Eleanor's smaller household numbered only a chaplain and a clerk or two who celebrated daily services for her, took care of the chapel equipment when they travelled, looked after her books, wrote letters at her dictation, and read to her when she wished. The only other important officer was her chamberlain, who was, in effect, her general manager, having charge of the other members of the household establishment and all details of household management. Heading the queen's kitchen was her chief cook, an important individual as always, with a numerous staff.

The needs of Eleanor's growing family were met by the purchase of familiar articles appropriate to their stages of development. A baby carriage early made its appearance, while the expenditures for clothes grew heavier and heavier. The royal children also had to have toys. The tops and dolls were harmless enough, but Eleanor half regretted buying mock shields for the boys. They immediately improvised swords and began fighting. Their mother was constantly being called on to make peace. It was a foreshadowing of the future, when the boys, become men, were to fight jealously over their inheritances.

The queen called in her Norman chaplain to teach the children reading and writing. But the boys were reluctant pupils. Vainly did Eleanor hold up before them the examples of their father and grandfather, both proficient readers of Latin and of their native French—the lads were more eager to play games, to ride their ponies, to learn to use real swords and lances. They liked stories, however, and songs and music. They loved to hear their mother sing, and they themselves soon learned to pick out tunes on the lute or hammer them out on the dulcimer. Richard fell in love with the harp and early acquired skill in its use. Eleanor's chief assistant in stimulating the children's interest in these things, in developing their tastes and entertaining them with stories, was Marie, a young half-sister of Henry's.

King Henry's father, Count Geoffrey the Fair, had had several illegitimate children. Henry had, besides his two legitimate brothers, William and Geoffrey, two half-brothers and two half-sisters. His half-brothers were endowed with fiefs and proved to be his loyal supporters through life; the elder half-sister, Emma, was married off and ultimately settled in England. Marie, like the others born of an unknown mother, was brought over to England and placed in the queen's care. Eleanor took an immediate fancy to the girl, a dozen years or so her junior, and their acquaintance ripened into a lifelong intimacy. The children adored their Aunt Marie; for she never tired of playing, singing, and dancing with them, and, above all, telling them stories, of which she had an unending supply. Upon this store, Marie, a born story-teller, drew for those tales which have delighted children down through the ages. Henry, Richard, Matilda, and the other children would listen intently as their aunt told about the lion and the ass, the

140 ~

fox and the crow, Philemon and Baucis, Pyramus and Thisbe; about giants, elves, and fairies. Eleanor, busy with some embroidery, was as interested a listener as the children. She was impressed by Marie's imaginative artistry and would often urge her to put the stories in writing. Under Eleanor's constant encouragement, Marie eventually did set to work. When the tales had been copied out by clerks, they were spread abroad by Eleanor's enthusiastic hand and soon attained popularity.

Nor was this Eleanor's only success as a literary patron. Among the minstrels drawn to her court was a certain Thomas. He attracted Eleanor's special attention by his recital of the tale of Tristan and Iseult. Eleanor recognized the minstrel's artistic gift and felt that his poem should be recorded and made more accessible. Consequently, she urged him to write it out. Thomas demurred at first, saying that the task would be long and arduous. But at last he consented to try, and went away strengthened in his determination by a handsome donation from the queen.

In these associations with literary artists Eleanor found pure delight, but the pursuit of these interests had to be subordinated to Henry's wishes and needs. These did not involve mutual love, as Eleanor realized with increasing bitterness. She must bear him children, she must aid him with her prestige as countess of Poitou and duchess of Aquitaine, she must loyally help him extend his territories. He did not demand or expect that she love him. He was proud of her appearance, and pleased that her intelligence matched his own. Yet after all, she was eleven years older than he. Eleanor, at thirty-two, was keenly conscious of this fact. She had tried with all her art to win from Henry something warmer than admiration for her beauty and respect for her intelligence. But she had failed, and the consciousness of failure rankled within her. Furthermore, the fact that Henry, like his father, pursued his amours when and where he listed did nothing to assuage her growing bitterness.

Despite her disappointments, Eleanor strove to meet her obligations as wife and queen. She helped her husband outwit Louis's constant efforts to stir up Henry's vassals and weaken his hold on his Continental territories. She was a willing associate at first in his plans for his sons. She coöperated in the use of his daughters as pawns in the game of diplomacy. And, up to its tragic dénouement, she gave him constant support in the great struggle with Thomas Becket.

During the first four years of his reign, the king's swift blows, coupled with a wise moderation, had inspired fear, respect, and varying degrees of loyalty among all those English barons who had at first sought to defy him. The Welsh princes and Malcolm, the young king of the Scots, had recognized his authority. To strengthen his position, he had had the great lords of the realm recognize as heirs to the throne his baby sons, William, aged a year and a half, and Henry, who had attained the advanced age of six weeks. As dignified bishops and barons knelt to do homage to the infant heirs, Eleanor strove artfully to preserve in the children a decorousness appropriate to the occasion. The wisdom of having little Henry included in the ceremony was shown when his elder brother soon died, leaving him as the heir prospective. The line of succession was strengthened, however, by the birth of Richard and Geoffrey in successive years.

Little Geoffrey's birth took place shortly after the death of Henry's brother, Geoffrey, Count of Nantes. King Henry immediately took possession of the county with the consent of his overlord, King Louis. He named the last baby Geoffrey to indicate his intention of later making him count of Nantes. Nor did his busy brain stop there. He already foresaw a possible marriage to the heiress of Brittany which might win for the boy, Geoffrey, direct control of that whole duchy.

Another bit of marriage diplomacy had secured, earlier in the year 1158, a temporary peace with King Louis. Henry induced the French king to agree to the betrothal of little Henry, now aged three, to Marguerite, scarcely a year old, first child born to Louis and his second wife, Constance of Castile. As the princess' dowry, Louis agreed to hand over to Henry, when the marriage should actually take place, a long-coveted portion of the Vexin, a narrow strip of borderland between Normandy and France, previously ceded to the French king by Geoffrey the Fair. The baby Marguerite was placed immediately in Henry's charge, in order that she might be brought up under his influence.

The following year, 1159, was marked by Henry's spectacular but unsuccessful attempt to secure Toulouse, an enterprise in which Eleanor took a personal interest.

In December, 1158, two months after the birth of Geoffrey, Eleanor gathered up all the children and made the short trip from Winchester to Southampton. Here her eyes were delighted by the sight of a large, new ship, built at her suggestion to make the Channel crossing more comfortable. The *Esnecca*, as the new royal vessel was called, bore them safely across to Barfleur, whence they moved on to Falaise to spend the days of the Christmas feast with Henry. From him Eleanor learned in more detail about the recent happenings.

The first negotiations for little Henry's betrothal to baby Marguerite had been entrusted to Thomas Becket. The embassy, in order to impress the French court, had been carried out on a scale of unparalleled magnificence. Henry laughed as he told of the astonishment of the French when the chancellor's cortege entered Paris. The citizens and courtiers alike gasped in amazement at the long column of knights and the hundred pages gorgeously dressed, walking two by two, followed by a long line of carts drawn by two-horse teams, with monkeys seated on the neck of each horse.

When the feast days were over, Henry suggested a tour through Aquitaine, since he had not been there for many months. Consequently, early in 1159 they all moved south, much to Eleanor's delight. Leaving the children at Poitiers, the royal couple set out on an inspection of their Aquitainian possessions. On this trip Henry learned that Count Berenger of Barcelona was at odds with Raymond of Toulouse over border territory. The quarrel brought to Eleanor's mind her long-standing claim to Toulouse, and she proposed to Henry that he compel Raymond to render homage for both the city and county. Henry, ever ready to assert his power, found his wife's suggestion well-timed. He got in touch with Berenger and arranged for a joint attack on Raymond in the spring. On the way back to Poitiers, Henry, assisted by his wife's prestige, found little difficulty in securing promises of aid from the barons of the South. Encouraged by their attitude, Henry returned to Anjou, whence he sent out summonses to all his vassals, Continental and English, to join him early in the summer, prepared for the expedition against Toulouse.

In consequence of these arrangements, a vast host gathered near Bordeaux in July. Never had such an assembly of fighting men been seen. Besides the thousands of lesser men, vassals and hired men-at-arms, many distinguished leaders were on hand. But it was Becket who outshone them all. The chancellor, zealous as ever in the service of his master, had not only squeezed large sums from Henry's English subjects to meet the expenses of the expedition, but at his own expense had equipped and provisioned a force of seven hundred knights.

Yet all resulted finally in no more than a gesture. Henry had just arrived with his magnificent army before the walls of Toulouse when he learned to his intense chagrin that his sovereign overlord, King Louis of France, was himself inside the city, though Louis had previously led Henry to believe that he would not interfere with the enterprise.

Raymond's wife was Louis's sister, and when his brother-in-law had made a despairing appeal that the king come to Constance's aid, Louis had suddenly decided to act. Louis, whatever his faults, was not without courage. He gathered a small force of knights, set off at full speed and succeeded in entering the city in the nick of time. For once, Louis had completely outwitted his rival. Henry dared not attack the sovereign whose life he had sworn to defend with his own. Henry himself was a sovereign to whom thousands of vassals were bound by the same oaths he had sworn to Louis. If he held his oaths of no account, so might they hold theirs. Then the moral cement, such as it was, which held the structure of his states together would crack open at every seam. The English king, faced by such possibilities, ordered the siege given up, in spite of Becket's violent protestations and the angry disappointment of the other leaders. Henry did not, however, give up the several strongholds already captured in the county. He left Chancellor Thomas there to preserve and extend his authority while he betook himself to Limoges where he rejoined his wife. Eleanor could not refrain from remarking on her consort's foolishness in withdrawing from Toulouse when he might have taken it as easily as one could pluck an apple. But, heedless of her sarcasms, Henry pushed rapidly northward where the ever-recurring warfare with King Louis kept him busy for the next year or two.

Eleanor seized this opportunity to go to Rouen to revisit Matilda, now mellowing somewhat under the influence of age and the successes of her son. The old empress was delighted to see her grandchildren—young Henry, her namesake Matilda, Richard, and the baby Geoffrey. Eleanor was interested to get a first glimpse of little Henry's fiancée, two-year-old Marguerite, who was happy to have some children to play with. This pleasant visit was brought to an end by Henry's desire to have Eleanor return to England to report on conditions, as well as to speed up the collection of money for his military expenses. Eleanor, therefore, gathered up the children and crossed back to England, where she spent the major part of the year 1160.

The queen was soon able to send a favorable report to her husband, telling him that fifty carts, loaded with coin, would shortly be rolling from Westminster and Winchester to Southampton. On their arrival at the latter port, Eleanor had the precious freight loaded on the *Esnecca,* boarded the vessel, saw the cargo safely landed at Barfleur, and then returned quickly to Southampton.

The queen busied herself with various domestic matters during the remainder of this sojourn in England. She dwelt partly at Wallingford and Salisbury, but mostly at Winchester. Her apartments here, in accordance with her orders, had been rendered more comfortable by the installation of a chimney and fireplace, as well as by the building of a cupboard, hollowed out of the thick stone wall, where she was enabled to keep some of her increasing store of manuscript volumes. Her clothes, some of which she had had sent to her from Oxford, were stored along with those of her maids and children in numerous chests. These chests, covered with rugs and cushions, also served as seats, supplemented by a clumsily-made chair or two. Food supplies had to be replenished: pepper, cumin, cinnamon, and above all, wine. The lack of Continental wine had been a sore trial to the queen during her previous residence, for she did not relish English ale. She now imported quantities of wine and had supplies of it deposited at the residences she most frequently visited. She caused her husband's drinking cups to be re-gilded, bought gold and silver plate for use on state occasions, as well as incense and chests for her chapel. For these purposes and to pay the expenses of her large household during the nine months of this visit, Eleanor issued writs on the treasury totalling over £370.

In September, Eleanor returned to the Continent where she remained with the children for more than two years, until January, 1163. During this period she was able to interest Henry, who was a great builder, in two projects dear to her heart: the remodeling of her old home at Poitiers, and the replacement of the old cathedral of St. Pierre, also at Poitiers. Her design for the castle was to modernize its living quarters and to equip it with a splendid hall, built in the current style and more suitable for large gatherings. The cathedral was to be rebuilt from the ground up, on a much larger scale. Bishop Laurentius had already partially outlined plans for it to the queen. Preparations were soon underway, the work of assembling men and materials was begun, and all Poitiers began to hum with activity.

Eleanor, interested as she was in these activities, was neverthe-less constrained by her husband's necessities to move about. Shortly after her arrival from England, she was summoned to Neubourg to attend the wedding of Prince Henry, aged five and a half, to Marguerite, aged two and a half. This ceremony enabled King Henry to possess himself at once of Marguerite's dowry, the eastern half of the Vexin, thereby enraging King Louis who had thought to retain this territory for some years longer. In the ravagings that immediately broke out along the border, Louis had the aid of Eleanor's acquaintances, Count Henri de Champagne and Count Thibaud de Blois, since Louis had just married their sister, Adela. This marriage had taken place within less than two weeks after the death of Louis's second wife, Constance, who had died in giving birth to a second daughter, Alais. The king had been hurried into the marriage by the anxiety of his council for a male heir to the kingdom. The alliance with the powerful house of Champagne-Blois was strengthened a few years later by two marriages that touched Eleanor's interest very closely. To Count Henri was given Marie, Eleanor's eldest daughter by Louis; her younger daughter by the same marriage, Adele, was given to Count Thibaud, Eleanor's frustrated abductor.

The following year, 1161, besides being marked by the birth of Eleanor's and Henry's second daughter, named at Henry's sug-gestion for Eleanor, was signalized by an event which held great significance for the future, namely, the death of Archbishop Theo-bald of Canterbury. His death removed the single greatest support of the king's authority in England. Henry's choice of a successor for Theobald proved to be the single greatest error of his whole reign.

Henry had but one thought from the moment of the primate's death: to replace him by the man who had stood closest to himself in the great work of reconstruction that he had been carrying on so successfully in England. That man was the chancellor, Thomas Becket. For seven years the two young men had worked harmon-iously together, and Henry loved Thomas like a brother. It seemed to the king that with his boon companion at the head of the Eng-lish Church he need fear no opposition from the one organization that rivaled the royal power. Henry kept his thought to himself for some months. It was not till the spring of 1162 that he broached the matter to the chancellor. Thomas drew back instinctively from the proposal. He knew that as archbishop of Canterbury he would have to protect the rights of the Church against interference from the state. He warned Henry that, in the event of his appointment, their friendship would be threatened. But his words fell on heedless ears, since to Henry's mind such a change in their relationship was unthinkable. The king persisted in his intention. Thomas was first ordained a priest and then consecrated archbishop. From that moment Thomas became a changed man: he ceased playing the courtier, began practicing monastic austerities, and devoted himself fanatically to the service of the Church. The tragedy began gradually to unfold. Its culmination was fraught with significance for Eleanor's future.

The first act of the drama, in which these strong-willed men were the protagonists, took place during 1163-64 in England. Thither in January, 1163, Henry and Eleanor followed Thomas, who welcomed them at Southampton with Prince Henry by his side. The latter's position, as his father's destined successor, had just been further emphasized. Thomas' last service as chancellor was bringing the eight-year-old boy to London and staging a grand ceremony in which the dignitaries of the realm, ecclesiastic and lay, once more rendered homage and swore fealty to the prince. Immediately after this ceremony, Thomas resigned the chancellorship, sending back to the king the seals of his office and giving Henry his first shock. Henry, in spite of his resentment at this act, greeted the archbishop cordially, and the two rode off to London still apparently on good terms.

Prince Henry accompanied the two men, while Eleanor remained at Winchester. During the succeeding months she resumed the accustomed tenor of her life, moving about from place to place and spending Christmas time with Henry. Her entourage included a relative or two of her own, as well as the charming Marie, to whose stories Richard, Matilda, and Geoffrey continued to listen with rapt attention. Baby Eleanor, just beginning to walk and talk, had her own circle of worshippers. King Henry once snatched Richard away to London where he arranged for him a party about which, on his return, the little six-year-old never tired of talking. But the theme which more and more absorbed the queen and her circle was the growing dissension between the king and the archbishop.

Thomas had widened the cleavage begun through his resignation of the chancellorship by claiming for the archbishopric one manor after another held by the king's friends. Henry took these acts as personal affronts. The final breach came when the king sought to have clerics accused of felony tried in his courts. Henry had a passion for law and order. He had been able largely to repress the violence of his barons. But the crimes of lesser men had been difficult to eliminate. Many of these crimes, even murder, were committed by clerics who constantly escaped from the hands of his justices by claiming the protection of the Church courts. In these they received generally only some mild form of discipline, after which they were released and could continue their career of crime. Over a dozen murderers of this class were still at large, so his justices told him.

Henry proposed a compromise: clerics found guilty of crime in the Church courts should be unfrocked, given over to the royal courts, and sentenced there as laymen. Thomas claimed that this would be equivalent to punishing a man twice for the same crime. Finally, Henry included his proposal in a list of customs alleged to have prevailed during the reign of his grandfather, Henry I. These were presented for approval to a council at Clarendon. Thomas' fellow bishops, fearing the king's anger, thronged about their leader and urged his acceptance of the customs. Thomas at last yielded to the compromisers and reluctantly gave a qualified promise to observe the customs, called later the Constitutions of Clarendon. But shortly afterward, Becket, feeling that he had betrayed the Church, withdrew his promise. He split his own party by this act. Many bishops and abbots, terrified by the king's rising wrath, abandoned Becket's cause. They felt that the archbishop was endangering not only his own life and theirs, but also the whole fabric of the ecclesiastical structure. Henry, in his bitterness, demanded from Thomas repayment of large sums alleged to have been misappropriated by him when chancellor. After many parleyings, Thomas was summoned to appear before the king's court at Northampton. Here, instead of suing for mercy, Thomas defied the king to arrest him by appearing dressed in full canonicals and holding his jewelled crozier before him. Henry was thrown into one of his uncontrollable fits of rage by this defiance. Yet, since none of the barons dared lay hands on the sacrosanct person of the archbishop, Thomas at last walked unmolested from the hall. He slipped quietly out of Northampton that night, made his way to Canterbury, and eventually succeeded in escaping to the Continent, where he was followed later by his kinsmen and personal intimates whom Henry drove out of England.

Becket's flight widened the conflict, because he appealed for aid not only to the king of the French, but also to the pope. The pious Louis warmly received the persecuted head of the English Church, rejoicing at the fresh opportunity of harassing his English rival. Pope Alexander III, simultaneously appealed to by both Thomas and Henry, was in a quandary: he was inclined to favor the archibishop, but he needed the king's support against Emperor Frederick Barbarossa of Germany, who was supporting a rival candidate for the papacy and who had driven Alexander from Italy to France. The news of Becket's flight and his appeal to Alexander suggested to Frederick the possibility of winning Henry to the support of Alexander's rival. He sent to Henry, who had followed Thomas to the Continent, an embassy proposing marriage between Frederick's cousin, Duke Henry the Lion, of Saxony, a forty-year-old widower, and Henry's nine-year-old daughter, Matilda. Henry, wishing to secure Eleanor's advice, sent the ambassadors on to the queen in England. In the course of the negotiations which resulted in the betrothal, Eleanor crossed to and from the Continent several times. While in Anjou she gave birth to her third daughter, Joan, in 1165; and on Christmas Eve at Oxford, in 1166, her last child was born: a boy who was christened John.

As soon as the marriage was definitely decided on, the queen began busying herself with preparing Matilda's trousseau. The clothes, plate, and miscellaneous articles reached such a bulk that there was required for their packing no less than forty coffers, as many more boxes, and several sacks. All this baggage was ultimately carried aboard the small fleet of vessels headed by the *Esnecca* which bore Matilda, her escort, and her suite safely across the Channel.

Not many days after Matilda's departure, Eleanor received a summons from Henry. He had pressing need for her aid. His mother, who had so long watched over his interests, had died. Affairs in Brittany constantly needed his attention. Above all, Archbishop Thomas, aided by King Louis and Pope Alexander, was harassing him increasingly with ecclesiastical fulminations and political intrigues. While he watched over the North, she must watch over the South. Let her gather up all her belongings and come prepared for a long stay.

Eleanor, delighted at the prospect of returning to her homeland, set to work energetically to prepare for the departure.

Clothes, toilette accessories, chapel equipment, and articles of every description were assembled. Her library of manuscripts was packed under her own eye. This now included a small volume of Marie's delightful tales, as well as the copy of Wace's *Brut* with its dedication to her. All this luggage made a veritable mountain when dumped on the pier at Southampton, along with money chests and a dozen hogsheads of ale (specifically commanded by Henry). After the vessels had been loaded, the queen and her household approached to board the *Esnecca*. Joan and John were in the arms of nurses, five-year-old Eleanor clung to the hand of her Aunt Marie, while eleven-year-old Richard escaped from his guardian to dash excitedly about the dock. At last the *Esnecca* was cast loose and began slowly moving down the Solent. As she stood gazing at the receding shore, Eleanor little realized under what circumstances she would return, seven years later.

King Versus Archbishop
1168-1170

HAPPILY FOR
ELEANOR,
HENRY WISH-
ED HER TO MAKE HER
headquarters at Poitiers for
the next few years. Arch-
bishop Thomas' efforts to
undermine the English
king's strength kept Henry
in the North, and he needed
Eleanor to watch over the
restless barons of the South.
Placed here as regent, Elea-
nor spent some of her happiest days. She was back in her old home
among kinsmen and friends; powerful and respected, free to enjoy
her large income as she chose.

The newly-completed hall of the castle was her especial pride.
Its just proportions enhanced the natural beauty of its cream-
white stone. Even within doors the structure's airy grace was not
obscured; for from high glazed windows sunlight fell gleaming
against wall and floor. Here at last was a reception hall where the
mistress of Aquitaine and Normandy, Anjou and England, could
fittingly hold her court. Eleanor resolved to make it the center of
a social life such as France had not yet seen—a life where woman's
influence should reign supreme, elevating the relations between

the sexes, refining manners, nourishing the arts of poetry and music, raising the whole tone of social intercourse. But there were battles imminent on the field of politics, and for three action-filled years, the arts of leisurely living had to wait.

Scarcely had Henry escorted Eleanor to Poitiers when the surly De Lusignans began stirring the embers of their ever-smouldering revolt. But Henry made one of those sudden dashes by which he kept his vassals in order, and though the fractious brothers escaped him, they left their castle in his hands. Eleanor's first duty after Henry left for the North was to inspect the garrison which he had put there.

On a pleasant day in April she set forth. With her went Earl Patrick of Salisbury, whom Henry had appointed guardian to his queen, and some half-dozen knights. Among them was the landless son of an hereditary English marshal, a strapping young man whose courtesy and valor had attracted Eleanor. His name was William Marshal. The party, finding all well at the castle, spent the night there. Early next morning they set out with their hawks.

As they rode carelessly across the plain in search of game, they suddenly saw a group of armed horsemen approaching at a gallop. Earl Patrick bade the queen make for the castle in all haste. He barely had time to seize his helmet from a squire's hand before the De Lusignans were upon them. During the fight that followed, Eleanor reached the fortress safely and sent out a relieving force. But Earl Patrick, trying to fend off half-a-dozen attackers without the protection of his mail, fell, mortally wounded by one of the De Lusignans. The others of the little group were either killed or captured. Young Marshal, unhorsed and backed up against a hedge, kept his enemies at bay with his broadsword until one of them, from behind the hedge, thrust a spear through his thigh. His captors hurriedly flung him on a horse and made off as Eleanor's men charged after them in vain pursuit.

The queen, back at Poitiers, anxiously awaited news of her captive protector. Soon the De Lusignans sent word that Marshal was alive. Eleanor paid the thirty-pound ransom they demanded, and a few days later welcomed William to Poitiers. His wound had grown worse because his captors, hoping to hasten his ransom, had not allowed it to be dressed. Eleanor pronounced it severe, but not dangerous; and as she bathed and bandaged it, William told how one night at table a young girl had pushed toward him a loaf of bread. Somewhat amazed, he had broken it open. "And I discovered," he said, "that she had hollowed it out and stuffed it with bandages for my poor leg."

"That was a kindly act," said Eleanor. "May the saints reward her."

"May the saints reward you, too, my lady Queen, for today you have shown me great kindness and great honor."

Indeed, Eleanor continued to show him honor. She retained him at her court and promised that when occasion offered, she would find him a position in the royal household.

Meanwhile, Henry was fighting to preserve the very bases of his power. Archbishop Thomas had become a dangerous foe. He was making fiery appeals to Pope Alexander III, and once he received authorization for an interdict, Henry would be in grave peril: his friends might hesitate to support him, while his enemies would certainly welcome the excuse to attack him. Hoping eventually to outwit or placate Thomas, Henry concentrated on strengthening his authority by means of his children. His central plan was to have Young Henry crowned king—a step rendered difficult and risky by the archbishop's enmity. While secretly making arrangements for this move, he met Louis of France at Montmirail to discuss the titular division of certain possessions among his sons. There, in January of 1169, the two kings signed a treaty whereby Prince Henry was to hold Brittany, Maine, and Anjou, with the seneschalship of France, directly from Louis; Geoffrey was to hold Brittany from Prince Henry; Richard was to hold Poitou and Aquitaine directly from King Louis and be betrothed to Alais, Louis's daughter by his second wife. It seemed that once again Henry had the best of the bargain.

As soon as the princes had rendered homage to Louis for their lands, Henry took Richard on a visit to Poitiers. Eleanor with gladness received them both, for her husband had brought her dream to reality: Richard was legally heir to her own ancestral fiefs. Trouble in the South kept Henry on a disciplinary tour for three months, but when he returned he found time to discuss with his wife his plans for the children.

On his trip, a Castilian nobleman, sent by young King Alfonso, had broached a proposal of marriage between his fourteen-year-old sovereign and little Eleanor, now eight. Henry was inclined to favor the alliance, for it would strengthen his influence on the southern borders, so Queen Eleanor assented. Then she spoke of her own plans for Richard. Now that he had rendered homage for Poitou and Aquitaine, it was high time that he be formally installed as count and duke. Henry was glad to leave this routine matter entirely in her hands: he had a more important coronation on his mind—Young Henry's.

He explained to Eleanor the delicacy of the situation. As archbishop of Canterbury, the exiled Thomas Becket would be outraged if any other ecclesiastic should perform the rite of anointment and coronation. If he should hear of the scheme, he would try to prevent it by forbidding any English bishop to perform the act on pain of excommunication. "Secrecy," Henry said, "will be well nigh impossible. We must keep Thomas from sending any message to England until the ceremony is over. I may need your help in this." Eleanor readily agreed to do whatever she could. She was always eager to advance the interests of her children and to coöperate with Henry as long as their interests and his coincided. And since she had no particular love for the archbishop, the thought of thwarting him, as well as his ally, King Louis, added zest to the venture.

But the culmination of this project was still some months off, and soon Henry was drawn north again by news that the papal nuncios commissioned to deal with Becket's case had arrived in France. The queen was left to prepare little Eleanor for her coming marriage and Richard for his installations. She was contented that spring: she could devote herself to her favorite son, teaching him the duties of authority, acquainting him with the castles, hamlets, and fields of Aquitaine. With Richard at her side she held court, adjusted disputes, signed charters, and conferred with seneschal, provost, and bailiff. Together the boy and his mother rode through the land, savoring its beauty and its strength, hunting along the way, stopping here and there to hear petitions and complaints.

When they returned to Poitiers at Pentecost, they found preparations for Richard's installation as count all but complete. On the next Sunday, Eleanor, her uncle Raoul de Faye, her nephew and constable, Hugh of Châtellerault, and many Poitevin nobles took their places in the abbey church of St. Hilaire. Soon the monks of St. Hilaire and Montierneuf came chanting down the center aisle; then the canons of St. Pierre, with solemn step. Last of all, the twelve-year-old Richard walked with great dignity between Bishop John of Poitiers and the resplendent Archbishop Bertram of Bordeaux. Eleanor did not restrain her pride. She smiled joyfully at her son and noted with pleasure how handsome he was in his gold-embroidered white satin robe, and how the scattered sunbeams touched up the gold of his hair. The climax of the service came as Archbishop Bertram, adjuring Richard to protect the Church and to rule justly, presented to him a white silken standard embroidered in scarlet with the hawk and the lilies of Poitou. Then Bishop John presented the great lance, and as the boy stood holding in either hand these symbolic emblems of the countship, the choirs chanted in unison the responsorium, *O princeps egregie.*

On the next day, after Richard's new vassals had all paid him homage, the whole party rode gaily to Limoges. Here, in similar rites, the boy was invested with the traditional symbol of authority of the dukes of Aquitaine: the sacred ring of the martyred maid, Ste. Valerie. As it was placed on Richard's finger, the choirs burst forth with the same glorious chant used at Poitiers, the music and words of which belonged peculiarly to St. Martial's, since they had been composed by a monk of that abbey.

Eleanor and Richard stayed at Limoges only a day or two. The queen had brought little Eleanor to meet an escort from King Alfonso, and as soon as the girl had set out for Castile and marriage, the ducal party hastened back to Poitiers. Just before the ceremonies, word had come that King Henry needed Eleanor's presence in Normandy. So, stopping at Poitiers just long enough to leave Richard in the care of her uncle, Raoul, the queen set out northward, taking in her entourage William Marshal. Henry had agreed to make him tutor in courtesy and the use of arms to the prince who was so shortly to become king.

Eleanor reached Caen the day before Prince Henry was to be spirited across the Channel. The conduct of this mission had been entrusted to Richard of Ilchester, archdeacon of Poitiers, and from him Eleanor learned the latest developments. The king's apprehensions had been justly grounded. His intentions had become known, and Archbishop Thomas had procured from Pope Alexander letters prohibiting English ecclesiastics from having anything to do with the coronation. One copy of these had been placed in the hands of Bishop Roger of Worcester who was even now on his way to deliver it. The Channel ports must all be closely guarded: the queen must see to that. No one was to put out from the coast without her authorization. Prince Henry's wife, Marguerite, was to remain at Caen with the queen. Ilchester himself, taking the prince with him, would depart for England on the morrow. William Marshal would make one of the party.

During the ensuing two weeks, Eleanor enjoyed herself in blocking Archbishop Thomas' attempted interference. She kept in touch with the constable of Normandy, who reported to her that all guards at the Channel ports were on the alert, and on the lookout especially for Bishop Roger, who was wandering helplessly from port to port, seeming none too anxious to carry out his commission. Eleanor herself politely detained with her at Caen Bishop Bernard of Nevers who was bearing a papal commission to seek an interview with King Henry.

The tension was relaxed at the end of two weeks by the arrival of King Henry bearing the news that all had gone off well. Prince Henry, aged fifteen years, was now the "Young King." There had been no trouble about the coronation. It had taken place on Sunday, the fourteenth of June, 1170, at Westminster. The ceremony had been performed by Archbishop Roger of York.

News of Henry's *coup de main* roused the expected reaction in Thomas. He was furious. But the king learned to his surprise that Louis also was incensed because his daughter, Marguerite, had not been crowned with her husband. Henry's pride in his victory was tempered by the knowledge that the archbishop still had power in his threats; so Henry decided to placate these enemies. In a series of meetings, he had by the end of July soothed both men by promising that Thomas should not only crown Marguerite, but also re-crown Young Henry.

Shortly after these transactions, King Henry was struck down at Domfront with an illness so severe that he vowed a pilgrimage to Ste. Marie de Rocamadour, should she intercede successfully for his recovery. The king recovered and kept his vow. By the time he was able to resume active participation in affairs, autumn was well advanced.

After two more quite friendly meetings, Archbishop Thomas finally received from the king the things for which he had so bitterly fought during six long years—permission to return to England and be fully restored to his position as head of its Church. The lever which forced these concessions from Henry's reluctant hand was the hope that, in return, Thomas might refrain from using the authority granted him in an ominous roll of parchment signed and sealed in the papal chancery—the right to excommunicate the bishops who had crowned the Young King.

Archbishop Thomas landed in England on December first, and the reports of his early conduct caused Henry no special disquietude. But the primate of all England was not one to leave unpunished the slightest infringement of his rights, and Canterbury's right to crown the king of England he guarded with an especial jealousy. He was enraged at Archbishop Roger of York for having dared consecrate Young Henry. The English bishops who had sanctioned the act by their presence he regarded as scarcely less culpable. He persisted therefore in his decision to suspend Archbishop Roger in spite of all counsels of moderation, and to excommunicate the others. These men, though they trembled at the wrath of their archbishop, feared that of the king more. In desperation, they finally decided to cross the Channel and seek out Henry.

On the day before Christmas the three bishops arrived at the hunting lodge of Bur-le-Roi, where the royal couple were celebrating the feast. They found Henry and Eleanor in the hall, surrounded by a crowd of courtiers. Hurriedly making their way to the royal couple, they threw themselves on their knees before the king and begged for protection against the wrath of the archbishop. Not only had he refused to remove the sentences imposed on them, they said, but he was determined to tear the Young King from his throne. As the full import of their words broke upon the astonished king, the blood rushed to his face and in ungovernable rage he burst out: "What a parcel of fools and dastards have I nourished in my house that none of them can be found to avenge me of this one upstart clerk?" Henry's violent outburst terrified his courtiers and even Eleanor was shaken, though she had seen her husband in similar paroxysms before. When he finally recovered himself sufficiently to withdraw from the hall, the queen retired to her own apartment wondering what the outcome of Henry's words would be. A few hours later four armed horsemen dashed out into the night.

In less than a week, news of the horrifying sequel reached Argentan, whither the court had removed. The four knights had hurried to cross the Channel and had halted at Saltwood Castle, occupied by an implacable enemy of the archbishop. From Saltwood, the four determined men proceeded to the archbishop's residence. Entering unannounced, they made their way to a private apartment where they rushed up to Becket, roughly demanding that he recall the excommunications. When Thomas, with quiet firmness, steadily refused to yield, they rushed away shouting menacingly.

His terrified clerks pressed around Thomas, beseeching him to flee. But nothing was further from the archbishop's mind. In exaltation of spirit, he prepared to die a martyr's death in his own cathedral. Calmly he vested himself and entered the church. As he approached the chancel in the midst of his weeping clerks, two monks, in spite of Thomas' orders, ran to shut the entrance doors. Just as these were about to close, they were thrust back by mailed hands. The knights had returned. Brandishing their swords, they rushed up the nave shouting, "Where is that false traitor, Thomas Becket?" Standing near the chancel steps, the archbishop drew himself up to his full height and replied in a firm voice, "Here am I, no traitor but a priest of God." The infuriated villains then rushed upon him, and beneath their sacrilegious blows the martyred Thomas sank to the pavement.

When the messenger disclosed this to Henry, the king turned deadly pale, as though he too had received a mortal wound. His knees bent beneath him and he would have fallen had not a retainer rushed to his support. Leaning on the arm of the man, the king turned and was led stumbling to his room. There he remained alone for three days.

During these nerve-racking days, Eleanor's mind was busied with new problems. What was going to happen? The murder of the archbishop in his cathedral, almost on the steps of the altar, would send a shudder through the whole of England, and Europe as well. Would the pope now excommunicate Henry? If so, his enemies everywhere would surely take occasion to attack him. Louis of France would take the lead, drawing after him many great nobles, restless under their suzerain's increasing restrictions on their activities. The king would have to fight as he had never fought before. He would need all the support she could give him. But what if she should not support him?

The thought had risen unbidden in her mind and its presence there startled her. Not support him? And yet—why should she? Certainly on the marital basis he had long since forfeited any claim to her loyalty. She reflected with disgust on his promiscuous relations with women of all classes. There was that woman of the streets, Ikenoi, who had persuaded Henry to acknowledge her baby as his son. Then there were the daughters of his vassals, hostages at his court, none of whom was safe from his lustful hands.

Fresh in her mind was the revolt of Eudo of Porhoet, angered at his daughter's shame.

Eleanor had indeed become hardened to these casual relations; but there was one affair that was more than casual, one that had aroused in her a deepening resentment. Whisperings about the court had for years breathed the name of Rosamond Clifford, Sir Walter de Clifford's fair daughter. Henry had met Rosamond, who was then hardly more than a child, twenty years ago during that first year after his marriage to Eleanor, when he had gone to England, leaving her in Poitiers. The gossip was that Henry never missed a chance to see the girl. Some said that he had lodged her near his favorite manor of Woodstock; some, that he had placed her in the care of nuns at the convent of Godstow Abbey to which he had made liberal grants. Now came word that on this very last trip to England the king had thrown off all concealment and openly flaunted the hussy at court. Worst of all, their young son was rivalling Henry's legitimate offspring in the king's affection.

As the queen reflected on the possible danger of this last development, her mind reverted to her own children's future. How fortunate it was that her eldest was already crowned! The Young King ought certainly to profit in some way from this present situation. Her unbidden thought no longer disturbed her. If it came to a choice in loyalties, she knew where hers would go. Lord Louis had confirmed her sons in their possessions, and even if her husband lost his, they must retain theirs. Above all, her own Aquitaine must be preserved for Richard. At the seat of her power she could serve her children best. Away, then, to Poitiers!

The Court of Love 1171

ELEANOR'S RE-
TURN TO POI-
TIERS EARLY
IN 1171 MARKED THE
beginning of a compara-
tively peaceful period in her
life. During part of this
time, King Henry was in
the North attempting to
stave off the issuance of an
interdict. Finally, the better
to protect himself against
having any such document
served on him personally, he fled to England and thence to Ireland. Eleanor was thus left to herself with leisure to develop her
design for living—the refinement and enrichment of social life.
She had abundant material with which to work.

To begin with, she was surrounded by a score or so of boys
and girls, heirs and heiresses of noble families, sent to enjoy the
educational and matrimonial advantages at the court of their suze-
rains, the queen-duchess and the young duke, Richard. Then, in
addition to the constant flux of ecclesiastics, nobles and suitors,
there came others—poets, singers, men of letters. Every man was
welcome, whether jongleur or troubadour, clerk or layman, wandering scholar or mime, provided only that he was able to contribute to the company's pleasure.

Eleanor already had with her, as an assistant in shaping the manners and tastes of the younger generation, the gifted and charming Marie the Authoress. Now she hoped to secure the aid of another Marie. This was none other than her own daughter and eldest child, the wife of Henri the Liberal, Count of Champagne.

Eleanor had long wished to have a visit from her daughter, whom she had not seen for over fifteen years, while, for her part, Marie was equally anxious to see her mother. She had scarcely turned eight at the time of her parents' divorce. Yet she had continued to cherish an indelible impression of her young mother as a being altogether delightful. She had never forgotten the two happy years between Eleanor's return from the crusade and her divorce. In this period they were much together, since Eleanor never seemed too busy to entertain her child. She would play and dance with her, sing songs, and tell her endless stories. In the ensuing years, Marie's tastes had reflected Eleanor's enthusiasm for music and literature. The girl had absorbed all the treasures of the past and all the creations of her own age. She had read Livy's charming *History*, knew pages of Horace by heart, loved Ovid's *Metamorphoses*, and had devoured his *Art of Love*, which Eleanor had sent her. For the *Chanson de Roland* she cared less than for the more modern *Roman de Eneas*, in which Lavinia analyzed in long monologues her passion for Aeneas, and Aeneas, overcome by love, fainted at the first sight of Lavinia. Above all, she delighted in listening to troubadour or jongleur sing the love lyrics of the South, or those composed in her own honor.

Eleanor had kept in touch with Marie during their separation by an exchange of letters and books. Among the books which Eleanor had sent her daughter was a copy of the stories of Marie the Authoress, or "Marie de France," as people were beginning to call her. When the queen wrote to Marie de Champagne requesting the pleasure of a visit, she held forth as an added inducement the prospect of meeting in person the writer whose stories Countess Marie had so much admired. Marie replied, expressing her delight at the thought of seeing her mother, and said that she would be able to come, since Count Henri was about to leave on a round of tournaments that would keep him from home for a number of months. She would bring with her, she added, some musicians, as well as two persons whose conversation she felt sure her mother would enjoy. One was her chaplain, Andreas, a scholar versed in theology, widely read in Latin authors, and above all devoted to the writings of Master Ovid. The other was the gifted poet, Chrétien de Troyes, who had lately written a story which Marie herself had suggested.

On reading this letter, Eleanor's heart was filled with a joy surpassed only when her eyes beheld and her arms embraced her lovely daughter.

As Eleanor led Countess Marie and her attendants to their quarters in Maubergeonne's Tower, the party paused to catch a glimpse of the queen's apartment. Marie had scarcely more than sensed the taste reflected in the furnishings when her eye was caught by the figure of a golden-haired boy stretched out on the magnificent lion-skin which Eleanor had brought back from Palestine years ago. Richard's head was propped on one hand while with a quill pen in the other he was laboriously trying to write down a song which he had composed. Aroused from absorption in his task by his mother's voice, the lad jumped up, advanced toward Marie, and, dropping on one knee, kissed the hand extended to him. Then Marie, to her mother's delight, drew the lad gently up and kissed him on both cheeks. Richard, from that moment, became the devoted slave of his beautiful sister. He bounded ahead to lead the way when the little procession resumed its upward course.

When they arrived at the apartment destined for Marie, Eleanor awaited with some uneasiness her daughter's comments on its furnishings. The middle-aged queen was acutely aware that Countess Marie was of the younger generation and represented the latest word in every department of the *beau monde*: she dreaded being considered old-fashioned. Her fears were groundless, for Marie was tactful. She said nothing of the wonders—the vaulted ceiling bright with the planets and signs of the zodiac, the floor designed to present a map of the world with cities, rivers, and a sea with creatures swimming in it—which she had seen a few days before in the new apartments of her sister, the Countess Adele, at Blois. Instead, she admired the rich rugs, hangings, and cushions, the fireplace and Syrian braziers, the carved chests, the small leaded window panes, and the window seats made in the thickness of the walls. Eleanor, pleased by this praise, bade her daughter sit beside her on the silken coverleted bed which served as a couch, and as they chatted, mother and daughter took appreciative stock of each other. Eleanor was pleased by the beauty, intelligence, and dignity of Marie; while Marie admired, with a touch of awe, the still handsome, imperious face of her mother. Feeling her magnetism and force, Marie understood what her mother must have been like in her youth when, at Antioch, she had set the tongues of the whole world wagging, and later had thrown away the crown of France.

Eleanor had to satisfy the countess' curiosity about all her half-brothers and -sisters. But when the conversation threatened to involve the recent troubles of state, the queen rebelled: "Come, away with politics! Let us enjoy ourselves in this quiet corner of the world while we can." Then she began unfolding her plans for her household.

She was too busy herself with the affairs of county and duchy to train properly the horde of young people, and she hoped Marie would be willing to assist her. The girls would not be difficult to manage, but the roisterous young cubs were interested only in hunting, jousting, and other rough sports. They had as yet little tincture of courtly ways. "To see them at table," the queen said, "you would think them a pack of young wolves. If one in five has remembered tonight to brush his hair and clean his fingernails, it will be a seven days' wonder. When they sit next to a girl at table, they have no idea of engaging her in conversation or even of offering to cut up her meat. They have yet to be taught that a true knight must learn other things than to fight."

"You are quite right," rejoined the countess. "It certainly behooves a true knight to make himself agreeable to the ladies; and it is just as necessary that girls should learn the ways of courtly love. Our poets of the North have woven into their romances the theme of resistless love and its power of developing in man all virtuous qualities. My clerk, Chrétien, is the best of all. He shows wonderfully how a woman should train a man, and how a true knight in love ought to act. But I am anxious to have the subject worked out in a systematic way. I have asked Andreas to try it, taking Master Ovid's fine treatise on love as his guide. But with these young people, why not keep on as you have begun and gradually work up to something more formal? Perhaps we might even hold a court of love—the kind you've told me they have in the South during the spring season."

That very afternoon Marie began her admonitions to the young lords and ladies. They must be sure to dip their fingers delicately in the water basins before and after the meal, remember to dry them on the napkins, and not on their clothes, and avoid spotting their clothes with gravy. When the pages passed the meat and the various messes, let each lad attend first the wants of his lady; and after drinking from the goblet they shared, let him wipe the rim clean. At supper, the countess was pleased to notice that the young people remained quietly standing until their elders were seated, that the boys were attentive to their lady companions, and that all of them ate quite slowly.

After the meal was finished, the company began taking their places near the great fire-place. Eleanor found the poet Chrétien the most interesting man of letters with whom she had yet talked. Andreas the Chaplain appealed to her somewhat less, though she could see that he had much to recommend him. Marie de Champagne was charmed with Marie de France. The talk naturally ranged over literary favorites. *Floire et Blancheflor,* with its glimpses of oriental life, its sultans and harems, turned the conversation to the *Roman d'Alexandre* and its Eastern marvels. Someone asked if the story had not been dedicated to Countess Marie's husband. "That is true," the countess replied. "And recently my husband's brother was honored in the same way. Sir Gautier d'Arras dedicated to Count Thibaud his *Eracle.* Have you read it? He takes the hero all the way to Constantinople. That would interest you, my lady mother."

"Oh—Sir Gautier! He will soon be with us," exclaimed Eleanor. "He is bringing Pétronille's daughter, Isabella, from Flanders. We can hear the story from his own lips. I'm hoping another Northerner will visit us also: I have invited Benoît de Sainte-Maure to come and bring his new work, the *Roman de Troie.* But why do we talk of absent writers with such eminent ones in our midst? Chrétien and Marie, you must honor us with a tale."

"Yes, yes!" cried Richard. "Please, Aunt Marie."

Richard begged so persistently for one of his favorites that Marie had to yield. She told of the silly ass who wished to compete with the little dog for their master's affection by jumping up and pawing the master. The poor animal was rebuffed for his pains and departed sadly, reflecting on the wholesome moral that one should not seek to claim a position in life for which he is not fitted.

After the applause had subsided, Marie continued with some of her more sophisticated tales, which showed that true love always finds a way. Her concluding story told of a young baron who had a mistress of unknown origin, supposedly beneath him socially.

His vassals insisted that he marry a noblewoman who could bear him heirs. The two lovers prepared to bow to the inevitable. While the baron looked around for a suitable wife, his mistress began arranging the house to receive her. A bride was selected, and when her relatives flocked to the wedding, they could not refrain from expressing their admiration for the amiability and beauty of the forsaken mistress. At the last moment before the ceremony, the mistress was discovered to be the intended bride's twin sister and hence a woman of noble birth. The two lovers were married and an excellent husband was found for the deserted bride. This finale brought a round of applause from the audience, which now broke up, though not before it had been arranged that Chrétien should recite something the following evening.

When Chrétien stood ready to recite the next night, Countess Marie insisted on hearing "Lancelot, the Knight of the Cart." This was the poem she had suggested to Chrétien, and she thought it the best he had ever done, even though it was in an unfinished state. The poet bowed to her wish, though his choice would have been "Yvan, the Knight of the Lion," which he had recently completed.

The story concerned Lancelot, who dared countless perils to rescue Guinevere, and who subjected himself to heart-breaking humiliations in obedience to her imperious whims. All listened tensely as Chrétien told how the goodly knight crawled on hands and knees along the edge of a great sword which bridged a torrent, and how he cut down the savage guardian who attempted to block his progress. But when he was compelled to ride in a filthy cart reserved for felons, the cheeks of the men in the audience flushed with rage. And later on, when Guinevere, to punish Lancelot for having hesitated a moment before mounting the cart, ordered that he allow himself to be defeated in a tournament, Raoul de Faye and the older knights expressed incredulous disgust. Grizzled Raoul said he was not surprised that Master Chrétien had never finished the tale: such nonsense he had never heard. No knight could ever be so lovesick as to act like a craven. But the young girls sighed in rapture to imagine having a man so ardently in love with them.

The dialectical Andreas took up the discussion: "After all, is not love a noble thing, a power resistless, a law unto itself? It is but right that love's devotees should obey its dictates. And where should a woman find love? Surely not in marriage, which is an alliance of fiefs and not of hearts."

"Well said, my good master Andreas," broke in Countess Marie; "we women have too long been used to cement alliances and breed heirs. We have a right to love, and have it we will."

"Do you imply then, my lady countess," asked a young heiress, "that one cannot have love in marriage?"

Before Marie could answer, Chrétien interrupted to ask, "What would happen when two lovers married? Must the wife immediately cease loving her husband and seek love elsewhere?"

The queen remarked that these were weighty questions which might well be made the subject of a formal discussion. In the coming spring they might essay a court of love in which problems like these could be submitted to a jury of ladies. Master Andreas might work up some hypothetical cases to cover various aspects of the subject. If there were any genuine ones, they could be presented by an advocate so that the identity of the questioner would not be revealed. The queen's words evoked an enthusiastic response, at least from the feminine members of the audience, and Eleanor promised to undertake the project.

The date for the court of love was set for the eve of St. John's festival, and heralds were sent out to announce the affair to the lords and ladies the country round. Countess Marie aided Andreas in improvising cases, and also counselled several lovesick maidens. Raoul de Faye, as seneschal, was charged with assigning lodgings for the guests and looking out for their comfort. Constable Saldebreuil was to supervise the carpenters in building the stagings, and providing the awnings, banners, and tents. Before long, in the meadows along the Clain, a gay village of tents—red, yellow, and green—was being erected to receive the overflow of guests. Harvey the Butler saw that wines and provisions of all sorts were on hand so that there should be no stinting in the ducal hospitality.

The preparations did not interfere with the usual evening entertainment. Indeed, more and more friends were added nightly to the circle around the fire. Eleanor's niece Isabella, Countess of Vermandois and Flanders, finally came with Sir Gautier d'Arras; then the poet-clerk Benoît de Sainte-Maure arrived, bringing as he had promised his new *Roman de Troie*. On his first night at Poitiers he presented to the queen a vellum copy of the romance, begging the honor of dedicating it to her. Eleanor, replying that she was the honored one, insisted on a narration of the story. And so, for several successive evenings, Benoît spun out his tale of marvels and adventure. Knights, monks, and pages followed with critical interest the ancient battles, while the ladies listened intently to the tales of love about Jason and Medea, Achilles, Polyxena, and, above all, the flirtatious Cressida.

The day of the court of love dawned auspiciously, with the sun glinting on the fresh verdure of grass and trees. At an early hour a gay procession headed by trumpeters and heralds moved slowly out of the courtyard and around the castle to a spot where there was a gentle slope. Here a semicircular amphitheatre had been built, consisting of a platform from which on either side several ranges of benches extended in a curve. The platform was sheltered by a green canvas awning, while varicolored banners fluttered from the window openings of Maubergeonne's Tower in the background. Ascending the steps to the platform was a rather delicate procedure for the ladies since their skirts not only swept the ground in front, but also trailed out a yard or two behind. But with the trained help of the pages, the feat was accomplished gracefully. Eleanor sat in the middle one of three throne-like chairs, with Countess Marie and Isabella in the other two. The remaining ladies and maids took seats near the platform, making a charming picture for the men who sat on the benches or on the ground, thus completing the circle.

When all were seated, a blast on the trumpets silenced the buzz of conversation. A herald then stepped forward and declared that they were met under the aegis of the god of love, whose laws would govern the proceedings. By his edicts were to be decided all matters brought up for discussion before the president of the court, Her Highness Eleanor, Queen of England, Countess of Poitou, and Duchess of Aquitaine. All anxious lovers, vassals of the god of love, were invited to submit their problems and rest assured of just judgment.

Andreas the Chaplain submitted the first case. A knight had complained of his mistress' unjust treatment in extorting from him a promise not to speak a good word of her to others, on pain of losing her love. The lover faithfully kept his promise till one day, in the company of other knights and ladies, he heard them speaking shamefully about his lady. He endured this for a while with an ill grace, but when they continued to disparage his love, he at last burst out violently in her defense. When the affair came to his lady's ears, she condemned him to lose her love because he had violated her commands.

The honorable court lost no time in reaching a decision. Its unanimous opinion adjudged the arrogant mistress to be entirely in the wrong. It was deemed both unseemly and unfair for any woman to have laid such a command on a lover and then to blame him for not carrying it out. The gentleman, on the other hand, was commended for having defended the reputation of his mistress.

The next case struck rather closely home to Queen Eleanor, reminding her of her first marriage. It appeared that a certain man had in ignorance joined in love with a woman who was related to him. When he discovered his fault, he sought to leave her. "But the woman," the advocate said, "was bound by the chain of love and tried to keep the man in love's observances, claiming that the crime was fully excused by the fact that when they began to enjoy their love it was without any sin."

Announcement of the judgment was awarded to Eleanor, who decisively said: "A woman who seeks to preserve an incestuous love under an excuse of any kind is clearly acting contrary to what is right and proper. We are always bound to oppose any of those incestuous and damnable actions which we know even human laws punish by heavy penalties."

Andreas now begged permission to present a problem involving the question of whether true love were possible between husband and wife. A certain knight, he said, was in love with a woman who had given her love to another man, but the suitor received from her this much hope—that if she should ever lose the love of her beloved, her love would go to this man. A little while later, the woman married her lover. The other knight then demanded that she give him the fruit of the hope she had granted, but this she refused to do, saying she had not lost the love of her lover. Eleanor, to whom the decision was again left, gave her response with evident reluctance: "We dare not oppose the opinion of the Countess of Champagne who once ruled in a lengthy letter that love can exert no power between husband and wife. Therefore, we recommend that the lady should grant the love which she has promised." Yet the tone in which she spoke, and the fact that she gave no command but only a recommendation, led some to suspect that her sympathies were with the woman.

Discussion in a lighter vein ensued when Chrétien stated the case of a knight who sought vainly the love of a lady. Not to be discouraged, he sent her one handsome present after another. She did not, however, yield him her love. The knight complained that this was not fair treatment, and asked for an opinion from the court. The response was curtly expressed: "Let a woman either decline gifts offered her with a view to love, or let her pay for them with her love."

This prompted a gentleman in the company to inquire what things were fitting for a lover to give that his lady might properly receive. The Countess Marie replied: "A woman who loves may freely accept the following: a handkerchief, a fillet for the hair, a wreath of gold or silver, a breastpin, a mirror, a girdle, a purse, a tassel, a comb, sleeves, gloves, a ring, a picture, a wash basin, little dishes, trays, a flag as a souvenir—any little gift which may be useful for the care of the person, or pleasing to look at, or which may recall the lover to mind, if it is clear that in accepting the gift she is free from all avarice. But we wish all of love's knights to be taught that if a woman receives a ring as a pledge of love she ought to put it on the little finger of her left hand, and should always keep the stone hidden on the inside of her hand. This is because the left hand is usually kept freer from dishonesty and shameful contacts, and a man's life and death are said to reside more in his little finger than in the others, and because lovers are bound to keep their love secret."

As this seemed a fitting conclusion for the day's proceedings, the queen signalled the heralds to proclaim the session over.

Eleanor and the Great Revolt 1171-1173

URING ALL THE GAIETIES AT THE CASTLE ELEANOR'S thoughts had not ceased to run on graver matters. There was latent discontent with her husband's iron rule among barons everywhere, and the crisis produced by the murder of Becket aroused their hopes. Louis of France, ever watchful for a chance to weaken Henry on the Continent, was hinting revolt to the French barons. Count Philip of Flanders and the brothers Henri de Champagne and Thibaud de Blois, all hoping to extend their territories, had already pledged their loyalty to Louis. In England, the influential Earl Hugh of Chester and Hugh Bigod, Earl of Suffolk, were ready to rise against their king; while young William the Lion, King of Scotland, watched developments with covetous eyes.

But the most poisonous fruits were ripening in Henry's own family. The sixteen-year-old son to whom he had so recently given the name of king was no longer content with a title. Young Henry had become arrogant since his coronation—so much so that he had haughtily remarked at the banquet where his father waited on him at table: "Such action is entirely fitting since I am the son of a king while my father is only the son of a count." But his vanity had suffered a severe shock when his father continued to treat him as a mere boy. Furthermore, he felt it unbefitting his dignity that he should continue to live on the sums of money doled out to him by the Old King. He wanted the power of actual rule and revenues of his own, and he wanted his bride crowned queen. Even his younger brothers, Richard and Geoffrey, had caught his discontent and were beginning to dream of authority.

The boys' mother understood their ambitions. For seven months she herself had been ruling her ancestral lands alone, and the feel of power was good. If Henry were to yield up to his sons the real control of the French territories to which he had already acknowledged their titular right, she might, through Richard, continue as practically independent ruler of the Southwest. Furthermore, she found the complaints of her eldest son completely justified. By keeping the reins and the purse strings in his tight fist, King Henry was not only being selfish, he was being foolish. If he were going to call Henry the Young King he had best treat him like one. Otherwise, the boy's natural longing to feel his own importance would be turned against his father; and the passions of youth can be molded by skilful handlers into formidable weapons.

No one was more aware of the explosive possibilities in this whole situation than Louis of France. He saw in Henry's sons the spark he needed, but he knew that to use them safely, he must have their mother's support. So to Eleanor, through their daughter Countess Marie, he sent his proposal. The main resources of the Northeast—Flanders, Champagne, and Blois—were at his disposal. English adherents and the king of Scotland were ready for action. If Eleanor could rouse the Southwest, they could, by a concerted attack, force Henry to relinquish at least some of his lands. Eleanor had decided on her position months ago: if this were the only way her sons could gain their rights, it was the way she would take. She promised to sound out the Aquitainian barons. But she reminded Marie that Henry had a habit of taking his enemies by surprise with sudden blows, while Louis's movements were apt to be dilatory. The allies must keep in constant touch and be ready to attack at the same moment. When the moment came, Louis must strike with speed and decisiveness. She agreed that matters must come to a head through Young Henry, so she immediately sent for him and his wife, Marguerite.

The couple's visit increased the customary gaiety of the Poitevin court. Yet in between the hunting and jousting, the singing, and dancing, and love-making, Marie and Eleanor found occasion to stimulate Young Henry's grievances against his father. He finally declared that he would endure his position no longer. He would demand full control in Normandy at least, and if that were denied, he would appeal to King Louis, to whom he had done homage for the duchy. As for Marguerite, King Henry had promised to have her crowned, and now he must keep the promise.

By the time the boy king and his wife left in September, they were thoroughly infected with the germs of rebellion. King Henry had ordered them to England, trusting that his son's presence there would help preserve the royal authority. But the conceited youth did his best to undermine it. He travelled through the Island, making himself the rallying point of all the discontent in the kingdom.

Then suddenly King Henry appeared in England. He had received in Ireland the news that papal delegates had arrived in Normandy. When he learned that they had come, not to excommunicate him, but merely to adjudicate his complicity in the Becket murder, he decided to meet them. The field was still open for diplomatic discussion, and at this Henry was a master. He might yet extricate himself from the vexing situation. Taking Young Henry and Marguerite with him, he crossed the Channel to Normandy in May, 1172. The negotiations with the cardinal legates were successful. Both Henry and the Young King swore to abolish the disputed Constitutions of Clarendon, and in return the legates absolved Henry of guilt in the archbishop's death, though they did exact penance for the consequences of his ill-timed words. The Old King felt secure for the first time in many months.

Henry's peace with the Church did indeed dampen the hopes of his antagonists, but it did not drown them. The intriguers had roused aspirations which would not be allayed. Young Henry, caught up in the business-like court of his father, felt his insignificance more than ever; for it was still to the Old King that courtiers looked for commands and favors. The boy, with increasing ill humor, plagued his father continually with his demands: provinces of his own to rule, money of his own to spend. Repeatedly he, Eleanor, and King Louis complained that Marguerite was still an uncrowned queen. Henry finally decided to grant what would cost least. Accordingly, he sent the young couple to Winchester, and there on August 27 Bishop Roger of Worcester placed the long-desired crown on Marguerite's head. The king made a further investment in his son's docility by giving the pleasure-loving boy and his whole entourage complete new wardrobes.

The royal pair had reluctantly rejoined Henry on the Continent when they were agreeably surprised by an invitation from King Louis to visit him in Paris. Henry thought it inadvisable to offend the French king, so he gave his consent to the trip. He had as yet no reason to suspect why Louis expressed a longing to see his daughter just at this time.

The Young King and Queen were welcomed to the French capital with excessive courtesy, and treated as if they were already reigning sovereigns. After the austerity of the English court, Young Henry found his father-in-law's solicitous attention both a balm to his pride and a spur to his ambition—as it was calculated to be. The scheme for wresting power from his own father was soon the concern of their every conversation. When Louis had learned from his guest the sentiments of the English noblemen, he perfected his plans. Simultaneous attack could be launched from north and east. William the Lion, supported by Earl Hugh of Chester and other northern barons, would invade in force from Scotland. From Flanders, Count Philip and the Young King would lead an army across the Channel and land on the east coast, where they would be aided by Earl Hugh of Suffolk. Then, while the main English forces marched to fight the king of Scotland, the expeditionary army could push down unopposed from Norfolk and capture London.

Young Henry became much excited at the prospect of action, and Louis goaded his already sensitized resentment into fury by revealing King Henry's pending shift of territory. Seeking to extend his control over the Alpine passes to Italy, Henry had arranged to betroth six-year-old John to Alice, daughter of Count Humbert of Maurienne who held two of the passes in Savoy. The needy count was willing to barter the hand of his heiress for money, but he was demanding in addition that John be endowed with lands. The implications of this report struck the Young King instantly on the sorest one of his grievances. Bursting into Louis's speech, he cried: "By the eyes of God, John shall have none of *my* fiefs!"

Louis had prepared his answer long before: "Of course he shan't! But your father may try to give him some. If he does, defy him and fly to me. Our allies will strike, and we will soon have the old fox at our mercy."

Louis's hope that King Henry's latest manoeuvre would provide the conspirators with the provocation for attack was shortly stimulated by Eleanor. The English royal family was together at Chinon in January, 1173. Here Eleanor learned from her son the details of Louis's plans, and she constantly exhorted him to follow the French king's advice. To her husband she carefully presented a deceptively calm picture of the Southwest. Aquitaine was, to be sure, quiet; but it was the oppressive quiet which precedes a storm. The duchess said nothing about holding out to her barons the prospect of freeing themselves from Henry's iron grasp, nothing about their enthusiasm for the coming revolt. Henry accepted her report without question, and, deeming the South secure, was all the more ready to push his plans for eastward expansion. And so, taking Young Henry with him, he rode off to his first meeting with Count Humbert at Montferrand.

This council was something of a disappointment to the intriguers. Henry delivered to the count the first of the five thousand marks he had agreed to pay for Alice. Then Humbert asked what lands John was to receive. But the crafty king answered only in general terms, assuring him that John would have enough for an ample income. Humbert was apparently satisfied for the moment; so the hoped-for crisis was postponed until February, when another council was to make final settlement at Limoges. Here, surely, Henry would have to declare his hand.

Several days before King Henry reached Limoges, most of the southern barons arrived to perfect, with Eleanor and Duke Richard, the plot to end the English king's rule. Eleanor informed them that the moment for their concerted effort was surely at hand, and warned them to be ready.

The council opened with a ceremony of homage. The reigning count of Toulouse, young Raymond of St. Gilles, knelt to both Henry and Richard in token of fealty to Aquitaine. It was a token also of Henry's diplomacy, for he had without a struggle won a claim which both he and King Louis had earlier tried vainly to enforce by war. After the exchange of oaths among the new vassal and his two lords, Count Humbert at last pressed for completion of his contract.

He was now ready, he said, to deliver Alice into King Henry's keeping and to receive the second installment of one thousand marks. He wished, however, to have the contract reduced to writing, and in that writing to have set forth in detail the landed possessions assigned to Prince John. In the momentary silence following this demand King Henry failed to notice the tenseness which gripped his eldest son. Though he knew that the Young King would probably object to giving up any of his possessions, King Henry had been so long used to carrying all before him that he expected to override easily any such boyish opposition. With scarcely a glance at his son, he announced that he would assign to Prince John the goodly castles of Loudun, Mirebeau, and Chinon. Young Henry sprang to his feet: "John shall have none of my castles, not one! If you must give him something, give him Richard's lands or some of your own. Mine he shall not have. Take witness, you assembled here! My father refuses me control of my rightful lands and seeks even to take them from me. My appeal shall be now to my liege lord, Louis, King of France." Before the astonished Henry could utter a word, the enraged youth stormed out of the hall, followed by his retainers. That night the Aquitainian barons took horse and made for their various strongholds.

The king made stumbling reassurances to Count Humbert and left the council. Next day the assembly at Limoges was bewildered by the news that King Henry had left on a hunting trip. Even Eleanor and Young Henry were surprised at his apparent unconcern. But Henry was not riding forth for sport. During the night Count Raymond of Toulouse, acting under the promptings of his newly-sworn fealty, had bared to his liege lord the widespread conspiracy against him. At Raymond's suggestion, Henry had sent warnings to his castellans in the other regions, and was even now making a personal round of his strongholds near Limoges. Within the city, the queen and her defiant son went ahead with their plot, unaware that they were being watched closely by Henry's most trusted men.

When Eleanor left with Richard and Geoffrey for Poitiers, William Maingot de Sugères and Porteclie de Mauzé, two Poitevin nobles loyal to Henry, rode with her under instructions to report to the king her every movement. Having returned to Limoges, Henry himself took his elder son in charge. In spite of violent protests, he replaced the Young King's most hot-headed companions with his own knights and led the whole party to Chinon. They reached the castle on March 5, and when they retired that night, the king compelled his son to sleep in the same chamber with him. The precaution was of no avail: the boy's pallet was empty in the morning. The lad had risen in the night, stepped over the body of the sleeping guard at the door and passed softly by the men-at-arms snoring in the hall. In the courtyard William Marshal and two other close friends were waiting with horses. The youths passed quietly across the drawbridge, mounted, and rode off at full speed for Alençon.

When King Henry discovered that his son had stolen away, he shouted for his horse and set out in mad chase after him. Arrived at Alençon, he found his son had left for Argentan. At Argentan he discovered that Young Henry had escaped him once more. Seeing now that the youth would make good his escape across the border to the French king, Henry gave up the chase and headed north to place his castles in a state of defense.

Young Henry and his friends did not slacken their pace until they had sighted the spires of Chartres, where King Louis awaited them. On the second day after their arrival, they were summoned to an audience given by Louis to two nobles sent by King Henry. The messengers had come to demand that King Louis return Young Henry to his father. When Louis inquired who made this demand, they replied that it was the king of England. Then he arose, placed his hand on the shoulder of the Young King, and replied, "What you say cannot be true, for the king of England is here and through you he has made no demands upon me. His father may indeed be living, but as king he is dead, for with his own mouth he has resigned the kingdom to his son." The noble ambassadors were obliged to be content with this mocking reply and to return empty-handed to their sovereign.

The French king decided on one more move to consolidate his advantage before touching off the revolt. He felt that with Richard and Geoffrey in his hands, most of their vassals in Aquitaine and Brittany would join the uprising. So he persuaded Young Henry to make a dash for Poitiers and bring them back. The Young King and his friends reached Poitiers in the dead of night. Having roused Eleanor and the boys, Henry infused his brothers with his own youthful enthusiasm: their liege lord had issued a call to arms; they must fly to his court and fight to save their lands from their father's miserly grasp. The sleepy children were wide awake in an instant. Whatever their love for their father, it was not enough to compete with their brother's dramatic appeal to their manhood. Eleanor was reluctant to part with her younger sons, but seeing their eager faces, she resigned herself, and played the Spartan mother to such perfection that both Richard and Geoffrey went off resolved to reflect honor upon themselves and the ancient house of Poitou.

The events of the night were soon related to King Henry by a message from William Maingot. The news convinced Henry of his wife's disloyalty. He broke out into curses against the woman who had alienated his sons from him, and swore to exact vengeance. But for the moment his hands were tied.

Everyone everywhere seemed to have risen against King Henry. Louis had made his usual sortie against Verneuil. Earl Hugh of Chester, returning from a pilgrimage to St. James of Compostella, had joined Ralph of Fougeres in attacking Dol in Brittany. William the Lion had called the barons of Scotland to his banner. Earl Robert of Leicester was preparing to join forces with Sir Hugh Bigod in Norfolk. Count Philip of Flanders was gathering troops and awaiting the arrival of the Young King. Many nobles in Anjou were either ravaging King Henry's lands or, abandoning their own castles, had led their followers to join the king of France. In northern Poitou Sir Raoul de Faye and Vicomte Hugh of Châtellerault were attacking the king's castles, while Eleanor's followers were doing the same in the West and South.

King Henry seemed strangely inactive. He had moved to Rouen, where apparently he was interested in nothing but hunting. What he was really doing, however, was gathering a force of mercenaries, chiefly Brabantine *routiers*—professional fighters always ready to follow a leader who paid well and promised booty. Henry had not hoarded treasure for nothing, and he knew when to spend it.

It was not till the end of August that he felt ready to take the offensive. Then with his accustomed rapidity he dashed against Louis, who had been conducting a leisurely siege of Verneuil, observing the canonical hours of prayer, doing a little fighting and more hunting. But Louis could retreat with celerity. This he did as soon as news reached him of Henry's headlong approach. King Henry then turned westward, after he had forced into submission several of the border vassals. He dashed across Normandy to fall on the attackers of Dol with such violence that he not only relieved that castle, but took an embarrassing number of prisoners, including Sir Ralph of Fougeres and the returned pilgrim, Earl Hugh of Chester. To teach the rebellious lords of Brittany a lesson, he turned the terrible *routiers* loose to plunder at will. Then, turning northeast again, he arrived toward the end of September at Gisors, where he had arranged an interview with Louis. He thought his successful campaign might induce the French king to cease hostilities. The interview was fruitless, and the sight of his disobedient sons standing at Louis's side served to increase Henry's rage against Eleanor. Then, thinking it time to move in her direction, the king directed his march southward into Anjou.

The same results followed his swift movements there. Castle after castle fell before him. Wavering vassals came over to his side and were compelled to give up hostages for good conduct. Being in need of money to pay his *routiers,* he next headed for his chief depository of treasure at the castle of Chinon. On the way, he had the satisfaction of settling scores with Sir Raoul de Faye by burning his castle and laying waste his manors.

The news of Henry's rapid successes was anything but cheering to Eleanor, left almost defenseless at Poitiers. Her chief vassals were engaged in looking out for their own interests. Some seized the occasion to attack a weaker neighbor; some plundered the lands of convents and monasteries; others laid siege to royal castles. There was not a thought of concerted action. Chief among the few warriors around the queen-duchess were the traitorous William Maingot and Porteclie de Mauzé. Eleanor had no suspicion of the part they were playing. Consequently, it was to the poisonous counsel of these two that she turned.

Both William and Porteclie showed great solicitude for Her Highness' safety. They pointed out the danger of her position, surrounded as she was mainly by women and children, with a mere handful of men-at-arms to defend the castle. The castle itself was in a sad state of repair. Would it not be wiser to join her sons at King Louis's court? The proposal of fleeing as a suppliant to her former husband was highly repugnant to the queen. She finally adopted Marguerite's suggestion that they make for Countess Adele's castle at Blois and then push on to Countess Marie at Troyes. William and Porteclie immediately dispatched a rider to inform Henry of their route.

Eleanor's preparations were quickly made. She would take with her only Marguerite, who wished to rejoin her husband. The other children—Joan, John, and his little fiancée, Alice of Maurienne—were to remain at Poitiers. She and Marguerite must assume men's garb, since speed was called for and some attempt at disguise would be desirable. In the grey of a November dawn, Eleanor and the Young Queen rode away, protected only by William, Porteclie, and a few men-at-arms. They followed the Clain to Châtellerault, then crossed the Vienne which guided their course for some twenty miles farther. Darkness had set in when a band of knights dashed out of the woods and surrounded them. Her protectors made a brief show of resistance, but soon allowed themselves to be disarmed. Eleanor found herself helpless in the hands of Henry's men.

For a few moments Eleanor was so dazed that it seemed as if her very life had been brought to an end. Gradually, however, she forced herself to master the thoughts whirling through her mind and began to adjust herself to the situation. She had been a fool to rely on Louis, hesitant and given to half-measures. She should have known that Henry would beat him: he always had and he always would. But Henry was not going to intimidate her. She had been right in fighting for her sons.

By the time they reached Chinon, Eleanor had regained her equanimity and felt ready to face Henry upon whatever ground he might choose to give battle. Nevertheless, she was not sorry to learn that her husband had not yet come. She thus had two days to rest and further prepare herself for the ordeal of facing Henry's wrath.

Immediately after his arrival, she was ordered to attend him in the hall. Rallying her forces as she descended the stairway, Eleanor swept into the room where her irate husband stood waiting to receive her. They were a strongly contrasting couple as they confronted each other. Eleanor, slender and elegant; Henry, stocky and dishevelled. But they each resembled the other in one thing—the bearing of both was regal.

The lion-like king glared at his recalcitrant wife silently for a few moments, enjoying his triumph. The imperious woman before him met the gaze of his piercing grey eyes steadily and proudly. At last he broke out mockingly: "So, my lady, you thought to escape the eagle's talons by seeking safety with the hare!"

"My lord Louis does indeed run well," retorted Eleanor,

~ 179

"but at least he insults not his wife by flaunting harlots in her face."

"Think not to justify your conduct by such foolish talk. Know you not that you stand before me guilty of treason? No betrayer of my trust shall live to glory in the deed. Treacherous sower of discord which has imperilled my very crown, subtle alienator of my sons, do you think to escape my vengeance?"

"For your vengeance I care little; for my sons I care much," cried the indignant queen. "Blame not me if your sons now fight against you. You thought to make a man a king and still keep him in swaddling clothes. Had you but given Young Henry some small portion of that land which you hold in your tight fist, some real authority; had you been more generous with him, you would have found in him a loyal supporter. As for Richard. . ."

"Enough, enough! Jibe on if you will, but I'll put you where no jibe of yours shall ever plague my ears again. I'll pack you off to the nuns of Fontevrault. By the eyes of God, I think a nun's habit would become you well."

"Quite as well as, if not better, my lord," Eleanor quickly retorted, "than a monk's cowl would become you." Then as Henry turned to leave she cried: "But by the Virgin's crown, I'll ne'er exchange mine for holy veil at the behest of any man, be he king or knave!"

Isolation at Salisbury Castle 1174-1183

ELEANOR HAD BEEN EXHILA-RATED BY HER DUEL OF WITS WITH Henry, but her exhilaration lessened with each step she took up the narrow winding stairway to her apartment. When she threw herself down on the cushioned window seat, her mind was intent on thoughts of the future. She had little hope that her allies would be able to defeat Henry now that the revolts against him on the Continent had been almost snuffed out. His enemies were too widely scattered and lacked effective leadership, though to be sure King William the Lion of Scotland had yet to be heard from. If they should all be defeated and she were to remain in her husband's hands, what could she look forward to?

The queen's faint hopes of being rescued faded away during the next eight months, as one piece of news after another reached her through the lips of her guardian, Sir Robert Malduit, a knight who had grown up in King Henry's service. Eleanor speedily discovered that Sir Robert was absolutely faithful to his king, and soon gave up attempts to alter his allegiance. He was courteous, however, toward both her and Marguerite and quite willing to tell of Henry's successes.

These were as usual due both to his ability as a negotiator and his skill as a warrior. The first report dealt with the failure of the allies' projected move on London through Norfolk and Suffolk. This had been checked by the justiciar, Richard de Lucy. He had repulsed Earl Hugh Bigod and captured Earl Robert of Leicester with his wife, both of whom had crossed over from Flanders ahead of Count Philip and the Young King. Philip and his companion, on hearing this news, had given up for the time being their plan of sailing to England and had turned their attention to making sallies into Normandy.

Eleanor spent a dreary Christmas season alone with Marguerite, and then was further depressed by hearing that Henry had negotiated Lenten truces with both Louis and the young king of Scotland, whose hoped-for invasion was thus still further delayed. Meanwhile her son Richard, just knighted at the age of sixteen by the king of France, had been sent off to give much needed leadership to the barons of the Southwest. Since, however, the lad had been excepted from the Lenten truces, his father was free to attack him. It was the young knight's first venture in real warfare. He fought bravely, but proved no match for his father. The town and stronghold of Saintes which Duke Richard, supported by the De Lusignans, elected to hold, soon fell before Henry's thunderbolt attack, though Richard himself escaped to the South.

Shortly after news of these events had reached Eleanor, Robert Malduit presented himself to announce that she was to leave Chinon. King Henry was preparing to cross the Channel to help repel invasions from Flanders and Scotland, where William the Lion was at last on the move. The Scottish king had crossed the border, and many nobles were reportedly joining him as he pushed southward. Henry had ordered his forces to gather at the port of Barfleur and had sent a company of men-at-arms to escort the two queens there. Eleanor was glad of any change after eight months of seclusion at Chinon. What a joy it would be, she exclaimed to Marguerite, to ride through the open country once more!

So, it was with heightened spirits that the two women

mounted their palfreys next morning and set off for the long ride to the Cotentin. As they descended a rocky hillside a few days later, they saw below them the village of Barfleur and its harbor crowded with a fleet of transports. When they drew near the docks, Eleanor beheld a group of prisoners in chains, huddled together in the foggy dampness. Among them she detected two of England's great earls, Hugh of Chester, and Robert of Leicester with his defiant wife. The queen longed to talk with them, but was prevented by Robert Malduit, acting on strict orders from the king.

While they stood there, Henry himself rode up and dismounted. For a few moments he gazed upon his captive enemies, then, without a word he turned and walked quickly toward the gangplank. He was followed by the children whom Eleanor had left at Poitiers, and Geoffrey's ten-year-old fiancée, Constance, the Duchess of Brittany. Eleanor looked for some sign of recognition from her children but neither John nor Joan, eyes fixed on the teetering gangplank, noticed their mother's face strained toward them. They were led from sight as Eleanor and her fellow prisoners boarded the vessel.

Fortunately for the noble prisoners, crowded uncomfortably on the deck, the July night was moderate, the Channel relatively quiet, and the wind favorable. They made a quick crossing and reached Southampton early in the morning of July eighth. The first to disembark were the king, the children, and their attendants, who quickly mounted and rode off on the way to Winchester. Then the prisoners disembarked and took the road toward Salisbury. Their way led them after an hour or so to the southern edge of a vast plain. For miles around nothing but wind-bent trees broke the horizon, but gradually the outline of a conical hill emerged before them. Soon they could see on its top Salisbury Castle, perched three hundred feet above the level of the plain. Eleanor viewed the fortress with some apprehension, hoping that it was not to become her prison. As the first of her fellow captives rode on past the road which branched up the hill, her fears subsided for the moment. But as she herself approached the roadway, Robert Malduit gently forced her horse to the left, toward the glowering castle. This, then, *was* her destination. Even her last faint hope—that she might at least have Marguerite's companionship—was shattered as she watched the Young Queen ride away northward. When Marguerite's figure at last faded into the distance, Eleanor with a sigh turned her horse's head upward.

About half-way up the long climb, the tiny cavalcade encountered the first of the encircling fortifications: a deep ditch, bordered in its inner edge by a mound a hundred feet in height, capped by a high stone wall twelve feet in thickness. A sharply inclined ramp led them upward across the ditch and through an entrance in the wall, out onto the level surface of a considerable enclosure, known as the outer bailey. From the center of this space there rose confronting Eleanor's eyes the conical summit of the hill crowned by the castle's towering keep. But between her and the castle's yard yawned a second ditch, backed by another earthwork and wall. The queen and her escort passed over the drawbridge, through the gatehouse with its heavy doors and overhanging portcullis, and finally, by way of a passage tunneled through the mound, entered the inner bailey. When they issued from the dark passageway, the soft evening light, filling the compressed circle of the inner bailey, brought a sense of relief to the wearied queen. And when the fragrance of linden blossoms came to remind her of the castle's garden, nourished by her care in years gone by, she felt better able to face the complete isolation which her husband seemed bent on imposing upon her. She was somewhat less depressed as she followed Sir Robert around to a doorway opening directly from the bailey level into a large ground-floor apartment abutting upon the base of the rectangular keep and extending the full length, fifty feet, of its shorter side.

Sir Robert assisted his queen to dismount and then led her into the apartment, apologizing the while: he was custodian, he said, but his long absence and the haste of their recent movements had prevented him from renovating the castle and making arrangements proper for her reception. He would remedy these defects as soon as possible. Eleanor replied that all she wished for the moment was something to eat and drink before she retired. Accordingly, Robert dispatched his squire to seek out what the castle larder afforded. Since the kitchen was close at hand, around the corner and separated from the queen's apartment only by the chapel, the squire soon returned followed by two attendants bearing half a cold fowl, a loaf of bread, a flask of wine and a goblet. After this refreshment, Eleanor thanked her attendants and dismissed them, then threw herself down on the good mattress with which, she thanked God, she had had the apartment equipped years ago.

The queen awoke the next morning, surprised at the brightness of her room. Then she remembered that she was no longer at Chinon. Salisbury Castle was still prison, but at least it was blessed with wide windows. The sunlight cheered her so that she arose full of plans for her restricted domain. First, of course, the filthy rushes must be swept out, and the floor spread with sweet clover hay. After she had washed her face and hands in a basin of fresh water brought by Robert Malduit, and refreshed herself on wine and bread, she took up with him the renovation and staffing of the castle.

Eleanor soon learned that Sir Robert, son of a royal chamberlain and himself chamberlain for some years, had already taken steps to satisfy most of her requirements. But when she exclaimed that it was outrageous of her husband to leave her without a single woman to wait on her, Robert came to the defense of his sovereign. She must remember that the lord king was hurrying to meet the foes who still imperilled his realm. Nevertheless, he had, before quitting the ship at Southampton, issued a writ authorizing drafts on the sheriff for all immediate needs. It was the king's desire, the chamberlain explained, to make the queen as comfortable as possible under the circumstances. But until all traces of the rebellion had been stamped out she must be kept from all contact with the outside world. For this reason no young woman of noble birth could be allowed near her for some time. Robert said, however, that he would soon find, among the villagers in the outer bailey, a young person suitable for an attendant.

The chamberlain went on to say that he himself would not always be present to attend to her wishes. He must, therefore, select some other man to act as deputy chamberlain or usher to serve her in his place, and asked if she had any preference. The queen replied that she would be glad to have Sir Roger de Gruze, who had once been a member of her household. Robert felt the choice would be entirely acceptable to the king, and promised that if, as he thought, Sir Roger was even now at Winchester, he would have him assigned to her service immediately. Just at this moment attendants made their appearance, prepared to clean the apartment; so Eleanor, at Robert's suggestion, went out to survey her garden.

The garden was rectangular in shape, fitted into an irregular space defined by the main wall surrounding the inner bailey and by a curving subsidiary defensive mound. Eleanor entered the garden through a gap in this mound. She was astonished at its well-kept appearance after her years of absence. She soon discovered the explanation when she spied in a far corner the familiar figure of Buistard, her former gardener. The wiry little man, when he heard a footstep on the gravel path, turned an inquiring face toward the intruder. With a cry of recognition he ran to greet his mistress. His ruddy, weatherbeaten face beamed as she praised him for the care he had bestowed on the flowers, shrubs, and trees. As they walked along the box-bordered path, Eleanor exclaimed over the blossoming phlox and roses. She was especially pleased to note how well-grown were some half-dozen chestnut trees planted at intervals around the garden's edge. She had had them sent down from Warwickshire fifteen years ago when they were young trees. They had been slow in starting on this dry, windy hilltop. Buistard said it had been a hard fight, but he had kept them well-watered as she had instructed him, though it was a long carry from the well in the castle yard.

At the end of the survey Eleanor found herself beneath an elm tree at one corner of the garden. Here she seated herself while Buistard returned to his work. Just then her eye was caught by the figure of a young girl entering the garden. After a moment's hesitation the maid sought out Buistard who took her by the hand and led her to the queen. Eleanor put the girl at her ease and found out that her name was Mary. She was eighteen and the niece of a freeman living in the village. She had lived in Winchester till the death of her father, an importer of wines. Since the girl was well-mannered and intelligent, and spoke French, Eleanor gladly accepted her. Mary brought word that the queen's apartment was now ready for occupancy. Eleanor arose with alacrity, for she had had no opportunity to change her clothes or to bathe since quitting Chinon.

Eleanor found the apartment much more livable. The chests containing her wardrobe and toilette accessories were soon opened and Mary laid out a robe, tunic, and chemise. A circular tin tub was brought in from the adjoining room and filled with water. After she had bathed, donned fresh clothes, and had her hair brushed and arranged, Eleanor felt more ready to face the lonely days that lay ahead.

For the next week or two, time did not hang heavily on the queen's hands. Her incarceration at Chinon had taught her that a prisoner's salvation lay in keeping engaged at some task or other, so she was glad that the ordering of her apartment and the provision of necessities demanded her attention. One concern—securing chapel equipment and the services of a priest—had to await the return of Robert Malduit. He had happily found De Gruze at Winchester and soon brought him to Salisbury along with several others to fill out the castle staff.

To Roger, Eleanor told her needs. There were a number of things in her chamber at Winchester which she wished to have brought up—a few books, her guitar and psaltery, and if possible her harp; also a set of chessmen, if none could be found in the castle. These, however, could wait: a priest to officiate in the chapel and act as her confessor and clerk was the first requirement. If none could be detached from the staff of the cathedral below, one must be brought from the cathedral at Winchester.

Sir Robert proceeded at once to discharge this commission. Late that afternoon, he introduced to the queen a canon by the name of Anselm. When she glanced up at the black-robed priest, Eleanor's first impression was of an alert intelligence which, combined with a quizzical cast of countenance, recommended the man instantly to her favor. Her favorable impression was deepened when inquiry revealed that he was widely read, not only in the works of the Roman writers, but also in those of recent times. He had begun his schooling at Winchester, studied at Chartres and her own Poitiers, then travelled to Paris to be stimulated by the famous Peter Abelard. All in all, Eleanor concluded that she had secured in Anselm not only a chaplain, but a companion whose resources of mind would help much to relieve the tedium of her isolation.

Underneath the surface occupations of Eleanor's mind there ran an insistent questioning during these early days: What was happening in the North? Had William the Lion and his Scots triumphed and were they even now driving southward? And what of her sons in France? She hardly dared hope for good news. It was not till the end of July that her suspense was ended and her faint hopes dashed. One day when Sir Robert was serving her at dinner, he told her of all that had happened since she had seen her husband riding away from Southampton toward Winchester.

Before leaving Normandy, the king had been warned by his confessor that his penance at the tomb of Thomas Becket had been too long delayed. Until he entreated for forgiveness the soul of the archbishop, murdered as a result of his hasty words, he could not hope for victory over his foes. Consequently, Henry had taken only a brief rest at Winchester, and had set out early the next morning for Canterbury, which he reached on the third day. The royal party halted before the west gate of the town at the church of St. Dunstan. Inside, the king was stripped of his garments and clothed with the woolen shirt of the pilgrim. Then he made his way barefooted over the rough stones to the cathedral entrance, followed by a gathering crowd of wondering townsfolk. He was received at the west doorway by the monks and a group of bishops hastily summoned for the occasion. Led by the prior, the king walked slowly along the center aisle of the nave and descended into the dark crypt, its gloom only partially relieved by the flickering light of tapers. The king uttered a cry at the sight of the holy martyr's tomb and threw himself prostrate before it. Deeply moved at this sight, the bishop of London declared the king guiltless of any intent to have the archbishop murdered, and asked the assembled bishops to absolve him. Absolution was granted, and the clergy proceeded to inflict penance.

When the king's shirt had been stripped off, he knelt at the tomb to receive the penitential blows. The thought of striking their king unnerved some of the monks so that their strokes fell but lightly. But others, remembering the murderous blows dealt their beloved leader, brought their rods down with such force that they bit into the flesh.

King Henry remained kneeling all night before the martyr's tomb. In the morning he arose and was taken above to the vestiary to be clothed before attending mass. After the ceremony, he presented treasure and other gifts to the cathedral, mounted his horse, and rode away, refusing to refresh himself with anything more than the bread and water which had been his only diet since quitting Winchester four days before. On the following day he dismounted at the royal palace of Westminster and withdrew at once to his apartment where he threw himself down on his couch utterly exhausted. He remained secluded for two days, gradually recovering his strength, though anxious thoughts preyed on his mind, for there was still no news from the North.

On the morning of the seventeenth of July before dawn, the king was aroused from fitful slumber by a man who had thrust aside the protesting chamberlains and burst into his room. Before the startled Henry could speak, the man gasped: "A message . . . from the North . . . from your faithful servant, Sir Ranulf de

Glanville. Good news. . . . your foes have been defeated. The king of Scots is in chains at Richmond Castle." King Henry could scarcely believe it until he read Glanville's letter describing the victory. Then he broke into thanksgiving: blessed Thomas had not been entreated in vain.

When Eleanor heard this, she tartly remarked that if the archbishop since his ascension to heaven had suffered a change of heart sufficiently to make him fight for, instead of against, her husband, it was indeed sure evidence that he had become a saint.

After the capture of William the Lion, the rebellion in England collapsed. Barons surrendered their castles without a fight as soon as they saw Henry approaching with forces which included five hundred carpenters and engineers bringing up siege materials: timber, battering rams, and ballistas. Wavering neutrals hurried from all sides to Henry's court at Northampton to assure him of their loyalty. All these, along with William the Lion, Constance of Brittany, and Marguerite, Henry sent to Portsmouth and Southampton. From these ports, forty vessels took them, as well as the king and his household, to the Continent. Here the many distinguished prisoners and the thousand or more of lesser note were distributed among Norman castles.

With the English situation thus taken care of, Henry turned to deal with his sons and their French supporters. A few swift dashes induced King Louis and the others to agree to a truce. Meanwhile, the waverers hastened, as they had in England, to join King Henry's side. Finally a gathering of all parties took place in October of this same year, 1174, at Falaise in Normandy. A final accord was written out and signed.

Eleanor was relieved to learn that her sons had been leniently treated. Their father, satisfied that he had taught them a lesson, received them back into his confidence, requiring only a renewal of their homage. They were awarded large annual incomes. For nine-year-old John, his doting father generously provided, again at the expense of his elder brother's prospective inheritance, two castles in England and several others scattered throughout the Continental possessions. This went much against the grain with the Young King, but he was compelled to swallow his chagrin and accompany his father to England, even occupying the same berth when they crossed the Channel. Immediately after landing, King Henry took his son to pray at the martyr's shrine at Canterbury, and then on to London, where they appeared before a grand council of prelates and barons, as public evidence of their reconciliation. Almost all the prisoners had given hostages and had been released by this time. But Henry felt that the score with his queen had not yet been settled to his satisfaction. He determined to rid himself of her.

At Henry's special request, Cardinal Ugoccione, legate *a latere,* paid a visit to England, nominally to settle certain affairs of state, but really to be consulted on the possibility of a royal divorce. If Henry could arrange a divorce, he planned to disinherit his sons and marry the French princess, Alais, long affianced to Duke Richard. Any heir born of such a marriage, so the king thought, would ensure the support of his grandfather, King Louis of France. But the cardinal crushed his hopes completely: divorce was out of the question. The news of Henry's design and its failure served to divert Eleanor for a whole day.

Yet reports from the outside world came only too rarely to relieve the monotony of the queen's life. Eleanor would have found her lot much harder to bear had she not delighted in reading. She had a fair store of books: some had been found in the chapel stored away with service books in a recess of its wall; others, in a similar press in her apartment. Additional volumes had been brought from her chamber in the palace at Winchester. Among these treasures was the volume given her by King Roger of Sicily when she was returning from the crusade. It was a copy of Boethius' *De consolatione philosophiae.* As Eleanor turned over the pages, beautifully illuminated in gold, blue, and crimson, she found some solace in this volume, written by a prisoner to console himself for his misfortunes.

Yet the monotony of her daily round weighed heavily on her spirits. She rose with the sun, dressed, breakfasted, and took a walk in the garden to consult with Buistard until Anselm's arrival to celebrate mass. At this ceremony Eleanor was joined not only by Mary but also by Sir Roger, his squire, and one or two others, while in the rear little old Buistard reverently listened to the familiar words of the sonorous service. After mass Eleanor would often detain Anselm for conversation, reading aloud, or a game of chess. The hours were consumed in this way until Roger or Robert Malduit himself would appear to announce the serving of dinner. Eleanor always drew out the mealtime as long as possible, dallying over each course, drawing her companions into conversation with the hope of obtaining news of the outside world.

The afternoon hours were usually spent in the garden over embroidery till time for vespers and supper. Then the queen might teach Mary to sing a favorite song while she played the melody on her guitar, or else they would set out for a walk around the circuit of the inner bailey wall. To reach this they proceeded to the gatehouse where a narrow stairway in the thickness of the wall enabled them to ascend to the broad pathway on its top. As they walked along this, they could see over the breast-high parapet the panorama of the plain. The sight of the golden sky was to Eleanor a never-ending source of pleasure, delightful in itself, but also recalling to her memory the sunsets of her own Poitiers.

One day, however, when the prospect of a third year of this complete isolation from the outside world seemed almost insupportable, there came a sudden break, as unexpected as it was welcome. Eleanor could scarcely believe the good news when Sir Robert Malduit told her that the king had ordered him to escort her the next day to Winchester. Robert could only guess the meaning of the order, but it might have been caused by the arrival there of the princess Joan, on her way to be joined in marriage to William, King of Sicily. Possibly Joan had induced Lord Henry to give her, before she left England, one last sight of her mother. Such indeed proved to be the case. When the queen dismounted the next day at the royal palace, her feet had scarcely touched the ground before Joan threw herself into her mother's arms. The loving embrace was a tonic for both mother and daughter.

Eleanor revelled in the days that followed. Her first care was the inspection of Joan's trousseau. She found this practically complete, since the procurement of it had been entrusted to the capable hands of her old acquaintance, Richard of Ilchester, recently made bishop of Winchester. She enjoyed being able to converse freely both with Bishop Richard and with the many other persons in the castle. Evidently the king, having been induced to release her, at least temporarily, had decided to place no restrictions on her.

Henry himself once strolled unexpectedly into the ladies' bower and found Eleanor and Joan together. The daughter was momentarily startled for fear that sparks might fly at this first meeting of her high-tempered parents after their long separation. During that time, however, much had happened to modify the attitude of both. Eleanor had concluded that the interests of her sons could henceforth be best served by coöperating with Henry. Her husband, for his part, since he had been able neither to force his wife to seclude herself as a nun nor to induce the ecclesiastical authorities to sanction a divorce, was perforce compelled to make what use of her he could in the furtherance of his future designs. But to win her coöperation he must conciliate her, at least to some degree. So Joan beheld no display of tempers. Both her parents were on their best behavior and, when they wished it, no couple could surpass them in graciousness. The meeting, though brief and a bit constrained, was affably maintained to its close.

The first week in September brought the day for Joan's departure. Eleanor enjoyed the ride to Southampton, the bracing air from the sea, and the sight of the *Esnecca* with the flotilla of seven ships provided for Joan's household and escort of bishops and barons. Eleanor remained at Winchester till early October. Then she found herself guiding her palfrey once more up the steep slopes leading to Salisbury Castle. She felt encouraged in spite of the fact that she was returning to her isolated life. Her meeting with Henry seemed to her to presage a relaxation of the restraints hitherto placed on her intercourse and movements. But the first sign of such a relaxation seemed an unconscionably long time in appearing.

Appear it finally did, though not till more than half a year had dragged itself out. Then one day Sir Robert brought word that he had been ordered to purchase clothes not only for the queen but for some maid of noble birth. The queen was to be allowed to select this companion, who must, however, be of a family of unimpeachable loyalty to the king. Eleanor's heart leaped up, for she now felt sure that she would be gradually restored to freedom of action. She began at once to talk over with Sir Robert the question of clothes and the choice of a suitable attendant. The matter of clothes was soon settled: an assortment of hoods, pelisses, mantles, and a few other articles would suffice. Who her companion should be was a graver matter. The queen's choice, approved by Robert, finally fell upon Sibyl de Lucy, a connection of the justiciar, Sir Richard de Lucy. Eleanor had become acquainted with Sibyl during her recent visit at Winchester, and the girl had recommended herself by her gaiety, her fondness for song, and her ability to read.

Robert said it would take some time for these matters to be arranged: the king's writ for clothes would have to be forwarded to Sir Edward Blunt, royal chamberlain in London. Sir Edward knew the shops there well and made many purchases for the royal household. Sibyl de Lucy had gone northward, and some weeks would elapse before she could be brought to Salisbury.

Sibyl, when she finally arrived, proved to be a great addition to the queen's circle. Eleanor felt that she had to apologize for the couch provided for the girl, since it had only a straw mattress. A new mattress, stuffed with hair and tufted, had been included in the orders sent to London: both the clothes and the mattress should arrive any day now. A week later, a bulky consignment of goods was brought into the queen's apartment and dumped on the floor by staggering attendants. The bundles were quickly undone and their treasures revealed. There were the goodly mattress and the new garments: scarlet cloaks and hoods, a set for both the queen and Sibyl, and two beautiful fur mantles of grey squirrel skin. Eleanor stroked the glossy fur, revelling in these welcome luxuries.

The next break in routine did not come until the winter and spring of the next year, 1179, had run their course. Late in July Sir Roger de Gruze came to announce that King Henry was at Winchester and wished the queen to meet him there at once. But that was not all: Prince Richard was to be there also.

On her arrival at Winchester late the next day, Eleanor was disappointed not to be greeted at once by her son. She was met instead by one of the chamberlains, who conducted her to her apartments. There King Henry soon appeared and told her his object in bringing her to meet Richard. He wished to reward the boy for reducing the barons of Aquitaine to order by restoring to him the titles of count of Poitou and duke of Aquitaine, forfeited when the lad had joined in the great revolt. The titles thus forfeited, Henry explained to Eleanor, had theoretically reverted to her. He therefore wished that she should return them formally to her son. The ceremony was to take place the next morning in the presence of the whole court, provided she consented. Eleanor, eager to do anything which would help Richard, readily agreed to the proposal which Henry had made. Nor was she at all displeased at the thought of appearing before the court after her years of seclusion. She hoped her appearance would create a sensation.

Eleanor was not disappointed in her hope. At her entrance next morning, a noticeable ripple of whisperings ran around the throng of courtiers. But Eleanor's attention was quickly centered on the blond young giant who came forward to kneel and kiss her hand. During the ceremony that followed, Eleanor's eyes drank in her son's every feature, followed his every gesture. When the court broke up, mother and son had opportunity for only a few moments of conversation, since Richard was setting out on his return journey that afternoon and Eleanor was to return to Salisbury Castle. Henry himself was leaving at the same time, followed as usual by the whole court. He had an appointment to meet an old acquaintance who was expected at Dover in a few days.

This old acquaintance was none other than Eleanor's former husband, King Louis of France. Louis's fifteen-year-old son, Philip, on whom the destinies of the French monarchy hung, had fallen dangerously ill. King Louis had anxiously sought the surest means for his recovery by obtaining from King Henry permission to intercede for the life of his only son at the shrine of the martyred Thomas. The aging Louis, none too well himself, was received at Dover in the most friendly fashion by Henry and escorted to Canterbury. There the pious king knelt at the shrine, thrust his head and hands through openings in the stone sarcophagus enclosing the sacred remains and invoked the intercession of the saint. Reassured by this devout act, Louis set out on his return trip the following day, but not without granting to Canterbury's monks trading privileges in his domains, and presenting for the ornamentation of the shrine a wonderous diamond, the very one given him on his return from the Holy Land by the pope himself.

The blessed martyr's aid had not been sought in vain. King Louis was soon cheered by the recovery of his son, whom he immediately caused to be anointed and crowned king of France. Then, as though he felt his work was done, King Louis sickened and died.

The chief instigators of discord for Henry the king were thus silenced: the one by confinement, the other by death. For Eleanor watched three more years limp by, with only occasional rides on the bleak Salisbury plain to break the dreary succession of days and nights.

Meanwhile the antagonism among the royal children had been growing. In the spring of 1183 it erupted, and Henry saw his southern French lands torn by the active jealousies of his sons. Richard, now vigorously ruling Aquitaine, had put down several uprisings. The barons, by appealing to Young Henry, gave him an excuse to attack Richard; and Geoffrey, as covetous as the Young

King of Richard's lands, joined in. Their father, feeling Richard to be in the right, led a large force into the South to relieve him. As he drew up to Limoges, he was very nearly killed by his eldest son's men. From the city walls they deluged him with arrows; and one shaft went clean through his surcoat.

Limoges held against all attacks; and then from within the city strange rumors came to the besiegers—rumors that Young Henry was lying crazed with fever, calling upon his father to come and forgive him. The king was not unmoved by this story, but he remembered the arrows and feared a trap. The penitence might be real, however, and he was ready to forgive. As a symbol of pardon he sent to his son a ring from his own finger.

On the night Eleanor heard of her son's sickness, she lay wakeful for hours, but finally fell into a fitful sleep. Into her dreams came a vision of her eldest son. On his head were two crowns, the lower one shining but dully: it was his earthly crown. But the upper, radiating more than earthly glory, assured her that he had passed in peace to heaven. It was a vision wrought of truth: Young Henry died in July. And after death no human force was able to wrench his father's ring from his finger—a sure sign that his heavenly Father, too, had forgiven him.

Father and Sons: Finale 1184-1189

WILLIAM MAR-SHAL HAD BEEN FAITH-FUL TO YOUNG HENRY to the last. And King Henry, never viciously vengeful, knew the rarity and worth of loyalty. He at once took William into his own service and sent him on a mission which he knew would please him. It was to bear a message of release to his benefactress, Queen Eleanor.

When William presented himself to Eleanor at Salisbury Castle, the unexpected sight of her son's closest friend moved her so that at first she could not utter her pleasure. But soon William was telling her all she wanted to hear: how her Richard was, where the other boys were, and, above all, the sad details of Young Henry's last moments. When he had recounted everything, including the burial at Rouen, William took a bundle from his squire's hands. He had saved till last the account of a sacred trust laid on him by Henry. The Young King, before his illness, had taken the crusader's cross. When he realized that he himself would not be able to discharge his vow, he had begged William to do it for him.

So William had knelt and received from the dying prince the cross-emblazoned cloak, and had promised to lay it on the sepulchre of the crucified Christ. Loosening his bundle, William spread the cloak on Eleanor's knees. She could not refrain from pressing her lips first to the garment and then, gravely, to William's cheek.

To help his sovereign regain her composure, William quickly told her of his order from King Henry: she was to be relieved of all restraint, that she might travel freely through her dower lands. The queen, although delighted at the news, confessed that she was puzzled at the direction her travels were to take. Since her confinement at Salisbury, she had almost forgotten that she had any dower lands. That was the point, William explained: others might have forgotten too. The one upon whom King Henry wished to impress her ownership by this trip was none other than King Philip of France. The eighteen-year-old monarch, far abler, thought William, than his royal father, had taken up with vigor King Louis's policy of persistently attempting to pry loose from Henry some piece of French soil. Philip's half-sister, Marguerite, widowed by the Young King's death, had received as her marriage portion the Vexin, a strip of land wedged between France and Normandy. Philip now demanded its return. The grasping young man had demanded in addition that Marguerite's English dower lands should also be given up. King Henry had countered by asserting that these manors had already been assigned to increase the dower of his own queen. To enforce the point, he now wished her to travel through them.

Eleanor, though amused at Henry's characteristic manner of parrying an unwelcome blow, was glad to win the freedom given her. But William continued with more news. The queen's eldest daughter, Matilda of Saxony, was in Normandy with her husband, Duke Henry the Lion. She was expecting the birth of another child and wished that it might be born in her native land. Her father had promised to bring her back with him as soon as he recrossed the Channel. Eleanor looked forward to this reunion with Matilda, whom she had not seen in fifteen years. After William's departure Eleanor began immediately her preparations to bid adieu to the castle eyrie of Salisbury. She left it with no regrets.

Early the next morning the "valiant and courteous" queen gaily led forth her small cortege through the dark passageway of the gatehouse, across the drawbridge, out into the bright sunlight of a September morning. In spite of her sixty-two years, she rode with shoulders straight and high, and would have brought her mount to a canter had the slope not been so steep. She chatted incessantly to Sibyl, pointing out the bronze and russet foliage of trees on the plain below, and when conversation gave out, she amused everyone by breaking into a *reverdie*. At the foot of the hill, she looked up once toward the castle, as though she were looking back upon a long illness, then set her horse's head toward Winchester and freedom.

She stayed a week in Winchester, walking happily through the fine palace, riding through the town, enlarging her household. Then late in September she set out on her tour. She first inspected two dower manors in Berkshire, then travelled to Reading where William, her eldest born, lay buried near the tomb of his grandfather, King Henry I. The monks of Reading, previous beneficiaries of the queen, gave her a hearty welcome. After a pleasant visit of some days, the queen and her household rode along the lovely, elm-bordered way beside the Thames to Wallingford, to Abingdon, to Oxford. From Oxford Castle the party pushed northward to the royal hunting lodge at Woodstock, one of her husband's favorite resorts. Nearby, in an embowered cottage, had dwelt the one woman whom King Henry had really loved: fair Rosamond Clifford. Shortly after she had been drawn from her seclusion to be flaunted before the court during the queen's absence on the Continent, she had been struck down with a mortal illness. Yet in spite of her sinful life, her body had been given honorable burial by the nuns of neighboring Godstow Abbey, who had been richly rewarded with gifts of land.

On the morning after her arrival, the queen decided to inspect Woodstock. At other manors, she had discovered that the royal stewards had been neglectful during her long absence. The wooden shutters in the hall needed repair, and the linen curtains in her apartment were faded and torn. She found the kitchen utensils greasy and battered, and the whole equipment much depleted. She told the steward to order a supply of soap from Bristol, and to secure another leaden vat, a couple of cauldrons, half-a-dozen pans and several stools, so that the cook and his assistants could do their work more conveniently. The royal housekeeper returned to the hall with much satisfaction, feeling that the royal lands were once again in capable hands.

Eleanor's continued progress carried her past Sulgrave Manor to her Cambridgeshire lands in the diocese of Ely. Then she moved south across Hertfordshire to Middlesex, where she halted at *Hethe Reginae*—the Queen's Manor of Hethe. Early in June Eleanor returned to Hertfordshire and settled at Berkhamstead where she soon welcomed Matilda. When the floodgates of speech were unloosed, Eleanor noticed that her daughter's French had acquired a German accent. This proved, however, no bar to the stream of question and answer that now ensued. Matilda gave a far from favorable picture of Eleanor's crusading acquaintance, Frederick Barbarossa, now king of Germany and emperor of the Holy Roman Empire. He had unjustly seized her husband's estates and driven him and his family into exile to live on the bounty of others. Matilda spoke warmly of her husband who, though many years older than she, had been most considerate to her.

About the middle of July, some weeks after the arrival of Duke Henry, the queen moved the whole of her court to Winchester. Here Matilda was delivered of a baby boy who was christened William, after Eleanor's first-born son. Eleanor took great delight in her grandson. She watched over him day and night, although she had provided him with two nurses as well as a laundress. Indeed, William of Winchester became the uncrowned king of the royal household for the next few months.

Toward the end of November, the queen, the duke and duchess of Saxony, and their two sons, Otto and Henry, were summoned to Westminster to attend the Christmas court, where Eleanor looked forward to seeing all her sons, especially Richard. When the queen's party reached Westminster palace, they found the members of the court struggling with the monks of Canterbury over the selection of the archbishop.

While this involved affair was being worked out, Richard took the occasion to pour out his heart to his mother. He was much disturbed by the course of events since the death of his brother, which had made him heir to the throne. He had expected his father to recognize him as such, but neither in public nor in private had the king made any declaration on the subject. On the contrary, he had begun at once to advance John's interests. His father had first commanded Richard to surrender to his brother the whole of Poitou and Aquitaine in return for John's homage. Richard had refused to do this, and had told his father that Aquitaine had come to him from his mother and that he would never yield it to anyone. Several months later the king had renewed the demand. When Richard again refused, his father had told John to call Geoffrey to his aid and make war on their brother till he yielded up at least a part of his lands.

"What an outrageous piece of folly!" exclaimed Eleanor. "How can a man as wise as your father in the ways of the world be such a fool in the treatment of his sons? As if there were not enough fighting in the world without setting his sons to hack at each other."

"Of course," resumed Richard, "Geoffrey and John were not behind-hand in accepting the invitation. So we've had a pretty time of it plundering and burning each other's villages and crops. I could never come up with the rascals, for they took good care never to meet me in combat. At last my lord father called off the boys, and bade us all three come here, where, no doubt, we'll soon be giving each other the kiss of peace!"

"If your father asks it of you, do so by all means; humor him when you can without endangering your rights, but be ever on your guard. He is so blinded by his fondness for John that one can never tell what he will do next. I have never seen such a man. Lord Henry dotes on his youngest child, thinks he loves his father and will always be loyal to him. I doubt if the boy has a loyal bone in his body. The king had best beware: John has not yet been tested."

The following day was a noteworthy one for the queen; for she, as well as Richard and John, was summoned to attend a full meeting of the council. The sight of the queen, sitting beside her husband, signified to all assembled there that Eleanor was once again to take her legitimate place in the affairs of the kingdom. After the dispatch of several preliminary matters, the king called upon Count Richard and Prince John to carry through the public reconciliation on which he had set his heart. Richard and John signed an agreement not to make war or infringe on each other's rights. After each had sworn an oath to keep his written pledge, the brothers gave each other the kiss of peace in final confirmation of their good faith. Then the court broke up, to reassemble shortly at Windsor for the Christmas feast.

Preparations for this festal gathering had long been going forward. The officers of the royal establishment had been busy for months securing great numbers of hogs, cattle, and sheep; quantities of wheat, barley, and honey; casks of wine and beer; supplies of pepper, cardamom, cinnamon, cloves, and other spices. The royal table equipment, bronze bowls and ewers, silver and gold goblets and platters, table cloths and napkins, had to be brought from Salisbury, Winchester, and Westminster to be added to the stock at Windsor. Thousands of pounds of wax were needed for making candles. Rings, jewels, and other "entertaining trifles suitable for feasts" had to be bought. Then, clothes must not be forgotten: robes for the king and queen, ornaments for a hood of samite for Eleanor, mantles of beaver. Finally, more than a hundred furred mantles, one to be presented to each of the greater vassals on his arrival.

The days of Christmas week passed all too rapidly for Eleanor. Richard took his leave before New Year's day, bound for Poitiers. Not much later King Henry set out for Winchester, where he was met by envoys who had been sent to Germany to intercede for the duke of Saxony. They brought back word that Frederick Barbarossa, wishing to retain the good will of the English king, had reinstated Henry the Lion in a portion of his estates. The good news soon brought the queen and the ducal family also to Winchester to celebrate the end of the duke's exile and the prospective return of himself and his family to their homeland.

Shortly thereafter, an embassy from the Christians in Palestine came to beg Henry to aid them in turning back the Muslim hordes. The patriarch of Jerusalem and the grand master of the Hospitallers laid at Henry's feet the royal standard of Jerusalem and the keys of the Holy Sepulchre, imploring him to carry these sacred symbols back at the head of a crusading force. Never since Eleanor and Louis had led their expedition had the Holy Land been in such peril. Henry was deeply moved, but after consultation with his council declined the invitation. The patriarch, though he bitterly denounced Henry, nevertheless accepted his escort to the Continent, where he hoped to obtain aid from the king of France.

The food supplies at Winchester, depleted by the court's visit, now began to run low, so the queen's party moved a few miles southward to Bishop's Waltham, a palatial residence built by the late luxury-loving bishop of Winchester. Here the queen soon received her husband's order to cross to the Continent, and to bring with her Duke Henry the Lion and his family, baby William excepted. Eleanor looked forward with eagerness to returning to the Continent after her years of absence. She had to delay their departure, however, until the arrival of new saddles and bridles recently ordered from London. But the whole party finally travelled to Portsmouth and crossed the Channel on a small fleet headed by the *Esnecca*.

The queen and her companions found Henry at Bayeux. King Henry soon told Eleanor the reason for her summons abroad. He was completely out of patience with Richard: the boy was fighting again in spite of his pledges to keep the peace. He and Geoffrey, whom Richard had never forgiven for siding against him with both Henry and John, had fallen into dispute over the ownership of fortresses along the border of Brittany and Poitou. The situation was intolerable, and he was determined to bear it no longer. When Eleanor asked what he proposed to do about it, Henry replied: "Since the title to Poitou and its dependencies lay in you, and you have transferred it to Richard, I shall demand that he come and formally return Poitou to you. If he should delay to obey me, I shall place you in command of a force of hired troops with which you are to lay waste his lands until he is willing to surrender them to you." Eleanor gazed at her spouse in open-eyed astonishment at these words. Considering her participation in the great revolt, could he really intend to send her at the head of an army to Aquitaine, where she might side with her son against him? It was unbelievable. Nevertheless, she said she was willing to coöperate, bizarre as the proposal was. She had little doubt, however, that the expedition would never take place, since Richard, she felt certain, would yield the lands to her. He would know without her assurance that Poitou and Aquitaine would be safe in her hands, and that she would never yield them to John.

The event proved the queen's surmise to be correct. When Richard received the order, he was as astonished as his mother had been. He controlled his anger and consulted his companions. They advised him to submit, saying he had nothing to lose by waiting. Turn and twist as he might, King Henry knew, as well as everybody else, that Richard was his natural heir, and that he must succeed not only to Aquitaine but to the whole of Henry's possessions, including the kingdom itself. Richard had only to bide his time, since the queen, as all knew, was on his side. Richard was convinced. He rode north, and before the court assembled at Alençon, resigned his rights to the queen. Richard and his mother enjoyed each other's company in the months that followed, while Henry, after being nursed through another one of his violent illnesses, started off on a tour of Aquitaine to replace Richard's castellans with his own men. He returned to celebrate the Christmas feast at Domfront, then early in the following year, 1186, released the energies of his restless heir by sending him to take vengeance on the count of Toulouse for siding with King Philip. Henry then took Eleanor to England.

The succeeding months were happy ones for the queen: she was once more on good terms with her husband, and she was confident that Richard would succeed to the throne. She added to little William's household a tutor and three young companions, and provided them all with new clothes. She reëngaged her former clerk, Jordan, and took him with her to London for a prolonged stay at Westminster palace. Here she busied herself buying clothes for herself and her maids, as well as for two royal wards: Isabel of Gloucester, affianced, since the death of Alice of Maurienne, to Prince John; and Richard's betrothed, the French Princess Alais.

Alais's life had been a sad one. Her mother, Constance of Castile, had died in giving birth to her. The motherless girl had been betrothed to Richard when she was nine years old and immediately given into King Henry's hands to be brought up. She was now a young woman of twenty-six, and ugly rumors had begun seeping through court circles about King Henry's relations with her, especially since Rosamond's death. These rumors, however, only served to arouse the queen's sympathy for the girl.

Early in 1187, Henry had crossed back to the Continent. In the preceding summer Geoffrey had been killed during a tournament at Paris. His death gave Philip fresh opportunity to harass King Henry. Geoffrey, who in 1181 had married Constance of Brittany, was survived by his wife and a baby daughter, heiress of the duchy. The custodianship of both was now being claimed by the king of France as overlord, but Henry had no intention of allowing such a prize to escape his grasp. In his next demand Philip was more successful, for Henry agreed to recall Richard from his war on the count of Toulouse. King Philip then renewed his prodding of Henry to return Marguerite's dowry, the Vexin, and also insisted on the immediate marriage of his sister Alais to Richard. When Henry continued to evade these issues, Philip declared war.

By May the opposing forces were confronting each other near Chateauroux in central France, south of the Loire. Richard and John were with their father when Henry called for another conference. Having exhausted all his other wiles, the English king finally made a proposal to Philip in writing which rebounded upon him with fatal effect. At a previous conference Philip had set a trap for Henry by offering to accept John instead of Richard as a husband for Alais. Henry had rejected the offer at that time, but now he seized the bait. He proposed that Alais should be given to John, to whom he would allot the counties of Poitou and Anjou, as well as all the other lands which he held from the realm of France, Normandy alone excepted. As soon as the quick-witted Philip had read this letter, he cried out that he had caught the old fox at last. He immediately summoned a trusted knight, gave into his hand the fatal letter, and charged him to deliver it to Count Richard and to him alone.

Though Richard was enraged when he read his father's offer, no open breach occurred till after Philip and Henry had met to conclude a two-year truce. At the close of this meeting, Richard left his father, withdrew with Philip and resisted for several weeks King Henry's appeals to rejoin him. Finally, after a raid on Chinon, whence he carried off his father's treasure chests, Richard did return, but only on King Henry's promise that Aquitaine should be restored to him.

Shortly after this hollow reconciliation, word came from Palestine that the Holy City had been wrenched from Christian hands by the Saracens, its king, Guy de Lusignan, captured, his army destroyed; and worst of all, the True Cross itself had fallen into heathen hands.

All other considerations were forgotten for the moment as the resolve swept through Europe to drive Saladin and his pagans from the Holy Land and to restore to Christian hands the sepulchre of the Saviour. The news had killed the reigning pope, but his successor immediately summoned the Christian world to a crusade. The crisis brought Richard to the front. He instantly took the cross without waiting to consult his father, much to the latter's disgust. The kings of France and England went on with their petty squabbles. But suddenly during a conference, the archbishop of Tyre rose up before them and put them to shame. Deeply sensible of his land's grief, he spoke from a heart so filled with despair and with a tongue so touched with fire that he set the souls of all aflame. When he ended his appeal, they rose as one man crying, "The crosses! The crosses!" Both Henry, the veteran politician, and the coolheaded young Philip were carried out of themselves and were the first to receive the crosses from the hands of the inspired man from Tyre.

On the following day the assembled ecclesiastics and barons turned to practical considerations. They decided that the tenants in chief of both sovereigns must be summoned to give their assent to the levying of an aid to meet the expenses of the expedition. King Henry obtained the consent of his Continental barons at Le Mans, and then set sail for England in January of 1188 to hear the decision of his barons there.

When Henry told Eleanor that he was going on the crusade, she could not refrain from wondering just how seriously this hard-headed man took his sacred vow. On his absolution for the death of Becket, he had agreed to go on a crusade within three years. He had later been allowed by the pope to delay the fulfillment of the promise on condition that he endow three religious foundations. Again, he had promised at Ivry to go with King Louis. This time, however, he had made the vow and accepted the cross, and Henry's actions soon convinced his queen that he had every intention of immediately journeying to the Holy Land.

In the first place, the king had obtained from his barons their consent to the necessary tax. In the second place, Henry told Eleanor that his departure raised the problem of the governance of the realm during his absence. So many of his trusted ministers had taken the cross that he had not a man left to whom he dared entrust supreme authority. "I have therefore decided," continued the king, looking gravely at his consort, "to entrust you with the regency." Eleanor, moved by this unexpected evidence of her husband's trust in her loyalty and ability, replied that she would do her best. Henry then indicated the men who would be her most capable advisers, bade her farewell, and left for the Continent. But King Henry was fated never to go on the crusade.

The scene on the Continent was a familiar one: Richard making war on the count of Toulouse, Philip making a war of revenge on Henry's possessions in the North. One futile conference after another followed, till finally both kings were at war, with all Europe scandalized at the sight of two crusaders fighting while Saladin held the Holy Sepulchre. Then in another conference, Richard, urged on by the crafty Philip, demanded that his father publicly acknowledge him as heir to all his dominions. Upon Henry's refusal, Richard threw down his sword at his father's feet and knelt before King Philip to do homage for all the Continental domains, excepting only all obligation to attack his father's person.

Thereafter, the drama drew rapidly to its close. Baron after baron left Henry's court to gather around Richard. King Henry, attacked by fever, dragged himself about, pursued by the forces of his two young opponents. Finally, as he lay ill at Chinon, he asked for their terms. Among them was a demand that he forego the allegiance of all those who had allied themselves with Richard. When he saw the name of John at the head of the list of those who had deserted him, he exclaimed, "Now let all things go as they will. I care no more for myself nor for aught in the world." With the words, "Shame, shame on a beaten king," he breathed his last.

Eleanor Protects the English Throne 1189-1193

IN DEATH THE VAL-
IANT HENRY WAS AT
LAST DEFENSELESS.
HIS ATTENDANTS DE-
spoiled him; left no shred of
majesty behind. William Marshal found the body of the English king lying naked and alone
upon a sheetless couch. He and
his friends clothed it in their own
garments, placed it on a bier,
and carried it on their shoulders
all the way to the abbey of
Fontevrault. The abbess and her
nuns watched over it in prayer
as it lay in state before the altar of their church. Here Richard
came, and stood for a long time staring down at his father's face.

William Marshal waited outside the church. He would face
this Richard whom he had lately fought, though he had reason to
fear him now. For once when he was guarding his late master's
retreat, Richard, unprotected by mail, had come dashing in hot
pursuit; and William had killed his horse with a lance thrust and
thrown the prince to the ground.

When Richard finally left the contemplation of his father's lifeless features, he drew William aside and said: "Marshal, good sir, the other day you wished to kill me, and you would have done it, if I had not turned your lance aside with my arm."

"Sire," William replied, "I had no intention of killing you, nor have I ever tried to do so. I am still strong enough to direct my lance. If I had wished, I could have struck your body as I did your horse. If I had slain you, I would not consider it a crime, and I still do not regret having slain your horse."

Disarmed by William's frankness, Richard instantly replied: "Marshal, I pardon you, and will bear you no rancor."

The signs of his pardon were not long in appearing. The chancellor, Lord Geoffrey, bastard son of the late king, came to Fontevrault for the funeral next day. He happened to remark to Richard that Henry had given William the hand of Isabel de Clare, heiress of Richard Strongbow, Earl of Strigul and Pembroke, and lord of Leinster in Ireland.

"By the legs of God!" exclaimed Richard, "Lord Henry did not give her to him. But I will give him freely both the lady and her lands."

To the promise of a bride and an earlship, Richard added another honor: he entrusted William with a message for the queen. One day in July, William presented to Eleanor at Winchester a written order appointing her governor of the realm till Richard should arrive.

The queen sat silent as Marshal left, savoring the love and trust which the formal words conveyed. Richard her dearest-born was king and she at last secure. She had spent no tears upon his father's death, and yet her mourning weeds were not mere pretence. Henry had killed her love and stifled the remnants of affection; but admiration for him Eleanor retained. His first attraction for her, all the bitter years between had not quite blotted out: he had been strong, yet knew how to be gentle, and Eleanor admired tempered strength. His stubborn will had held together, like an iron hoop round barrel staves, the disparate family lands. Though she hated his selfishness and pitied his frequent blindness, Eleanor felt a force snap with her husband's death—the consolidating tension was relaxed. Richard had his father's fighting temper, and, with her help, he must prove heir to his father's virtue—strength.

The thought brought her to action. She issued proclamations

on Henry's death, Richard's accession, and her appointment; she ordered the magnates to assemble at Winchester for the king's arrival; she gave donations—by no means extravagant—for masses to shorten Henry's stay in purgatory. Richard, for the good of his father's soul, had also ordered that all captives be liberated: an order that gave his mother peculiar pleasure, for she had learned from experience that "confinement was distasteful and that it was a most delightful refreshment to the spirits to be liberated therefrom." Then Eleanor travelled with her court to cities and castles, making sure that men everywhere swore allegiance to the new king. She returned to Winchester in time to see Richard greeted by its citizens and the summoned magnates on the fourteenth of August. But Richard was also greeted by report of a revolt that had broken out in South Wales. He wished to leave at once to suppress it, but his mother pointed out the folly of a campaign before his consecration as king. Furthermore, she had already commanded the sheriffs of the neighboring counties to send reinforcements to the threatened area, and the rebels would be defeated before he could get there. So, while Eleanor set out for London to perfect arrangements for the coronation, Richard took John to Marlborough Castle and saw him married to his third cousin, Isabel of Gloucester. In order to carry out further his father's intentions, Richard gave to his brother several estates, three castles, and the two counties of Derby and Nottingham.

Richard returned to London shortly before time for his coronation, which Eleanor had determined to make the most brilliant occasion of its kind. On the appointed day, Eleanor and Alais proceeded to the places reserved for them in Westminster Abbey, where they watched the long procession as it entered at the west end of the church.

First the lesser clergy bearing the Holy Water, the Cross, and lighted tapers came slowly up the aisle. After them came the higher ecclesiastics from all the king's realms, and the abbot of St. Denis as the representative of the king of France. Then two barons, one bearing a cap, the other a pair of gold spurs. Next, the new Earl of Pembroke, William Marshal, bearing the scepter with its golden cross, followed by other earls bearing the three swords of state in their heavily embossed scabbards of gold. Then six barons carrying a chest containing the regalia and royal robes, and after them the earl of Essex carrying a golden crown sparkling with jewels. Then, accompanied by two bishops, came Richard, walking under a canopy of silk supported by lances held by four barons of the Cinque Ports.

Eleanor saw her son kneel before the altar to take and swear to keep the coronation oath. The king was then led behind a screen and stripped of his clothes in preparation for his consecration. This rite was performed by the Archbishop of Canterbury, Baldwin, who poured the sacred oil on Richard's head and with the same holy chrism made a cross on his forehead, breast, and arms to signify knowledge, glory, and valor. Last of all, a consecrated linen cloth was bound around the king's locks to contain the dripping oil, and the consecrated cap pressed firmly down over all. After being clothed in his coronation garments the king stepped forth to receive from the archbishop the Sword of Rule with which to crush opponents of the Church, and to have the gold spurs buckled on by two earls. The archbishop now led him to the altar where he was adjured not to take up the crown unless he had the full intention of observing the vows previously made. Richard replied that, with God's assistance, he would observe all his pledges without reservation. He then lifted the heavy crown from the altar and presented it to the archbishop who, with the aid of two earls, placed it on the king's head. Richard, grasping the scepter in one hand and the rod of royalty in the other, was led back to his throne by the bishops.

When mass had been celebrated, Richard was conducted out of the minster to the palace, where he willingly exchanged the heavy ceremonial crown and stiff robes for ordinary clothes and a lighter crown. Richard then proceeded to the banqueting hall where three of the greatest barons of the realm were waiting to act as royal server of the basin and towel, cup-bearer, and roast-carver. Richard first slaked his thirst and then prepared to enjoy his share of the roasts, messes, and two thousand fowls provided for the feast.

Richard began his reign with efforts to amass money for the crusade. At the end of three months he journeyed to Canterbury where he found his mother awaiting him. He insured her financial independence by adding to her own dowers those formerly held by the queens of Henry I and Stephen. He also authorized her to draw on the public treasury. He continued in his determination to bring John's income up to the amount promised by his father by turning over to him the control of a solid block of territory formed by the four counties in the southwest corner of the Island. The possession of this area, added to the lands and castles previously allotted to him, placed in John's hands an influence that he was later to use to his generous brother's disadvantage.

On the twelfth of December, 1189, Richard set out for the Continent, leaving his mother to act as a balance wheel between two justiciars: Hugh, Bishop of Durham, long experienced in English affairs; and William Longchamp, newly created Bishop of Ely, a stranger to English ways. Longchamp, who had been Richard's chancellor and devoted friend on the Continent, was a lame, ill-favored person, unscrupulous in his master's service. In the contest for complete control which immediately arose between the two justiciars, Longchamp won the first rounds. When jealous officials ran to Richard with complaints, he ordered his mother and the two justiciars to the Continent. At a conference in Normandy, Chancellor Longchamp secured the chief justiciarship, while Bishop Hugh's authority was confined to the North, from the Humber to the Scottish border. In a further effort to forestall trouble, Richard exacted from John and his half-brother Geoffrey an oath not to enter England for three years from the time of his departure for the crusade. When Eleanor backed up John's protests, however, Richard gave him leave to return to England if he could secure Chancellor Longchamp's permission.

Eleanor travelled with Richard to Tours. Here she saw him receive his pilgrim's staff and scrip, and was amused to see the staff break under his weight as he was playfully testing it. In June she bade him farewell. This parting was not to be final, however, for she had received a commission to bring a bride for her son to Sicily.

The bride was not to be Alais. Since Richard had refused to marry her, his mother had suggested Berengaria, daughter of Sancho VI, king of Navarre. She was reputedly more learned than beautiful, but she had been brought up in a court famed for its poetical and musical culture, just as Richard had. Richard had agreed that Eleanor should communicate with Sancho, and that if he approved the match, she should escort Berengaria to Messina. Richard undertook to secure from King Philip, by the time of their arrival at Messina, a release from his promise to marry the French princess. When Eleanor sent her messenger to King Sancho, she found the way open for her son's marriage; for the Southern ruler had even thought of proposing the alliance himself. So she went to Bordeaux early in December and was joined there by her future daughter-in-law, Berengaria, who seemed in every way a suitable consort for Richard.

When the party set forth from Bordeaux Eleanor, though in her sixty-ninth year, scorned the use of a litter: she would ride her palfrey, for they must make haste if they were to catch the king before he sailed from Sicily. Their route led them up the Garonne past Toulouse, Carcassonne, Montpellier, and across the Rhône at Avignon. From there, the road, guided by the Durance, grew gradually steeper as they approached the pass of Mont Genèvre. It was now mid-winter, the cold intense, and the snow deep. Before crossing the pass, the party halted at a monastic hostelry where everyone mounted sure-footed mules. Long before this, the septuagenarian queen, remembering her youthful experiences in the mountains of Asia Minor, had donned breeches in order to ride astride, and had forced all her feminine companions to do the same. The crossing was effected without any more serious discomforts than numbed fingers and feet, though there were several narrow escapes from snowslides. By the twentieth of January, the party reached Lodi, southeast of Milan, where they joined forces with a group attendant upon Henry of Hohenstaufen.

Eleanor was not surprised to find this German prince in southern lands. She had lately heard news of him from her daughter Joan. The girl who at the age of eleven had gone to Sicily to marry its king, William II, had recently been left a childless widow of twenty-five. King William had bequeathed the kingdom of Sicily to his sister Constance, the wife of Henry of Hohenstaufen. But Tancred, an illegitimate member of the Sicilian line, had seized the government before Henry could arrive. Eleanor learned now, however, that Henry had given up his wife's claim. He was travelling south not to fight Tancred, but to be crowned emperor. His father, Frederick Barbarossa, who had taken the cross at the same time as Philip and Richard, had perished on the overland route through Asia Minor; and Prince Henry was now King Henry VI of Germany. Eleanor was sorry to hear of the death of her old crusading companion; and very glad she had made Richard travel by sea.

At Rome Eleanor's party left this future ruler of the Holy Roman Empire to his coronation and hurried on to Naples. Here the queen was relieved to learn that Richard was still in Sicily. He had sent a fleet to bring her there, but Eleanor, preferring land travel, sent only the baggage by water. She found, however, that Tancred had sent his admiral to meet her at Brindisi; and not wishing to offend the new Sicilian ruler, she sailed from that port down to Regio Calabria. Richard crossed the straits here and escorted Eleanor and Berengaria back across the water to Messina, where Joan was waiting to receive her mother.

Richard had easily escaped his obligations toward Alais by simply telling Philip that he could not marry a girl who was suspected of improper relations with his own father. Philip was satisfied with a money payment and the return of his sister to the French court. Even her dowry, Gisors Castle, was to be retained unless Richard died without male issue, in which case it was to be returned, together with the Vexin. The way for marriage with Berengaria was thus open, but the ceremony would have to be postponed until the Lenten season was over. This would not affect the crusaders' plans, however, for Berengaria was to sail with them under the protection of the widowed Joan.

Eleanor was off again on her travels even before Richard's forces sailed. Pope Clement III had just died, and Richard wanted her to win from the new pope confirmation of Geoffrey's election as archbishop of York and of Longchamp's appointment as legate. Furthermore, England's affairs were running none too smoothly under the unpopular chancellor. The queen and Walter of Coutances, the archbishop of Rouen, must hurry on to the Island and restore amity. So the valiant lady, taking only four days' rest, set out on April 2. Eleanor found it hard to part with Richard; but she entrusted him to the care of the Lord, bade him a courageous farewell, and stepped firmly aboard a waiting vessel. As the sails filled with wind, Eleanor kept her eyes on the little group on the dock until they were lost to view.

The queen's party arrived at Rome to find that the new pope had already been elected. He proved to be the Cardinal Hyacinth who had acted as Eleanor's escort on the return from her crusading adventures forty years earlier. The queen was able to attend his consecration as Celestine III on Easter Day, April 14, 1191. A few days later, Eleanor obtained from her friend the two favors she asked, and set out for Normandy.

From Rouen, Archbishop Walter went on to England, while Eleanor stayed to keep order in the French lands. The archbishop soon quarreled with the imperious Longchamp and finally forced him to flee to the Continent. For Eleanor, summer and fall went by peacefully. But the Christmas season was marred by disquieting news: King Philip had returned to France! This unexplained move by the supposed crusader could mean, felt Eleanor, nothing but trouble. She was right.

King Philip began by trying to persuade the seneschal of Normandy to give up Alais, together with Gisors and the rest of the territories comprising her marriage portion. But the seneschal claimed that the purported order from Richard to this effect was a forgery. The seneschal would surrender neither the girl nor her dowry. At this, the French king called on his barons to help him take the lands by force. When they refused to have any part in such a business, Philip began to court Prince John, whom Longchamp had allowed to go back to England. Philip proposed to recognize him as lord of all Richard's Continental possessions and to help him secure control of them, provided he would discard his present wife and marry Alais.

When Eleanor heard of the proposal, she took the first ship for England. The hours on the Channel seemed interminable to the anxious mother, who feared that her light-minded son would seize the bait dangled before him. At last the boat docked at Portsmouth and Eleanor hurried to Winchester. John had not yet left, but he had ordered a vessel to be made ready at Southampton. Eleanor instantly countermanded his order and summoned him to her. Then she bade Archbishop Walter bring the members of the royal council to meet her at Windsor.

Her interview with John was disheartening. In explanation of his conduct, he charged that Richard had broken faith with him. When his astonished mother asked what he meant, he claimed that his brother had tried to block his rightful succession to the crown. Before leaving Sicily, Richard had written to several persons, so John asserted, indicating that his nephew, Count Arthur of Brittany, should be recognized as king in case he should not return from the Holy Land.

"And no one here," said John, "really believes that England will ever see him more. I certainly do not. I am determined to have my rights, and if Philip alone will help me to secure them, I shall ally myself with him."

Eleanor argued that even if the accusation against Richard were true, John would gain nothing from Philip. Every liegeman of Richard would repudiate him, and he would be left at the mercy of the French king who was only using him as a cat's-paw to secure the Continental lands for himself. But John remained obdurate.

The queen finally ended the meeting with: "Begone, sir! If your sense of honor and decency will not persuade you to follow a better course, I will try force. Every castle you possess shall be wrenched from you." Then she rode off to Windsor.

Archbishop Walter and others of the governing council, relieved to have their hands strengthened by Eleanor's powerful presence, joined with her in ordering Earl John to come before them at once and not to leave England under penalty of having his castles seized and placed in their hands. While waiting for John to appear, the council moved to London, later to Oxford, and finally back to Winchester. Here John finally met them and yielded to their demands, but not till he had won his point, namely, that they should formally recognize him as heir to the crown. The queen and the council were congratulating themselves on their victory when they were startled by the news that John, after his departure, had bribed the royal castellans of Windsor and Wallingford to deliver their castles into his hands. Eleanor and her companions immediately took horse and rode off for London to make sure of the Tower. From this vantage point they sent message after message to John demanding that he give up the castles at once and appear before them. But Earl John did neither the one nor the other.

The harassed council members were now disturbed further by the appearance of messengers from William Longchamp who had chosen this moment to return to England. From Dover he sent a demand that he be allowed to resume his chancellorship. This demand threw the council into an uproar. Eleanor alone spoke in favor of allowing Longchamp to return. Knowing that he and John had been bitter adversaries, she hoped he might help to restrain her rebellious son.

She was soon disillusioned. John abruptly entered the council chamber and to her astonishment championed the chancellor's reinstatement. The earl significantly revealed the reason for his stand as he casually announced that Longchamp had offered him a good round sum for his support. With this intimation that he could be bought off, John withdrew. The members of the council allowed their hatred of the low-born chancellor to prevail over their fear of John, and offered the earl an equivalent sum to withdraw his support. John accepted the bribe, and the council ordered Longchamp to leave England. Furthermore, they dropped the matter of the castles. Thus John, though thwarted for a while in his attempt to join forces with the French king, had actually strengthened his position.

Eleanor took advantage of the expulsion of Longchamp, who was also bishop of Ely, to inspect the condition of her dower lands in his diocese. But in the bitter struggle for supremacy waged between Longchamp and Archbishop Walter of Rouen, each had placed the lands of the other under an interdict which forbade priests in these regions to perform their offices. Consequently, the queen encountered pitiful scenes as she rode through the diocese. "Wherever she passed there came out to meet her from all the hamlets and vills, men with their wives and children, not all of the lowest class,—a populace weeping and tearful, their feet bare, garments unwashed, hair dishevelled. Words failed them through grief: they spoke with tears; nor did they need an interpreter, since one might read in a page plain to all more than their words could have expressed. Human bodies lay everywhere through the fields unburied, . . . Queen Eleanor, a matron worthy of all mention over and over again, . . . understanding the cause of this great severity, and being of a pitying disposition, compassionating the painful feelings of the inhabitants at the sight of their dead, forthwith giving up her own affairs . . . went to London."

Eleanor bent all to her will on her arrival at the capital. She shamed Walter of Rouen into lifting the interdict from Longchamp's diocese. She then sent messengers to the chancellor to inform him of this move, and to bid him in his turn raise the interdict from Walter's archdiocese of Rouen. Bishop Longchamp immediately obeyed. So the merciful queen won the devotion of the distressed populace in both lands.

During the rest of the year Eleanor's peace of mind remained relatively undisturbed, save for the fact that John was moving restlessly about in the west and attaching to himself whatever barons he could. But disquieting rumors about Richard began seeping into England. Returning pilgrims said that the king had left the Holy Land at the same time as themselves, but nothing had been heard from him since his ship had been reported at Brindisi. Eleanor's anxiety was further increased in the middle of January, 1193, by a report that Richard had been shipwrecked on the northern shores of the Adriatic and was being held a prisoner by Archduke Leopold of Austria, whom he had offended in the Holy Land.

While the queen and the council were discussing this news, they were startled by a report that Earl John had sailed from Southampton to join Philip. Eleanor promptly sent out three men to search for Richard—the abbots of Boxley and Roberts-bridge, and Bishop Savaric de Rohun of Bath, a close friend of Richard's who had high connections in Germany. Then she decreed an emergency council of barons for February 28 at Oxford, and sent summonses to all tenants in chief.

When the council met, it immediately decreed that oaths of fealty to King Richard should be renewed throughout the land. While the members were debating further action an usher threw open the door of the chamber to announce Earl John. The heir apparent strode into the room and stood for a moment glaring around. Then he truculently announced that Richard was dead and demanded that he be immediately recognized as king in his brother's place.

The astonishment of the barons at these words soon gave way to suspicion and then to anger. But before anyone else could find speech, the queen's voice rang out: "By the Virgin's crown, my lord John, you proclaim weighty news and such as can scarce be believed. King Richard's death must have indeed been sudden, for word has reached us but recently that he was in excellent health. Surely you bring us some sure proof, some token—perhaps my ring which lord Richard swore would never leave his hand except in death."

As John shrank back, William Marshal started up, shouting: "This is the devil's work! He would make us traitors to our king. Seize him before he does more evil."

As the barons sprang to their feet, the queen's voice held them back: "Quiet, my lords, you forget yourselves. Let Earl John depart in peace, for he can do but little harm. By the sword of St. George, we'll hold the kingdom safe till Richard, please God, returns to take it into his own strong hands."

Seeing his ruse foiled by his mother's resolute words, the chagrined earl left the hall, mumbling that King Philip would soon set him on the throne of England.

When order had been restored, Eleanor spoke out sharply: "My lords, let us instantly to work. Earl John must be confined to the west and his castles taken from him. Have our own provisioned and their garrisons strengthened. And thou, my lord justiciar," she said, turning to Walter of Rouen, "see that all commands for this purpose be issued at once."

The magnates of the realm, spurred on by the energy of the queen mother, soon had the traitorous John on the defensive. Supported mainly by Welsh troops and mercenaries, he was penned up in the west while he saw his castles elsewhere attacked by the supporters of the king. His half-brother Geoffrey laid siege to Doncaster; Walter of Rouen marshalled forces against Windsor; the vigourous old bishop of Durham invested the strong castle at Tickhill. Eleanor undertook as her special charge the defense of the eastern coasts against invasion.

John's threat that Philip would aid him had proved to be no idle one. News soon reached England that the French king was gathering a fleet at Wissant opposite Dover. In response to the queen's urgent orders, all the coastal inhabitants, "noble and ignoble, knights and rustics, rushed to arms to defend the coast that looked toward Flanders." Sometimes Eleanor overrode jurisdictional rights by ordering out for construction work those over whom the Crown had no direct authority. After the tension eased, she sent apologies to those lords and monasteries whose privileges had been infringed: she assured them that what she had done under stress of necessity would in no way be regarded as a precedent.

Eleanor's anxiety for Richard's safety was finally relieved at the end of April. The abbots of Boxley and Robertsbridge returned, bringing with them Bishop Hubert Walter of Salisbury. The bishop had landed in France on his return from the crusade, learned that Richard had been captured, and sought out and found the king.

A King's Ransom
1193-1195

THE RUMORS THAT RICHARD HAD BEEN CAPTURED BY LEOPOLD of Austria proved to be true. Confined in Castle Dürrenstein, he had spent a dreary period of waiting until one never-to-be-forgotten day when a song struck his ear. His heart began to beat more quickly, for it was no ordinary song, but one known only to its joint composers, himself and a well-loved minstrel, Blondel de Nesle. Could it be Blondel? The king leaped to his feet to peer out the barred window of his tower. Yes, there below he saw the figure of his old friend. After the completion of the first stanza, the king sang the response. The minstrel shouted and waved his hand, but before Richard could reply he was forced by the entrance of his keeper to turn from the window. Though that was the last he saw of Blondel, the captive took the visit as a happy augury. And rightly, for on the very next day the king was informed by Archduke Leopold that he would soon be delivered from the castle into the hands of the archduke's overlord, the king of Germany and Holy Roman Emperor, Henry VI.

Bishop Hubert explained to Eleanor that Richard's long imprisonment had been occasioned by Leopold's efforts to wring from the shifty Emperor Henry guarantees that the archduke would receive a proper share of whatever ransom might be paid by Richard's subjects for his release. Terms had at last been agreed upon, and the emperor now held the English king at Speyer on the Rhine. Henry VI had at first demanded as ransom the preposterous sum of 150,000 marks (£100,000), claiming that King Philip had offered to pay him even more than that if he would surrender Richard to him, or else hold him prisoner indefinitely. The emperor had gradually modified his demands, however, and had finally settled for 100,000 marks. Furthermore, he had agreed to set King Richard free on the delivery in Germany of 70,000 marks of pure silver, these to be counted and tested by German agents sent to England.

His most exciting news, Bishop Hubert kept till last: he bore a letter from Richard. Eleanor broke the seal with tremulous hands and read:

"Richard by the grace of God, King of England . . . to his most revered Lady and dearest mother Eleanor, by the same grace, Queen of England, greeting, and every happiness which a devoted son could wish for his mother. In the first place to God and afterwards to your serenity, sweetest mother, we render whatsoever thanks are in our power, although we are in no wise able to make them suffice for actions so worthy of gratitude, for the fealty which you have preserved toward us, and for the faithful and diligent care which you have so devotedly and effectively expended for the peace and defense of our lands. For though we have been only partially informed, we are quite certain that it has been through the mercy of God and your counsel and aid that the defense of our lands has been, and will be, in greatest part provided. For our greatest reliance in the maintaining of peace, until our own arrival in the land, is on your prudence and discretion."

The remainder of the letter was taken up with Richard's request that the vacancy in the See of Canterbury, caused by the death of Archbishop Baldwin in the Holy Land, should be filled by Bishop Hubert Walter. On the crusade Hubert had shown himself so devoted and so efficient in every way that the king wished him to be placed at the head of the Church of England. He begged his mother to use her great influence in securing Hubert's election from the prior and monks of Canterbury, to whom he had written on the subject. The queen turned with a gracious smile to Hubert and assured him that she would make every effort promptly to carry out the king's wishes. Hubert was duly elected, and Eleanor quickly saw the wisdom of Richard's choice; the new archbishop was a forceful addition to her council.

Before the king's ransom could be collected, there had to be peace in the land. So Eleanor renewed negotiations with John. His affairs had not prospered. Philip had failed to help him; no English nobles of importance had come over to his side; the castles of Nottingham and Tickhill were closely besieged; and Windsor's garrison was on the point of surrender. Under these circumstances John consented to a truce, in which he agreed to yield into his mother's hands the castles of Windsor, Wallingford, and the Peak, while retaining Nottingham and Tickhill. With the cessation of civil war, Eleanor and her advisors took up the matter of the ransom.

The amount was so large that it could not be obtained by the ordinary aid owed by tenants in chief for the ransom of an overlord. In consequence, the council decided on levying in addition a combination income and personal property tax calling for one-fourth of all rents and movables, not excepting Church plate. Over and above this minimum, all were urged to give as much more as their devotion to the king prompted them. Moreover, there was to be kept a list of all contributors and the amounts given, so that the king on his return might be able properly to reward each according to his merit. Then the efficient administrative machinery was set in motion: in each shire the bishops, abbots, barons, knights, freeholders, and representatives of every town and village were called together. The justices made their circuits, and the property of each was assessed—by juries of neighbors if necessary. Then followed the task of collection, arduous enough, since, though all loved their king, no one loved taxes.

The driving force in the tedious operation was that "incomparable woman," Queen Eleanor, who drew on all her energy, persuasive charm, and commanding force to see that the work never flagged, and that everyone gave what he could. Yet she tempered justice with mercy, as when Abbot Samson and the monks of St. Edmund's Abbey turned in as part of their contribution a certain chalice which had been presented to the abbey by the queen herself. Eleanor sent it back, thanking the abbot and his monks for their generosity, but saying that she would pay into the ransom chest a sum equivalent to its value.

The collection was greatly hastened when Eleanor made public a song which the waiting Richard had composed and sent to one of his sisters. It began:

> Feeble the words and faltering the tongue
>   Wherewith a prisoner moans his doleful plight;
> Yet for his comfort he may make a song.
>   Friends have I many, but their gifts are slight;
>   Shame to them if unransomed I, poor wight,
>   Two winters languish here!
>
> English and Normans, men of Aquitaine,
>   Well know they all who homage owe to me
> That not my lowliest comrade in campaign
>   Should pine thus, had I gold to set him free;
>   To none of them would I reproachful be—
>   Yet—I am prisoner here.

As the money trickled in, provision for its storage and safe-keeping was made at a council held in the first days of June at St. Albans. It was agreed that Archbishop Hubert Walter and four others should take charge of the money chests, which were to bear the seals of Queen Eleanor and Archbishop Walter of Rouen. At the same meeting the detested William Longchamp presented himself, bearing letters from King Richard and Emperor Henry. The latter's ornate bull urged the people of England to contribute freely to their king's ransom, and declared that Henry was the king's friend, ready to help him against all enemies. Richard's letter asked the council to send in Longchamp's charge some hostages for the payment of any balance lacking in the first ship-ment of the ransom. The council agreed to send hostages, but not in the charge of Longchamp, who returned empty-handed except for a letter assuring Richard that the money would soon be on its way.

When rumors reached John that the money chests were piling up at Westminster, the scheming earl had a letter written ordering the ransom money delivered to him, sealed the document with an imitation of Richard's seal, and presented it to Hubert Walter. But the archbishop merely laughed at his childish scheme and sent him away. Shortly after this there was placed in John's hands a missive consisting of one line: "Look out for yourself, the Devil is loose." John needed no help to decipher this code. The craven prince fled to the king of France.

At the end of October, German agents came to London and tested the 70,000 marks in silver pennies which had been amassed. When they were satisfied, the pennies were all repacked and a goodly number of carts transported the twenty tons of silver to Dover, whence they were shipped to Antwerp. When Richard learned that the ransom money was in the emperor's territory, he informed his mother that the date for his liberation had been set and bade her come with Walter of Rouen to attend the ceremony.

Queen and archbishop soon landed at Antwerp and reached Cologne by January 6. Here Richard's friend, Archbishop Adolf de Altena, joined them in their trip up the Rhine. To Eleanor the river's current seemed to beat malignantly against their ship's prow, slowing the hours as well as their progress. But at last they reached Speyer, and she forgot the journey in the joy of embracing her adored Richard.

Lion-hearted though he might be, it was well for King Richard that he had his incomparable mother to help free him from the snares with which the greedy emperor sought to keep him captive.

On the seventeenth of January, the date originally set for Richard's liberation, an imperial council was held, to which neither the king nor his mother was invited. Archbishop Adolf attended, however, and brought them a disturbing report. The emperor had wavered between freeing the king and finding pretexts for not doing so. He had put forth various specious reasons for delay: the ransom had not been paid in full; there were too few hostages, and their rank was not sufficiently high; Archbishop Walter of Rouen and more lay barons of importance must be added. When many German bishops and barons had protested at such dishonorable conduct, the emperor had agreed to call another council two weeks later at Mainz. He swore that the king would be set free at this time. Eleanor and Richard, though depressed at the prospect of delay, were encouraged by the anger of Adolf, who assured them that he and the others had sworn on the emperor's soul that the agreements should be carried out and would force Henry to live up to his word.

Nevertheless, Richard and his mother awaited with mounting suspense the day set for the council. On that day, the second of February, they took seats at the end of the hall opposite the throne. Richard waited tensely for the emperor's first words. It was not possible, the captive thought, for Henry to delay longer.

He was stunned by the emperor's opening announcement: Henry could not set his cousin of England free, much as he loved him. Messengers had just arrived from the noble king of France and his ally, the great Earl John, offering much money if he would retain the English king in his power. "Here are their letters," shamelessly continued Henry, "which you may read for yourself."

Richard, in his rage, could scarce grasp the letters thrust into his hand. Before he had time to glance at them, a tumult broke out in the room. The great vassals of the German crown rose to demand the expulsion of John's and Philip's messengers and the immediate liberation of the king. They pressed so threateningly around the throne that Henry hastily agreed to their demands.

He was pleased, he averred, that his subjects had so unanimously shown their devotion to his well-loved cousin. There was one small favor he would ask of lord Richard before his departure. Since he had just renounced a munificent offer, perhaps the king of England would compensate him by giving into his hands the kingdom as a fief of the Empire, to receive it back in return for homage. Richard, furious at this impudent demand, started up to hurl defiance at his captor; but his mother's restraining hand forced him back while she whispered: "Consent, consent! 'Tis only a meaningless gesture. The knavish fool will win naught thereby; thou wilt lose naught but gain much: thy freedom and thy land!"

She and the whole assembly gazed intently on the English king as he slowly rose and stood silent for a moment. Then, matching the emperor's suavity, with just the barest hint of mockery, he expressed pleasure at the opportunity so considerately afforded him by his loving cousin to show him this little favor. He would gladly render the desired homage. Eleanor and the German barons visibly relaxed at the words. The vain Henry rose with alacrity to announce that he would accept the homage on the day after the morrow, and that King Richard would be then free to set out for his kingdom.

On the appointed day Eleanor and Richard reëntered the hall, not knowing just what to expect. But Richard went through with his part of the bargain. The flattered emperor gave Richard a double cross of gold as a sign of reinvestiture with his own kingdom. Agonizing seconds passed. Then the emperor stepped forward, gave Richard the kiss of peace, and declared him liberated from all restraint. Eleanor threw herself into Richard's arms with the cry, "Richard, my son, my son, thou art free at last!"

Eleanor and Richard had no desire to linger at Mainz. They

set out promptly with Archbishop Adolf down the Rhine. Adolf insisted that they rest at Cologne a few days, and while they were there, he designed a delicate compliment for the newly liberated prisoner. At mass one day he led the choir himself, and displaced the Introit proper for the day with one whose words began: *Nunc scio vere quia misit Dominus angelum Suum, et eripuit me de manu Herodis*—Now know I truly that the Lord sent His angel and snatched me from the hand of Herod. When the choir had finished singing these words, the archbishop stole a glance at his guests and was delighted to perceive by their smiles and nods that his compliment had been appreciated.

The long-absent Richard was impatient with delay: he made for England with what speed the wind would allow. He landed on the tenth day at Sandwich, and it is said that the sun shone forth with unwonted brilliance as the king set foot once more on the soil of his own kingdom.

The royal party went at once to Canterbury, to kneel in gratitude at the shrine of the Blessed Thomas. Three days later Richard and Eleanor made triumphal entry into London and proceeded to a service of thanksgiving at St. Paul's. But Richard could not delay in London, for John's adherents were still holding Tickhill and Nottingham. The following day he pushed northward, and after stopping at St. Edmund's shrine, arrived before the frowning castles. He had come prepared for battle, but the defenders, as soon as they were convinced that Richard himself was leading the attack, immediately surrendered.

During the weeks that followed, Eleanor remained by Richard's side while he was settling the affairs of the kingdom. His chief concern was to raise money both for completing the ransom —thus releasing the hostages—and for troops to fight Philip of France, who was attacking the Norman barons. The members of the council forced another matter on the king's attention. They felt that the homage enforced by the German emperor had impugned the independence of the Island kingdom, and tarnished its crown. This stain must be removed by a ceremonial crown-wearing. So on Low Sunday, April 17, Richard, wearing his crown and heavy coronation vestments, walked through much pagentry up the aisle of Winchester Cathedral, while the organist struck with his fists thunderous notes from the clumsy keys of the organ.

In less than a month, Richard and Eleanor went to the Continent. Before they reached Lisieux, Eleanor had won Richard's consent to forgive his brother, provided only that John should instantly forsake Philip. The French king had already dismissed him as useless, and John, learning of his brother's arrival, hurried to Normandy. He reached Lisieux shortly after the king had retired for the night.

Richard, worried by reports of Philip's successes, was tossing wakefully on his couch when Jean d'Alençon entered the chamber. The king, perceiving his host's embarrassment, exclaimed: "What is the matter? Has John come? If he is afraid, tell him to enter without fear, for he is my brother. I'll not reproach him for acting like a fool. But as for those who have pushed him to it, they have already paid the penalty or they soon will."

When John was brought in, he burst into tears, grovelling at his brother's feet and begging for mercy. Richard kept back his own tears with some difficulty, then gently raised John from his knees, saying: "John, do not be afraid, thou art only a child who hath been badly advised. Those who have counseled you shall pay for it. Come, get up and let us have something to eat."

Reassured by his brother's words, John's sobs gradually subsided. Not long afterwards, he sat down at table and gorged himself on the salmon that Richard had had cooked for him. On the following morning, Eleanor had the satisfaction of seeing her two sons ride off side by side on their way to exact vengeance on the faithless Philip.

No sooner had their figures disappeared in the distance than the queen mother turned to the next business at hand. She must go to Berengaria and Joan, whom she had not seen since the parting at Messina three years earlier. Eleanor thought it high time that Richard and his queen, now that they were both back in Europe, should see something of each other. Since their marriage in Cyprus, Richard had been so constantly engaged in fighting that he had had scant opportunity to pay attention to his wife. He had promised to seek out Berengaria, however, as soon as he could attend to Philip and restore order in his possessions. Eleanor was determined to hold her son to his promise. She set out for Poitiers where the two young women had been living for a year, ever since their return from the Holy Land.

For the first few weeks the three women had so much to talk about that the time passed swiftly. But as the weeks passed into months Berengaria could not help expressing wonder that her husband had not found opportunity to make her a brief visit, at least. Philip had been forced back into his own territories, a long truce had been arranged, Alais handed back to her brother and at last actually married. Eleanor soon discovered the reason for the delay, but she kept it from Berengaria. She knew what it was to suffer from a husband's promiscuity; she prayed urgently that Richard might reform. Nor did her prayers go unanswered; for not long after Easter Richard rode up the narrow street and threw himself off his horse in the castle yard.

In Normandy some weeks before, a hermit had been ushered into the king's presence. The holy man adjured him to forsake loose women and cleave only to his wife. If he did not, God would inflict on him a terrible vengeance. Richard scornfully told the man of God that he would wait for some sign of divine wrath before he would change his ways. A few days later he was smitten with a violent illness. Convinced that this was a punishment for his sins, Richard summoned his chaplain and confessed the foulness of his ways. He declared his contrition and vowed he would give up his concubines and return to his wife, to whom he would strive in every way to make up for his past conduct. The holy man filled the chamber with his praises to the Lord for the miracle He had wrought.

So the days at Poitiers were happy again, especially for Berengaria.

The Dowager Queen
1195-1204

RICHARD PROVED TO BE AN ATTENTIVE HUSBAND. HE AND BERENGARIA SPENT whole days together following the falcons, and in the evenings he was wont to entertain the whole court with tales of his adventures: how, after his shipwreck on the return from Palestine, he had tried to avoid recognition by posing as a turnspit at an inn where he was hiding near Vienna; how at Dürrenstein he entertained himself by wrestling with his hulking German guards, or playing tricks on them and getting them drunk. When the supply of such stories ran out, Richard would vie with Berengaria in singing favorite troubadour lyrics. Or if they were too tired from the day's hunt, Richard's ever-present minstrels would sing their lays of love and war.

The king was mindful of his religious duties now, too, and was fond of attending Notre Dame la Grande, whose main entrance had been recently decorated with exquisite sculpture. Once when they rode down to the cathedral, Richard guided Berengaria up a long, narrow stairway in the wall to point out the kneeling figures of his mother and father in the bottom panel of the apse window which they had donated. Richard, unlike his father, was a reverent listener at the services, although he could not refrain from occasionally leaping up and seizing the baton from the precentor to lead the choir. The temptation to do this was especially strong at the cathedral, for its large choir, splendidly trained by Richard's old master, often sang the sonorous sequences of Adam of St. Victor which Richard had loved since his student days.

Despite Berengaria's happiness at Poitiers, Eleanor sensed her desire for a home of her own, and suggested to her son that he provide one. They agreed from the outset that none of the royal residences would do. Something smaller, and built in the newest style, more for convenience of living than for defense, should be the aim. They were unable to discover in the country around Poitiers any suitable site, so to Berengaria's intense delight Richard took her northward to look for one. In the county of Maine, they found the land they liked near the village of Thorée, close to the river Sarthe. They settled themselves in a nearby manor house while Richard threw himself into the congenial task of planning the residence and providing materials for its construction. He secured a master mason with a number of skilled craftsmen and saw the work started before the necessities of government called him away. He was able to return frequently enough to join Berengaria in keeping an eye on the progress of the work, and toward the end of the year they moved into the new residence.

Richard found he enjoyed playing architect and builder. He decided he would plan a fortress to his own private and particular liking. He chose a spot on the Norman border and took time out from fighting Philip to watch it being erected. At the end of three years, the imposing stronghold was finished. Immensely proud of himself and the castle, Richard christened it Château Gaillard.

In the late winter of 1199 the king became involved in a petty quarrel. A peasant ploughing in the Limousin had unearthed what was rumored to be a treasure trove of fabulous value: the figures of an emperor and his family, all of pure gold, seated round a golden table, and also a fund of ancient coins. The land belonged to Achard of Châlus who held from Aimar, Vicomte of Limoges. Aimar had received most of the treasure, and had sent a portion of it to King Richard as supreme overlord. But Richard demanded the whole of it, and on being refused, attacked the castle of Châlus. As he, protected only by a steel cap and small square shield, rode around making a survey of the walls, an arrow struck his left shoulder back of the neck, glanced downward and became fixed in his side. Richard made light of his wound and rode back to his lodging. Too impatient to wait for a surgeon, he tugged at the arrow and broke off the shaft without extracting the head. The surgeon, operating by lantern light, finally removed the head, but only with the greatest difficulty. The wound soon became painfully fevered and swollen.

Convinced at last of his danger, Richard sent a message to his mother, who was resting at Fontevrault Abbey. Eleanor, frenzied at the thought of his death, took horse at once and, spurring unmercifully, led her escort the hundred and thirty miles to Châlus in three days. At dusk of the third day she dashed through the village streets, slipped from her mount at Richard's lodgings, and walked unsteadily into the room where he lay. The king still breathed, but consciousness was nearly gone. Eleanor fell on her knees beside the couch, crying out: "Richard, Richard my son, I am here." At the sound of his mother's voice, Richard roused himself to whisper: "Mother, dearest mother, I leave my realms, after God, in thy care." With these words, Richard the Lion Heart closed his life with the close of day.

The septuagenarian mother would have liked to keep a night-long vigil by her son's body. But sorrow, added to her years and her fatigue, weighed her own body down. After prayers had been murmured and tears had come and gone, she resigned her still fair Richard to the surgeon. Helped to another chamber, she dropped on a couch and slept deeply, still dressed in her dusty riding habit.

In accordance with the late king's wishes, his heart was removed and placed in a gilt casket to be sent to Rouen, while his body was prepared for burial beside that of his father at Fontevrault. The funeral cortege arrived at the abbey in time for the interment to take place on Palm Sunday.

Even before Richard was laid in the vault Eleanor discovered that she had no time to indulge her grief. The duties he had bequeathed her demanded action without delay. Her first concern was the succession, for Richard had died childless. John was of course the heir apparent, but the king had once hoped to make his brother Geoffrey's posthumous son Arthur his successor. However, when the boy's mother had sent him to be brought up at the French court, Richard had abandoned the idea. Eleanor knew that she

must get John crowned, unstable as he was, before King Philip
could use Arthur's feeble claim to contest the earl's right to the
kingdom. Meanwhile, news of the king's death brought persons of
all conditions flocking to the queen mother as the symbol of continuing power. One of these was the keeper of the royal treasure
at Chinon. Eleanor wearily told him to yield his charge to John.
She knew her youngest son well: before coming to Fontevrault,
John made straight for Chinon and claimed the treasure. Eleanor
kept him at Fontevrault till after Easter, trying by force of words
and will to make of him a worthy king. He understood well
enough that he must secure Normandy and England, but he rode
off with no more sense of responsibility than ever.

John was crowned king of England in the late spring; Eleanor
stayed on the Continent. She cowed the barons of Anjou, Maine,
Brittany, and Touraine, whom King Philip had gotten to recognize Arthur. Then she made the round of Aquitainian castles,
taking care that the vassals swore allegiance to her rather than to
John. In August she sought out her overlord, King Philip, at
Tours, renewed her homage to him, and received confirmation of
her rights. As the final step in her scheme, she had John render
homage to her for the duchy and regrant to her all his interest during her lifetime. In this way, she made sure that if her son died
before she did, Aquitaine would revert to her and not to Philip.

Eleanor stayed by John's side during the fall of 1199 and the
following winter, helping to keep his lands peaceful. She wanted
him especially to avoid conflict with Philip. Fortunately, Philip
was entangled in matrimonial difficulties which had brought with
them the threat of an interdict, so he was disposed to friendship at
the moment.

About the middle of January a marriage was arranged between Philip's heir, the twelve-year-old Louis, and Queen Eleanor's
granddaughter, Blanche of Castile, of about the same age. Eleanor
was anxious to cement the pact and, since there was no one
else of sufficient importance available, the seventy-eight-year-old
queen volunteered for the task of fetching the little girl. Consequently, the indomitable lady, "the admiration of her age," set out
to cross the Pyrenees in winter. As some compensation for the
rigors of this trip, Eleanor had a happy reunion with her daughter
Eleanor—the first in thirty years.

Blanche was at first rather awed by her stately grandmother,
but soon became her devoted companion. On the exacting journey

homeward, Eleanor detected in the child those qualities of courage, determination, and good sense which were to make Blanche of Castile one of the greatest queens ever to occupy the throne of France and a wise guide to her son, its most illustrious king.

Eleanor decided not to return all the way to Normandy. She stopped at Fontevrault and sent Blanche the rest of the way in the care of Archbishop Helie of Bordeaux. Before the end of the month she had the satisfaction of learning that the children had been married, though the ceremony had had to be celebrated on Norman soil; for Pope Innocent III had placed King Philip's territories under an interdict because of his bigamous marriage with Agnes of Meran. Now that the treaty of peace with Philip had been sealed, Queen Eleanor breathed more easily. She felt that John's path had been cleared of its chief difficulties. But she had underrated her youngest son's tendency to squander good fortune by folly.

On a tour through Aquitaine, John fell violently in love with Isabel, heiress of Count Ademar of Angoulême. Fortunately or unfortunately, John was unmarried. A few months previously he had secured the dissolution of the marriage with his cousin, Isabel of Gloucester, who in ten years had borne him no children. Isabel of Angoulême, who was scarcely more than twelve years old, was already betrothed to Hugh le Brun de la Marche, a member of the turbulent De Lusignan family; but her father was quite willing to exchange a count for a king as son-in-law.

The news caused Eleanor to throw up her hands in despair. One consolation and one only could she find in this latest evidence of John's selfish, headlong nature: he had at least won the friendship of the count of Angoulême, a vassal only slightly less troublesome than the De Lusignans. The De Lusignan family, furious at the loss of both honor and the lady's inheritance, brought up before the king of France this glaring usurpation of Count Hugh's rights.

King Philip was overjoyed at the excuse to berate John, but just then he himself was undergoing chastisement from his spiritual overlord, Pope Innocent III. The interdict had been lifted when Philip had made a show of taking back Ingeborg, his legitimate wife, but Agnes of Meran was still living, and the pope was suspicious. It was not till Agnes had died and Innocent had legitimized her children that Philip felt free to take action against John, early in 1202. From that moment, the drama moved swiftly on to a dénouement which all Eleanor's wisdom and energy, in the face of John's vacillation, could not prevent.

Philip's first step was to cite John as his vassal to appear on April 28 before the royal court to answer the charges preferred by the count De la Marche. When John failed to appear at the appointed time, the court declared all his fiefs forfeited. King Philip lost no time in attempting to enforce the decision. He began by invading Normandy.

In the first two months the French king swept victoriously through the long-contested border territory of the Vexin, and then took castle after castle till he came almost to Rouen, where John was idly sojourning with his young bride. When Philip laid siege to Radeport, only ten miles away, King John bestirred himself sufficiently to force a retreat. The French king soon renewed his attacks in the North, but not before sending the sixteen-year-old Arthur to make trouble in the South.

Philip first knighted Arthur, now duke of Brittany since his mother's death, and invested him with all of John's French fiefs, Normandy excepted, with the promise of putting him in possession of them when, God willing, they should be conquered. Finally, he placed under Arthur's charge a force of two hundred men-at-arms, gave him a goodly sum of money, and dispatched the young knight to win his spurs. At Tours, Arthur met the De Lusignans, led by the count De la Marche and his brother. They agreed that no more telling blow could be delivered to John's interests than the capture of the queen mother. Arthur hesitated to lead an attack on his aged grandmother, but the De Lusignans taunted him with childishness and he finally rode off at the head of the column.

Rumors of the intended invasion roused the indomitable old queen from the quiet of Fontevrault. She set out in haste for the defense of her lands. Escorted by a few men-at-arms, she rode southward, and succeeded before night in reaching Mirebeau's encircling walls. To get to the towering keep, she had to go through a gate in the village wall, past the tiny, red-tiled cottages, on across a drawbridge to the castle's outer wall, and through another gate into the outer bailey. Here the party ascended a ramp, and by another drawbridge over a second ditch, reached the inner bailey. Eleanor dismounted with difficulty and climbed an outside stairway guarded by a heavy iron gate at the top, which led to the great hall. Her resting place that night was a small chamber constructed in the wall, which was some twenty feet thick.

But the queen's rest was not destined to be long. Before dawn she was awakened by the hurried entrance of her chamberlain with the announcement that Duke Arthur and the De Lusignans had forced an entrance into the town and were demanding the surrender of the castle. "Tell them," said the valiant queen, "tell them I'll see them damned in hell first!" She gave orders for the garrison to put up the stoutest resistance in its power, then summoned a trusted servant of her house. She commanded him to seek out King John and bid him come in all haste to the rescue. She showed him a secret passageway reached by a circular stairway leading down to the keep's base. A trapdoor gave entrance to a tunnel, the exit of which opened into the floor of a forester's hut situated well beyond the village walls. Let him seize there the first horse he could find, dash for Loudun, procure a good mount, and speed on to the king.

The queen's next order was for the watchman on the top of the keep to send her word the moment he should see a horseman ride away from the forester's hut. The minutes seemed like hours before she was relieved by word that a man had been seen to emerge from a patch of woods surrounding the hut and ride off at a gallop toward Loudun. Eleanor breathed a prayer to the Virgin for his safety and then addressed herself to the problem of holding the castle till John's arrival.

Eleanor now took stock of her forces. These were scanty enough, not more than thirty or forty fighting men at most. To the half-dozen knights and men-at-arms she had brought with her, there could be added a dozen or more sergeants and an equal number of cross-bowmen. A well in the keep assured them of water, but their supply of provisions was not sufficient to enable them to withstand a long siege—perhaps no more than a week or ten days, at the most. Nor could she hope to hold the extensive circuit of the outer wall for any length of time. The smaller circuit of the inner bailey could be longer defended, and if worse came to worst they could hold the keep indefinitely, or at least till supplies failed. Everything depended on John! Would he come? If he did, all would be well, for he was nearly Richard's equal as a fighter. But those strange fits of indifference which seemed almost like a disease: suppose her message found him possessed by one of these! She could only invoke the Virgin's aid to avert such a mischance.

Eleanor hoped to delay the attackers before the gate of the outer bailey long enough to remove whatever supplies it contained. The enemy would be compelled to fill up the moat, install a battering ram, and smash through the uplifted drawbridge, as well as the immense barred doors blocking the entrance. When these appeared about to give way, she would order the defenders to withdraw quickly into the inner bailey, where her slender force would be able to put up a stouter defense from the smaller circumference of its walls. Then if needs must, she would order a second retreat, this time into the keep itself.

Eleanor disposed her forces in accordance with this plan, and awaited the attack which the enemy was slow in developing because they had come unequipped with proper siege machines. However, they soon began to fill up the moat opposite the drawbridge with stones and whatever debris could be gathered. They also dragged up a huge tree trunk for a battering ram, and began the construction of its framework. Their progress was disconcertingly rapid in spite of the arrows, bolts, and rocks showered upon them by the defenders. Yet night interrupted their work before the machine was ready for action. Eleanor, thankful for the respite, posted her guards and retired to snatch what rest she could. Come what might, she had wrested one day from fate.

Early the next morning Eleanor descended from the keep, walked across the inner bailey and ascended a short stairway to its parapeted wall, where she could watch the effects of the battering ram when it should come into action. She had not long to wait, for the attackers soon had the tree trunk thundering against the upraised drawbridge. The drawbridge was soon smashed to pieces, leaving the doors of the gateway exposed to attack. When Eleanor saw the heavy ram being slowly swung back once more, she turned to the trumpeter beside her and ordered him to sound the retreat. As soon as the trumpet's piercing notes reached the ears of the defenders, they began running across the inner drawbridge. Just as this began to tremble on the rise, a blow from the battering ram brought down the doors of the outer gate.

From her station on the wall Eleanor saw some foot-soldiers push their way through the wreckage of the outer gateway and begin peering around. When they had made sure that the defenders had withdrawn to the inner bailey, a crowd of others came flocking in. Then three figures detached themselves from the general mass and began walking slowly around the enclosure, apparently making a survey for the next attack. As the three men drew abreast of her position, Eleanor saw that they were the two

De Lusignans and Arthur. Cursing her grandson for his bold disrespect, she commanded the crossbowmen to try a shot at him. Though the bolts fell short, the leaders soon withdrew, followed by the others. Somewhat later the watchers on the wall saw men dragging logs and stones through the gateway for use in filling up the ditch in front of the inner gate, but they ceased working without making any further effort that night. Eleanor thanked God that she had gained yet another day.

On the following morning the attackers began in earnest to fill the great ditch, to haul up the cumbersome battering ram and to install its supports. They found the task more difficult than before; the ditch was deeper, and the slope of the ramp leading up to the drawbridge entrance made it harder to place firmly the framework supporting the ram. In addition, the fire from the wall was much more concentrated than in their attack on the first gateway. Yet in spite of everything, the work went steadily forward, so that when night came the ram stood menacingly before the gateway, ready for use in the morning. Though a third day had been won, Eleanor realized that she would probably be compelled during the next day to withdraw her forces into the keep, diminished as they were by the loss of several men and the wounding of others. She was as determined as ever to hold out to the end; but would John never come! Had the message failed to reach him? Had her rider been killed?

The rider had travelled at top speed through the first day, and from Saumur had pressed steadily on through the night. Just as dawn was breaking, he sighted the king's encampment near Le Mans, having covered the hundred miles in twenty-four hours. He guided his horse to the royal tent, slid to the ground, and in a voice faltering from fatigue relayed his message. Fortunately John was in a fighting mood. He instantly called his men and set off. John and his fifteen hundred men were unable to equal the messenger's speed, yet they covered the hundred miles in less than forty-eight hours, to come in sight of Mirebeau's lofty keep just as Eleanor was awakening to face the critical fourth day of the siege.

The queen was on the point of entering the great hall when a squire excitedly announced that a column of horse had been sighted riding rapidly toward the castle. Praying that John had arrived, Eleanor hastily descended the outside stairway and ascended the wall of the inner bailey. Her first glance assured her that it was indeed John coming to her relief. Eleanor almost collapsed at this sudden release from the strain of the last three days, but her faintness was only momentary, for the sight of the activities going on below was too enjoyable to miss.

John and his men had taken the enemy completely by surprise and were cutting down their foes in the narrow village street as they were trying to arm. Most of the knights surrendered without a struggle. Geoffrey de Lusignan was taken while finishing off a dish of pigeons which he had refused to abandon when the alarm sounded. As soon as John saw that the struggle was over, he rode up the hill to greet his mother. She welcomed him as she had never welcomed her youngest son before.

Two days later King John and his men rode triumphantly away, followed by a long train of manacled prisoners, chief among whom were the two De Lusignans and the young duke Arthur. Eleanor quit the castle and rode slowly southward toward her old home at Poitiers. She was at last almost ready to admit, at the age of eighty, that she was growing old.

From its flaming climax at Mirebeau, Eleanor's life declined in the next two years to a peaceful, if saddened, close. Almost to the day of her death, however, she exerted herself, by personal interviews and by letters, to maintain John's influence over his vassals. But the suspicious and treacherous king remained faithful to none, alienating baron after baron. And when the ghastly rumor spread abroad that John had with his own hands stabbed the youthful Arthur and thrown him into the Seine, public opinion turned rapidly against the English king. So when the persistent Philip resumed his attacks, scarcely a man held out against him. Nor would John come to the support of the few loyal men who did attempt to defend their castles. Instead, he withdrew to England, replying to their appeals for help only by saying that they must look out for themselves. Maine, Anjou, and Brittany passed almost completely into Philip's hands: in Normandy, only Rouen and Château Gaillard, the great border fortress which Richard had built and loved, held out. At last the defenders of this castle, the finest in Europe, were compelled to do what its lionhearted builder would have scorned—surrender.

The report that Richard's "Saucy Castle," the darling of his heart, had passed into Philip's hands, gave Eleanor her death blow. She retired to her bed, declaring that she no longer had any wish to live. To the abbess of Fontevrault she expressed the wish to be clothed in nun's garb and buried by Richard's side in the abbey; and there the great queen was laid to rest. Although the northern lands had been lost, her own dominions remained under the English crown for generation upon generation after her death, as though protected by her mighty shade.

EXPLANATORY NOTES AND
SOURCE REFERENCES

GENEALOGICAL
TABLES

INDEX

Explanatory Notes and Source References

THE purpose of the following section is, first, to indicate the extent and nature of the research on which the preceding text rests; and second, to enable those who may wish to do so to separate fact from fiction: that is to say, to determine in any specific instance whether a statement is an imaginary reconstruction. Furthermore, where it seems essential to justify an interpretation of some source passage, a brief critical discussion is given.

The book rests on a study, extending over a period of a dozen years or more, of practically all the original material in print. The bulk of this, provided by the twelfth century chronicles, is readily available in the *Rolls Series,* in the publications of the Société de l'Histoire de France, and in the *Patrologia latina* of J. P. Migne. For the information supplied by charters, I have relied mainly on the summaries supplied by Alfred Richard's excellent, detailed *Histoire des Comtes de Poitou,* (1903), 2 vols. Richard, an archivist long resident at Poitiers, devotes to Eleanor almost the whole of the five hundred and twelve quarto pages of his second volume. Additional charter material is provided by R. W. Eyton in his *Court, Household and Itinerary of Henry II* (1878).

The publications of the Pipe Roll Society, over fifty volumes recording royal expenditures during the reigns of Henry II, Richard I, and John, have yielded much information. They have been particularly helpful in shedding light on the darkest period in Eleanor's life, the period of her protective custody, 1174-1189. They show the gradual relaxation of the restraints placed upon her, and indicate that, several years before Henry's death, Eleanor was allowed to move about England with comparative freedom, and even to cross to the Continent.

For the sources in Old French, I have had to depend entirely on translations and on the works of numerous specialists in this field.

A five months' residence at Poitiers in 1937 enabled me not only to familiarize myself with the lay of the land in and around Poitiers, but also to study the many structures in the town surviving from Eleanor's day, particularly the remains of the old castle— Maubergeonne's Tower and the Great Hall.

The best full account of Eleanor's life to date is that by Alfred Richard, noted above. The best brief sketch is by T. A. Archer in the *Dictionary of National Biography,* XVII (1889), 175-78, which contains full source references. This article is superior to the more recent one (1933) by J. Salvini in the *Dictionnaire de biographie française,* fascicule VII, 2-4. All the full-scale biographies that I have seen, the older as well as the more recent, including Rosenberg's (1937), but excluding Richard's, are so uncritically misleading, especially in their acceptance of the mythical accretions clinging to Eleanor's name, that they are practically worthless. An extremely able article is Amy Kelly's "Eleanor of Aquitaine and her Courts of Love," *Speculum,* XII (1937), 3-19.

Brief discussions of the legendary elements are given at the appropriate places in the succeeding notes. T. A. Archer's article on Rosamond Clifford (Fair Rosamond), in the *D. N. B.,* XI (1887), 75-77, deals fully with the growth of this legend, which is also treated, along with several others, by F. M. Chambers in his article, "Some Legends Concerning Eleanor of Aquitaine," *Speculum,* XVI (1941), 459-68. One or two additional stories are given by Elie Berger, "Les aventures de la reine Eléanor. Histoire et legende," *Comptes rendus de l'Académie des inscriptions et belles-lettres,* séance du 16 nov., 1906, pp. 702-12.

Explanatory Notes and Source References

INTRODUCTION

P. x. For the quotation from Stubbs, see his edition of Walter of Coventry, *Memorials,* etc., II, xxviii.

P. x. Gervaise of Canterbury, *Chronica,* ed. William Stubbs, Vol. I, chap. xiii, 149; and Roger of Hoveden, *Chronica,* ed. Stubbs, I, 214 are the sources for the charges that the real basis for the divorce was adultery.

P. xi. *English and Scottish Ballads,* ed. F. J. Child (1864), VII, 210-16, contains the ballad about Eleanor and William Marshal.

P. xi. The Saladin story is from Natalis de Wailly, *Récits d'un menestrel de Rheims au trezième siecle,* Société de l'histoire de France (1876), pp. 1-7.

P. xi. Berger (cited in Introductory Note) is the source for Eleanor's words to her barons.

P. xi. This song of the wandering student may be found in Helen Waddel, *The Wandering Scholars* (1926), p. 216.

CHAPTER I

P. 3. The opening scene is an imaginative reconstruction based on summaries of two charters given in A. Richard, *Histoire,* II, 10-11, 18. The finger-printing is authentic. For chronological and genealogical data in this chapter and succeeding ones, I generally follow Richard.

P. 4. *Dux . . . erat nempe vehemens amator feminarum. . . .* (Geoffrey de Vigeois, ed. Philippe Labbe, p. 297). Geoffrey (b. *circa* 1140, d. *post* 1184) was prior of the abbey of Vigeois near Limoges.

P. 5. William's elopement with Dangereuse and their continued life together are authentic; the details are imaginary. Dangereuse was a real name, not a nickname. A. Richard, I, p. 472, n. 2, identifies her with a "Dangerosa" mentioned in a late 11th century charter. The story and the characterizations of William are most fully given by William of Malmsbury (d. *circa* 1142), *Gesta regum*, ed. William Stubbs, II, 510-11; and by Orderic Vitalis (d. *circa* 1142), *Historia ecclesiastica*, ed. Auguste Le Prevost, Vol. IV, Bk. X, chaps. xix, xx. William's poem (trans. Barbara Smythe, *Trobador Poets*, pp. 3-4) is one of the eleven of his preserved. The text of all eleven, accompanied by translation into modern French, is given by A. Jeanroy, *Les Chansons de Guillaume IX*.

P. 6. William the Toulousan was trained in music by the cathedral's subcantor. See Richard, I, 466.

P. 6. For Bleheris' visit to Poitiers during Eleanor's girlhood, see R. S. Loomis, "Bleheris and the Tristram Story," *Modern Language Notes*, XXXIX (1924), 319-29.

P. 6. This sketch of Eleanor's training is inferential: it follows that of Iseult as described by Gottfried von Strassburg (H. O. Taylor, *The Mediaeval Mind*, I, 595). Eleanor is called *diserta* by Richard of Devizes (*Chronicles of the Reigns of Stephen, Henry II, and Richard I*, ed. Richard Howlett, III, 402); translated "learned" by Joseph Stevenson, *Church Historians of England* (Pre-Reformation series), Vol. V, Part I, 258.

P. 7. In 1937, these waxen hearts were still being offered for sale to visitors as they approached the church's entrance.

P. 9. The presence of Eleanor at Parthenay is suppositious.

P. 10. Quotations are from a contemporary guide book. For the Latin text of the guide and a translation into French, see Jeanne Vielliard, *Le guide du pèlèrin de Saint-Jacques de Compostelle* (1938).

P. 11. For the account of William's death, see Orderic Vitalis, Vol. V, Bk. XIII, chap. xxx, p. 81. For the legend and much else about St. James of Compostella, see G. G. King, *The Way of St. James* (1920), 3 vols.

P. 12. The words *nobilissima puella* are Suger's in his *Vie de Louis VI le Gros*, ed. Henri Waquet, p. 280. This passage (pp. 280-82) forms the basis for the narrative up to Young Louis's departure from Paris. A few added details (King Louis's taxation, summonses to attend the wedding, munificence of the preparations at Bordeaux) are given in *La Chronique de Morigny*, ed. Léon Mirot, Bk. III, sec. ii, pp. 66-70.

CHAPTER II

P. 15. In the chronicle of Morigny, Louis is described as follows: *juvenis erat, corporis elegancia clarus, morum honestate et religione magnifice preditus, sensus et sapiencie vivacitate acutus.* John of Salisbury's actual words are: *Regi uisa est placuisse plurimum constitutio, eo quod reginam uehementer amabat et fere puerili modo.*, written in connection with the interview with the pope (*Historia pontificalis,* ed. R. L. Poole, p. 62). *Quae nimirum ita sibi in principio juvenis animum formae suae venustate praestrictum devinxerat.* . . .: "This princess [Eleanor] . . . had been married to the king of France. . . . She had at first so bewitched the young man's affections by the beauty of her person . . ." (William of Newburgh, *Historia rerum anglicarum,* Bk. I, chap. xxxi, 92, in *Chronicles of the Reigns of Stephen, Henry II, and Richard I,* ed. Howlett, Vol. I).

P. 16. The quotation is from the chronicle of Morigny. The details of the menu are in part borrowed from Salimbene's description of a feast served in 1248 at Sens to Louis IX of France, given in Taylor, *The Mediaeval Mind,* I, 525.

P. 17. The details of Eleanor's presentation of the cup are imaginary. The cup itself was still in existence in 1938, at which time I saw it in the Louvre. Louis later gave it to Suger who had engraved upon it the inscription described at the close of the next chapter.

P. 19. For Adelaide's interference and retirement, see Suger, *L'Histoire du roi Louis VII,* ed. Auguste Molinier, chap. iv, p. 150.

P. 19. Gustave Reese, *Music in the Middle Ages* (1940), pp. 265-67: "The earliest known applications in goodly number of what may be called the sustained-tone style are contained in four early 12th-century MSS originating from the monastery of St. Martial in Limoges. . . . it seems altogether likely that there was a connection between the St. Martial organa and the famous Parisian contrapuntal works of the latter part of the 12th century." Farther on (pp. 295-96), Reese says: "It was about the second third of the 12th century (1133-1166) that the school of Notre Dame de Paris assumed the leadership in musical development . . . it includes Leonin who flourished possibly before . . . 1163." At an unknown date before 1172, St. Martial compositions were being sung at St. Hilaire in Poitiers. (See Chapter XIV, p. 155 and note.)

P. 21. For Eleanor's visit and her confirmation of the grants to the abbey of Nieuil, see A. Richard, II, 77 and n. 3.

P. 22. Eleanor's vigorous championship of her sister's cause is, I believe, generally accepted. Only some of the details in my account that follows are imaginary: see A. Richard, II, 78 ff. E. Vacandard, *Vie de saint Bernard,* II, 180-206, gives the full details. Quotations are from Vacandard.

P. 26. The account of Eleanor's interview with Bernard rests on the authority of two biographies of the saint. They are found in Migne, *Patrologia latina,* Vol. 185, Part IV, col. 332, no. 18; and *ibid.,* col. 527, no. VIII. They give Eleanor's touching plea and the words of Bernard's promise as quoted in my text, and state it was at Eleanor's prompting that Louis later sought out Bernard and begged him to fulfill his part of the bargain. The two accounts combined give us the most intimate picture of Eleanor to be found anywhere in the sources.

CHAPTER III

The bulk of the first-hand information about the Second Crusade, from its inception till Louis's arrival at Antioch, is given by Odo de Deuil in his *De Profectione Ludovici VII in orientem* (Migne, Vol. 185, Part II, col. 1201 ff.; trans. Guizot, *Collection des mémoires relatifs à l'histoire de France*, Vol. 24). An excellent, new edition of Odo's work (text, translation, notes) by Virginia G. Berry, appeared too late for my use. Odo, a monk of St. Denis, as chaplain-confessor, stayed close by Louis as far as Antioch. His account, written for Suger, ends with the arrival at Antioch. All source quotations up to that point in my narrative are taken from Odo unless otherwise noted.

P. 29. The dialogue between Eleanor and Louis is an imaginative reconstruction representing my conception of how it came about that Eleanor went on the Crusade. Louis was deeply in love with her and hated the idea of a long separation. Eleanor was probably less moved either by religious motives or by devotion to Louis than she was by the thought of being left desolately behind when her husband was about to start off on the most exciting adventure that anyone at that time could conceive. I do not think that Louis, because of jealous love, was afraid to leave her behind. To be sure, the unknown author of the *Historia Francorum,* ed. Martin Bouquet, *Recueil*, XII, 116-17, writing about 1154, says that Louis, *inflammatus zelotypiae spiritu jurata consanguinitate, uxorem suam dimisit . . . Hac quippe occasione, Ducatum Aquitaniae Rex amissit.* The ordinary meaning of *zelotypia* is "jealousy," but in this connection it seems to me that the author is criticizing Louis's over-zealousness in breaking off his marriage because of a supposed infraction of canonical law.

William of Newburgh (*circa* 1136-*circa* 1198; began writing about 1196) says (Bk. I, chap. xxxi, 92-93) that Louis loved Eleanor so much that he decided to take her with him, and that "many nobles following his example, also took their wives with them; who, unable to exist without female attendants, introduced a multitude of women into those Christian camps, which ought to be chaste, but which had become a scandal to our army as it has been shown above [*i.e.*, in chap. xx]." In Odo's account, women are conspicuous by their absence: even Eleanor's presence is not mentioned until the expedition is approaching Constantinople, and it is never again alluded to by him.

P. 30. Louis's speech is given in *La Chronique de Morigny,* p. 85.

P. 31. Eleanor's presence at Vézelay seems to me altogether probable, though I have found no mention of it in any of the chronicles. Her preparation of the crosses is imaginary.

P. 32. I transpose this incident. Thibaud did once actually send hyacinths, but he sent them to Suger at the time of the conference at St. Denis. See Vacandard, *op. cit.,* for source passage.

P. 33. For the presence of Eleanor on Louis's sweep through Aquitaine, see A. Richard, II, 85-88, where also will be found details of bargains struck with the monastic institutions.

P. 37. That both Eleanor and Louis's mother walked in the procession is stated by Odo, who also says that in the church they were "nearly suffocated by their tears and the heat."

P. 38. The details connected with the presentation of the goblet are imaginary. It is not known when this took place.

CHAPTER IV

P. 39. The presence of Louis's cousin is mentioned by Odo when speaking of events immediately after the army's crossing of the Bosphorus. I have supplied the name, Elaine.

P. 39. Louis left Paris at Pentecost, June 8, according to Odo, but he seems not to have left till the thirteenth. Odo says they reached Worms on the twenty-ninth, so that a little over two weeks were occupied by this stage of the journey. At Metz they may have remained three or four days. All the main incidents narrated in this chapter are recorded by Odo unless otherwise noted. Eleanor's participation in them is imaginary until Empress Irene's letter reaches her at Adrianople: it is not until this point in his narrative that Odo reveals that Eleanor is accompanying her husband.

P. 41. Eleanor's share in the riot scene, as well as the introduction at this point of Thierry Gualeran, is imaginary. Thierry got his revenge at Antioch. John of Salisbury, *Historia pontificalis*, p. 53, is the authority for Eleanor's dislike and derisive treatment of the eunuch.

CHAPTER V

P. 49. Odo does not say that Blachernae was the palace assigned to Louis and Eleanor, but since he gives a detailed description of it such as he gives to no other, I conclude that it was. The chaplain says not a word about Eleanor during her stay at Constantinople, yet I hold it certain that the empress, especially since she had several times written to Eleanor, would extend to the queen attentions similar to those shown by the emperor to Louis. If Eleanor was not present at the banquet, as I have represented her in the text, she undoubtedly was at others given her by Irene.

P. 54. I am indebted for the translation of "Fair Yolanth" to the kindness of my colleague at Vanderbilt University, Maxwell Lancaster. The whole scene, of course, is an imaginative reconstruction.

P. 55. Odo describes Count Robert's snatching away of Louis's cousin for whom I have supplied the name "Elaine." Eleanor's share in it is imaginary but highly probable, considering all the circumstances: she would naturally wish to protect the girl, and Robert would have found difficulty in running off with Elaine without the queen's consent. Eleanor, being of a mischievous disposition—*novercali forte natura* (Giraldus Cambrensis, *Opera,* ed. J. S. Brewer, IV, 373)— would have loved such an affair.

CHAPTER VI

All the chief events recounted in this chapter, and the quotations, are found in Odo de Deuil's narrative. In substantial agreement with Odo's story are the much briefer accounts given by Bishop Otto of Freising and by William of Tyre. Eleanor's presence is nowhere mentioned by Odo in this section of his account: her participation in events as I have represented it is, therefore, imaginary.

P. 60. There is no mention in the sources that Eleanor and the other women rode astride. That women in case of necessity would do so, however, is evidenced by the story told of Henry II's mother, the Empress Matilda. Once when she was being pursued, her escort compelled her, for the sake of speed, to abandon the side-saddle and ride "after the fashion of men." (Sidney Painter, *William Marshal* [1933], p. 7.) I feel confident, therefore, that during most of the journey through Asia Minor, if not earlier, the women rode astride. Furthermore, I believe their doing so provided the basis for the Amazon myth. It is possible that Greek officials along the route, struck by the sight of women riding like men, spoke of the amazing sight. The story, ornamented as it was passed along by word of mouth for two generations, finally reached the Greek historian Nicetas who wrote after 1204. He says, in speaking of the *Germans* and "races related to them," that among them there were women riding "not with their feet close together but astride after the fashion of men, armed, and dressed like men, with martial countenance, bolder than Amazons, among whom there was one who excelled all the rest, like another Penthesilea, who, because her sandals and greaves were interwoven with gold, was called Golden Foot." For the Greek original of this passage, with Latin translation, see *Nicetae Choniatae historia,* Bk. I, chap. iv, p. 80 (*Corpus scriptorum historiae Byzantinae,* ed. Emmanuel Bekker, Bonn: 1835).

P. 61. The representation of Eleanor and Frederick Barbarossa passing the time of day in this way is, of course, imaginary. For his French lyrics, see Robert Briffault, *Les troubadours et le sentiment romanesque* (Paris: 1945).

P. 63. Ever since the end of the seventeenth century, French writers have placed on Eleanor's shoulders the blame for the disaster at Cadmos Mountain. There is not a shred of evidence supporting this position. Bernhard Kugler in his *Studien zur Geschichte des Zweiten Kreuzuges*

(1866), p. 170, n. 76, traces the beginning of this legend to Maimbourg's account written in 1685. It is still found in 1903 in the generally critical account by Richard, trained archivist though he is. The position of Eleanor in the line of march is not known, but to assume, as does Richard, that she and the other women would be riding near Geoffrey de Rancon at the head of the column, in a position of the greatest danger, is absurd.

The agreement about Cadmos had been, according to Odo who was on the spot, that the army was to halt and encamp at its foot. His statement is to be followed rather than that of William of Tyre, who, writing at least thirty years after the event, says that the agreement called for a halt and encampment on the summit. It is this statement of William that has helped nourish the fanciful account of the French writers. My own account is, of course, imaginary, but it has something to justify it, both from the conditions as described by Odo, and from Eleanor's character as revealed in her later life.

P. 69. The eating of horse-flesh and meal cakes cooked over coals is related by Odo; the details of the scene are imaginary.

CHAPTER VII

The basic account of the events narrated in this chapter is found in William of Tyre's chronicle, Bk. XVI, chap. xxvii (Migne, *Patrologia latina*, Vol. 201, cols. 670 ff.). William's whole chronicle is now available in the highly satisfactory English translation by Babcock and Krey, *A History of Deeds Done beyond the Sea* (1943), 2 vols. William (*circa* 1130-*circa* 1185) did not begin to write this section of his work until 1180, though he may have used notes written as early as 1167. When Louis and Eleanor were at Antioch, William was a lad of eighteen living at Jerusalem. His final account of these events was written over thirty years after they took place.

William's narrative is supplemented in important particulars by that of John of Salisbury. John was at the papal court when Louis and Eleanor returned from the crusade. Poole thinks that John's account of the affair at Antioch was written before 1153 and rests on things told him by some member either of the papal court or of Louis's entourage.

Brief excerpts from the two accounts follow: that from William of Tyre is given in Babcock's translation (II, 179 ff.); that from John of Salisbury (*Historia pontificalis,* pp. 53-54), in a rather free translation of my own.

William of Tyre: "He [Raymond] also counted greatly on the interest of the queen with the lord king, for she had been his inseparable companion on his pilgrimage. . . . When Raymond found that he could not induce the king to join him, his attitude changed. Frustrated in his ambitious designs, he began to hate the king's ways; he openly plotted against him and took means to do him injury. He resolved also to deprive him of his wife, either by force or by secret intrigue. The queen readily assented to this design, for she was a foolish woman. Her conduct before and after this time showed her to be, as we have said, far from circumspect. Contrary to her royal dignity, she disregarded her marriage vows and was unfaithful to her husband."

John of Salisbury: "But while they were delaying there . . . the familiarity [*familiaritas*] of the prince's bearing toward the queen and his constant conversations with her, almost without intermission, aroused suspicion in the king. This was intensified by the queen's desire to remain there when the king was preparing to withdraw; and the prince was anxious to retain her, if it could be done with the consent of the king. But when the king was on the point of tearing her away, the queen herself, calling to mind their kinship, said that it was unlawful for them longer to live together because they were related either in the fourth or fifth degree. . . . By this the king was very much disturbed, and, although he loved the queen with an almost immoderate passion, nevertheless he would have acquiesced in her remaining if his counselors and the French magnates had permitted. There was among the secretaries of the king a knight who was a eunuch whom the queen always had detested and whom she had been accustomed to deride, a faithful intimate of the king . . . Thierry Gualeran by name. At the council, Thierry persuaded the king that it would not do to suffer the queen to delay longer at Antioch . . . because it would be a perpetual source of opprobrium for the realm of the Franks if, among other misfortunes, it could be said that the king had been either deprived of his wife or abandoned by her. This Thierry said, either because he hated the queen, or because he really thought so, moved perchance by common opinion."

P. 80. William of Newburgh (Bk. I, chap. xxxi), attributes these words to Eleanor as giving her reasons for desiring a divorce from Louis: *illa maxime moribus regiis offensa, et causante se monacho non regi nupsisse.*

P. 81. For conditions of life among the crusaders who settled in the East, I have relied mainly on D. C. Munro's *Kingdom of the Crusaders* (1935).

P. 87. The drama at Antioch took place in a relatively short space of time. The accepted date for Louis's arrival at Antioch is March 19, 1148, and he reached Jerusalem in time to celebrate Easter, which fell on April 11, 1148. (John of Salisbury, *Historia pontificalis,* p. 57 n.)

CHAPTER VIII

My account of Eleanor's year in the Holy Land is wholly imaginary, since for this period no mention of her is made in the sources. I have acquired some knowledge of the geographic conditions from George Adam Smith's remarkable work, *The Historical Geography of the Holy Land* (20th ed., 1919).

P. 91. Eleanor's adventure with the lion was suggested by a somewhat similar one recounted in that entertaining and instructive work, *The Autobiography of Ousama,* trans. G. R. Potter (1929).

P. 91. Louis's letter expressing his anger over Eleanor's behavior at Antioch is known only through Suger's reference to it in this letter to Louis. The passage is as follows: *De regina conjuge vestra audemus vobis laudare, si tamen placet, quatenus rancorem animi vestri, si est, operiatis, donec Deo volente ad proprium reversus regnum et super his et super aliis provideatis.* (Migne, Vol. 186, col. 1378).

P. 92. The attack by the emperor's fleet and the rescue by King Roger's admiral are recounted by the anonymous author of the *Historia francorum,* ed. Bouquet, *Recueil,* XII, 116-17, written about 1154. A fuller account is given by John of Salisbury *(Historia pontificalis,* pp. 61-62), who also describes Pope Eugenius' efforts at reconciling Louis and Eleanor, relieving Louis's anxiety about the illegality of their marriage, and his causing them to sleep in the same bed: *Fecit eos in eodem lecto decumbere. . . .*

Pp. 93 and 94. The gifts to Eleanor by King Roger and by the monk at Cassino are imaginary.

Louis himself, in two letters to Suger (Migne, Vol. 186, cols. 1394-96), gives further details of the sojourn in Italy, including those concerning Eleanor's sickness at Monte Cassino. Their stay at Cassino is noted in the *Chronica Casinensi,* cited in Migne, *op. cit.,* n. 65.

CHAPTER IX

P. 97. Eugenius' gifts to Louis and Eleanor are imaginary. The psaltery, ordinarily plucked, could also be used like a dulcimer, in the manner indicated in the text.

P. 98. For the reception at Rome, see John of Salisbury, *Historia pontificalis,* pp. 61-62.

P. 98. Louis's request that Suger meet him at Cluny is contained in the second of the two letters cited above in the note to Chapter VIII. Eleanor's stroll and conversation with Peter the Venerable are imaginary.

P. 100. My representation of Eleanor as being much more anxious for the divorce than Louis is based partly on her conduct at Antioch, partly on John of Salisbury's statement that Louis was still passionately in love with his wife. Furthermore, two English chroniclers, Gervaise of Canterbury *(circa* 1143-1210) and William of Newburgh, both indicate a widely-held contemporary belief that Eleanor was the one who wished and worked for the divorce. Gervaise, who began writing about

1188, says, speaking of the divorce (*Chronica*, Vol. I, chap. xiii, p. 149): *Dicebatur enim artificiosam repudiationem illam ex ipsius processisse ingenio:* "For it is said that that specious repudiation had proceeded from her own [Eleanor's] inclination." William, who began writing about 1196, says (Bk. I, chap. xxxi, p. 93): *Dicitur etiam, quod in ipso regis Francorum conjugio ad ducis Normannici nuptias, suis magis moribus congruas, aspiraverit, atque ideo praeoptaverit procuraveritque discidum. Itaque . . . illa . . . multum instante, illo vero vel non vel remissius obluctante . . . solutum est inter eos vinculum copulae conjugalis:* "For it is said that while she was still married to the king of the Franks she had aspired to a marriage with the Norman duke whose manner of life suited better with her own, and for this reason she had desired and procured the divorce. And so, the queen urging it constantly, the king opposing it not at all or only very feebly, the marriage tie was dissolved."

P. 101. I follow Richard in dating the meeting at Paris, and in considering it the first time that Eleanor and Henry met. It is also, I think, the only provable meeting between Geoffrey the Fair and Eleanor. For a description and characterization of Henry, see Walter Map, *De nugis curialium (Courtiers' Trifles)*, trans. Tupper and Ogle, pp. 297-98 and 302-3.

P. 102. That Eleanor, as William of Newburgh says, began intriguing with Henry before the divorce had taken place is confirmed by the speed with which their marriage took place after the divorce. Walter Map (*circa* 1140-*circa* 1210) says (p. 297) that Eleanor "cast glances of unholy love" on Henry, and that "she managed to secure an unlawful divorce" and married him. The imaginary dialogue at the chess table represents one of the possible ways in which Eleanor revealed to Henry her designs on him.

P. 105. Years later, the embittered Henry used to assert that Eleanor had been too free in her relations with his own father. Walter Map, in the passage referred to above, tells the story in abbreviated form. It is told more fully by Map's fellow gossip, Giraldus Cambrensis, who apparently received it from Hugh, Bishop of Lincoln, who said it was told him by Henry himself. Giraldus writes: "Also Geoffrey, earl of Anjou, when seneschal of France, had carnally known Queen Eleanor: of which, as it is said, he frequently forewarned his son Henry, cautioning him and forbidding him in any wise to touch her, both because she was the wife of his lord, and because she had been known by his own father." (*Opera,* VIII, 300).

P. 106. About fifty years after this period, the monk Helinand (d. after 1215) said in his *Universal Chronicle* (Migne, *Patrologia latina*, Vol. 212, col. 1057, under the year 1152) that Louis divorced Eleanor on account of her incontinence and because she behaved herself not like a queen but almost like a courtesan (*fere sicut meretrix*). If there is any justification for such a statement, it might be found in Eleanor's conduct at this time in trying to hurry on the divorce.

CHAPTER X

The events described in this chapter took place between March 21, date of the divorce, and May 18, date of Eleanor's marriage to Henry: a period just short of two months.

P. 109. The story of Count Thibaud of Blois's attempt to force Eleanor to marry him rests solely on the authority of a chronicle written at Tours about 1210, two generations after the event, but supposedly based on an earlier account (*The Great Chronicle of Tours,* under the year 1152, in André Salmon, *Recueil de chroniques de Touraine,* pp. 135-36). The details of the interview and the escape are imaginary. The story of Geoffrey's attempt to win Eleanor for himself is recounted by the same chronicler. The details are imaginary.

P. 113. I think there is no doubt that Eleanor wrote to Henry, though I have been unable to find any trace of a letter. Mary Bateson, *Medieval England,* p. 159, says it was an impassioned one, but she gives no reference. I have found no trace of any written reply from Henry. William the Troubadour refers to his writing nook in these terms:

I wish the world at large to hear
A poem toned to please the ear
That's coming from my workshop here:
In this trade surely it is clear
 The palm is mine;
For proof the piece will soon appear
 In binding fine.

(Translated by J. H. Smith, *The Troubadours at Home,* II, 353.)

P. 115. For Eleanor's seals, see A. Richard, II, 439, n. 2; and F. Eygun, *Sigillographie du Poitou* (1938), pp. 159-60 and Plate 1.

P. 117. There is no record of Eleanor's speech.

CHAPTER XI

P. 119. Robert de Torigny (also known as Robert de Monte) supplies most of the details of Henry's campaign: "The Chronicle of Robert of Torigny" in *Chronicles of the Reigns of Stephen, Henry II, and Richard I,* ed. Howlett, IV, 164 ff.

P. 122. For the affair at Limoges, see Richard, II, 113-14.

P. 123. The translation of the first song is that of J. H. Smith (*op. cit.,* II, 165).

P. 124. The prose translations of Bernard's poems are by Barbara Smythe (*Trobador Poets,* pp. 46-49). It is quite possible that Bernard was not thinking at all of Eleanor when he wrote these poems. The problem of what particular lady provided the inspiration for them is one on which the specialists are not agreed. I have assumed that these three were inspired by Eleanor, and that they tell part of the story of Bernard's relations with her. That Bernard stayed for some time at Eleanor's court has long been accepted on the authority of his thirteenth century biographer: "He betook himself to the Duchess of Normandy, who was illustrious and much admired, and well versed in matters of fame and honor, and knew how to award praise. And the songs of Bernard pleased her mightily, wherefore she gave him a most cordial welcome, and he resided at her court a long time, and was in love with her, and she with him; and he made many fine songs about it. But while he was staying with her, the King of England, her husband, removed her from Normandy, and Bernard remained here, sad and sorrowful." (Translated by H. W. Preston in *Troubadours and Trouvères*, p. 180).

P. 126. The story of Henry's gift to Eleanor is imaginary.

CHAPTER XII

P. 129. Robert de Torigny reports (p. 179) the meeting at which Henry confirmed his election. He does not mention Eleanor. I have assumed that she came north with Henry, was present at this meeting, and remained in Normandy until, as recorded by Robert, she left with Henry for England six months later.

P. 129. Robert's possession of Geoffrey of Monmouth's *History of the Kings of Britain* as early as 1139 is attested both by Henry of Huntingdon, to whose attention in that year Robert called it, and by Robert himself. For the reference, see Henry of Huntingdon, *Historia Anglorum,* ed. Thomas Arnold, pp. xx-xxiv.

P. 130. Eleanor's conversations with Matilda are imaginary, but the ride from Winchester to Devizes and the escape from Oxford are related in Painter, *William Marshal,* p. 7; and in Norgate, *England under the Angevin Kings* (1887), I, 333 ff.

P. 131. Henry's sickness at this time is factual; the rest of the scene is fictional. Zumbro's speech on blood-letting is taken from Lynn Thorndike's *History of Magic and Experimental Science,* I, 728. The recipes for purge and febrifuge were gathered from various passages in *Leechdoms, Wortcunning, and Starcraft,* ed. Oswald Cockayne, 3 vols.

P. 132. In "Cligés" (*Arthurian Romances by Chrétien de Troyes,* trans. W. W. Comfort, p. 130), great medical skill is attributed to Thessalia, Fenice's nurse.

P. 133. For a translation of the whole poem, see Barbara Smythe, *op. cit.,* p. 6.

P. 134. For the various details involved in bookmaking in the Middle Ages, the rate of copying, etc., see J. W. Thompson, *The Mediaeval Library,* pp. 594-646.

P. 134. Wace (*circa* 1100-*circa* 1175) completed in 1155 his translating and paraphrasing of Geoffrey's work. His dedication of the work to Eleanor (generally assumed) and the fact that he was later commissioned by Henry to write a history of the dukes of Normandy, have suggested the imaginary scene just described.

CHAPTER XIII

The most detailed narrative of Henry II's reign is to be found in Kate Norgate's *England under the Angevin Kings,* 2 vols. She gives full references to the chronicles. The chronology for Henry's reign has been worked out by R. W. Eyton in his *Itinerary* (see Introductory Note). He includes references to Eleanor when he can find them.

P. 136. In 1156 and for several succeeding years Ralph de Hastings appears constantly in the Pipe Rolls as handling the disbursements for Eleanor and her household. See, for example, the entry in 2 Henry II, p. 4.

P. 137. Some of the details of this coronation have been gathered from J. H. Round's *The King's Serjeants,* chap. vi, "Coronation Services." On p. 133, he cites the chamberlain's right to carry off the basins, etc., as his fee.

P. 139. For a full list of the royal household, together with the emoluments of each officer, see the twelfth century document, "The Constitution of the King's Household," translated in Carl Stephenson and F. G. Marcham, *Sources of English Constitutional History* (1937), pp. 65-70.

P. 140. Expenditures for Eleanor's household are entered in the Pipe Rolls from time to time. Characteristic are the following entries for the year 1155-56, taken from Pipe Roll 2 Henry II, p. 4:

For goods purchased for the Queen 68s. 4d. by the writ of the Queen and the Justiciar.

And for allowance for the Queen £40. And for the allowance for Henry the son of the King, and for his Sister and his Aunt £34.

And for wine for the use of these (i.e., the persons just mentioned) £7. by Ralph de Hastings. And for the allowance for these same persons £6. 6s.

P. 140. The "baby carriage" entry is found among purchases for 1156-57 (Pipe Roll 3 Henry II, p. 71): *Et per Rusca portata Lundoniam ad opus filii Regis.* In C. T. Martin's *Record Interpreter,* "Rusca" is translated as "skep." A definition of this word given in the *Century Dictionary and Encyclopedia* reads as follows: "A vehicle consisting of a large wicker basket mounted on wheels, used to convey cops, etc. about a factory." The shields are mentioned in an interesting group of expenditures entered in the Winchester accounts for the year 1159-60 (Pipe Roll 6 Henry II, p. 49):

For the repair of the Chapel and of the houses and of the walls and of the garden of the Queen . . . And for the transport of the Queen's robe and of her wine and of her Incense, and of the Chests of her Chapel, and for the boys' shields . . . And for the Queen's chamber and chimney and cellar £22. 13s. 2d.

The tops are fictitious but possible: "for he turns faster than a top driven and lashed by the whip" ("Cligés," *Arthurian Romances by Chrétien de Troyes,* trans. W. W. Comfort, p. 140.)

P. 140. One of several references to the king's sister is as follows:

And for clothes for the maid of the king's sister 52s. And for clothes for the king's sister and his children £12. 3s. And for pans, basins, and towels for the use of the Queen 13s.—(Pipe Roll 4 Henry II, 1157-58, p. 111)

Some scholars consider that the sister referred to here is Emma. I have preferred to follow R. S. Loomis (*The Romance of Tristram and Ysolt,* pp. x-xii), and J. C. Fox ("Marie de France," *English Historical Review,* XXV [1910], 303 ff.), who seem inclined to identify this sister as Marie de France.

P. 141. R. S. Loomis (*The Romance of Tristram and Ysolt,* Chap. 1, note 5) adduces evidence strongly suggesting that Eleanor all her life had a special interest in the story of Tristan, which led, directly or indirectly, to the writings on that subject by Marie de France, Thomas, and Chrétien de Troyes.

P. 142. That the *Esnecca* was built at Eleanor's suggestion is a mere guess. "Esnecca" is probably the term for a type of vessel, but in the Pipe Rolls the word seems to be used as a proper noun.

P. 143. For the details of Becket's magnificent expedition, see Norgate, *England under the Angevin Kings,* I, 446-48, and the references there given.

P. 144. For Eleanor's voyage with the treasure and her quick return, see Eyton, *Itinerary,* pp. 50-51, and n. 1. For the improvements in her quarters at Winchester, see above, the Pipe Roll selection about the shields. An example of some of Eleanor's expenditures at this time is found below. In modern currency they would amount roughly to $100,000.

London: For wine for the Queen, £4. 16s. 4d. by her own writ. And for 2 ounces of gold for gilding the King's cups, 2 marks of silver. And for 2 tuns of wine, 34s. for the Queen's use. . . . And for an allowance for the King's son, £13. 4s. 7d.

Southampton: And for an allowance for the Queen by her own writ, 23s. 3d. . . . And in carriage of the Queen's wine and for loading and unloading, 7s. 3d. . . . And for carriage of the wine to Wallingford by writ of the Queen, 4s. 6d. And in transportation of the wine from Brittany 104s. 2d.

Hampshire: And in allowance for the Queen by her own writ, £226. 3s. 9d. in 13 tallies. And for allowance to Henry, the King's son, £56. 13s. in 4 tallies.—(Pipe Roll 6 Henry II, 1159-60.)

P. 145. That Eleanor was influential in interesting Henry in both these building projects is inferential but highly probable. The cathedral's apse, containing the great stained glass window at the bottom of which Henry and Eleanor are represented as donors, is thought to have been completed by 1162.

P. 147. Under London, in the year 1162-63 (Pipe Roll 9 Henry II) there is an allowance for Richard, by the king's writ, of £10. 6s. 8d.; also an item of 100s. spent for pork, mutton, and "little trifles" (*minutis rebus*) for the feast of the king's son.

P. 149. For Matilda's luggage, see Pipe Roll 13 Henry II, under "London and Middlesex." For the vessels carrying Eleanor and her household, see Pipe Roll 14 Henry II, under "Hampshire."

CHAPTER XIV

P. 153. For the William Marshal episode, see Painter, *William Marshal*, pp. 25-29.

P. 155. Geoffrey of Vigeois, then a monk at St. Martial's, says that the *O princeps egregie* originated at St. Martial's and from there passed to the monks at St. Hilaire (A. Richard, *Histoire*, II, 151, n. 1).

P. 157. That Eleanor was with the king at Christmas time is stated by Roger of Hoveden, *Chronica*, ed. Stubbs, II, 14.

P. 157. For Henry's passionate outburst on hearing of Becket's actions, see Norgate, *England under the Angevin Kings*, II, 78.

P. 158. Walter Map is the authority for the Ikenoi story (*De nugis curialium*, p. 299).

P. 159. For "Fair Rosamond," see Archer's article cited in my Introductory Note.

CHAPTER XV

P. 161. The correspondence between Eleanor and her daughter is imaginary. I follow Miss Kelly in her article (cited in my Introductory Note) in thinking that the two were together at this time. The description of Adele's apartment is taken from the same article.

P. 164. In the imaginary discussions of "current literature" described in these pages, I have had in mind the probable dates of composition as given in U. T. Holmes's highly useful *History of Old French Literature*.

P. 167. The chief source of information on the Courts of Love is the late twelfth century (1180?) work by Marie de Champagne's chaplain, Andreas, entitled *De amore*, Latin text edited by A. Pagès (1929); translated with useful introduction and notes by J. J. Parry, *The Art of Courtly Love* (1941). See also Miss Kelly's article and Sidney Painter's excellent *French Chivalry* (1940).

CHAPTER XVI

Much of my account of the manner in which the details of the plot against King Henry were worked out is suppositious. The motivation of Eleanor's conduct, however, is based on assertions contained in numerous passages of the chroniclers. These passages are, for the most part, given either in Norgate, or *England under the Angevin Kings,* or in Richard.

P. 176. For Young Henry's trip to Poitiers, see William of Newburgh, I, 169-72, where is also found the dialogue between Henry's messengers and Louis. For the part presumably played by William and Porteclie in the betrayal of Eleanor, see A. Richard, II, 170, n. 2. Gervaise of Canterbury, *Chronica,* I, 242, says about Eleanor's change of costume: *mutata veste muliebri.*

CHAPTER XVII

The reconstruction of Eleanor's life at Salisbury, 1173-83, is based mainly on data from the Pipe Rolls. Giraldus is the authority for Henry's attempt to force her to become a nun. His attempts to secure a divorce from her are referred to by both Giraldus and Gervaise of Canterbury. It is clear that the restrictions of her custody began to be relaxed from the time of Joan's arrival at Winchester, 1176.

P. 182. Robert Malduit had charge of Eleanor from the time of arrival in England and for several years thereafter. That he had charge of her at Chinon is not clear, but charters show that he was frequently on the Continent.

P. 184. For a description of Salisbury, *i. e.,* Old Sarum, as it was in Eleanor's day, and for plans of the twelfth century castle, see J. P. Bushe-Fox, *Old Sarum* (Ancient Monuments and Historic Buildings, H. M. Office of Works, H. M. Stationery Office, London, 1930). Also, *The Illustrated Guide,* etc. (Brown's series of *Strangers' Handbooks,* no. 3).

P. 185. Robert expended, between July 8 and September 29, 1174, for the queen's food, clothing, and general expenses, a little over £37; see Pipe Roll 20 Henry II (1173-74), pp. 29, 34. Roger de Gruze does not appear in the Pipe Rolls as one of Eleanor's attendants till some years later.

P. 186. During the year 1158-59, Eleanor caused some chestnut trees to be transported from Warwickshire to Salisbury (Pipe Roll 5 Henry II, p. 25). Though there must have been a gardener and, I think, a maid also, no mention is made of them in the records, nor of a chaplain.

P. 190. The reference to Henry's attempt to secure a divorce is as follows: *Rex enim suam exosam habens reginam, . . . eo quod supradicta persecutio ex ipsius reginae consilio emanasse dicebatur, omni conatu divortium moliri videbatur* (Gervaise of Canterbury, *Chronica,* I, 256). Also, to the same effect, see Giraldus Cambrensis, "Instruction of Princes," trans. J. Stevenson, *Church Historians of England,* Vol. V, Part I, 183-84. Later (p. 227) he records Henry's attempt to force Eleanor to take the veil: ". . . where [Fontevrault] he [King Henry] had eagerly striven with so great a desire and such earnest endeavours, to shut up Queen Eleanor, in the dress of a nun. . . ."

P. 192. Two entries suggest that Eleanor not only came to Winchester when Joan was there in the summer of 1176, but also that she went with Joan to Southampton:

1) Robert Malduit paid for the queen's expenses while at Winchester (Pipe Roll 22 Henry II, 1175-76, under *Civitas Wintonie,* p. 198).

2) Hugh de Gundevill appears in 23 Henry II (1176-77), p. 166, as paying out of the Southampton revenue to the queen's sergeants a certain sum for her allowance.

The meeting between Henry and Eleanor is both possible and probable, but I have found no record of it. Not many months after Joan's departure, Eleanor was provided with a proper maid of honor and a lot of new clothes—that they came because Joan interceded for them is a fair guess.

P. 192. The entry about the maid, clothes, and mattress applies to the year 1177-78 (Pipe Roll 24 Henry II, p. 128), and states that Edward Blunt, a chamberlain who was constantly making purchases at London for the royal household, had spent £28 (equivalent to about $3,000 today) to procure for the use of the queen and her maid (*puelle sue*), *.ij. palliis de escarlata . . . et .ij. pelliciis grisiis et .j. culcitra perpuncta. . . .*

P. 194. *Henricus rex et Alienor regina reconciliati fuerunt:* "Waverly Annals" under the year 1179, in *Annales monastici,* ed. H. R. Luard, II, 241.

P. 194. For details of Louis's visit to St. Thomas' shrine, see Giraldus, "Instruction of Princes," p. 178. For Louis's diamond, see J. C. Wall, *Shrines of British Saints,* pp. 156, 161, and 167.

P. 195. The dream is told by Thomas Agnellus, archdeacon of Wells, who says that it was related to him by Eleanor herself: *sicut ex ejus relatione didicimus* (Ralph of Coggeshall, *Chronicon anglicanum,* ed. Joseph Stevenson, pp. 272-73).

CHAPTER XVIII

P. 197. For Eleanor's release so that she might travel through these dower lands, see Benedict of Peterborough, *Chronicles of the Reigns of Henry II and Richard I,* ed. William Stubbs, I, 305.

P. 197. For William Marshal's promise to carry Prince Henry's cross to the Holy Sepulchre and for his visit to England, see Painter, *William Marshal,* p. 55. That William visited Eleanor then is not stated but seems highly probable. The characterization of Eleanor as "valiant and courteous" is that of the thirteenth century author of *L'Histoire de Guillaume le Marechal,* ed. Paul Meyer (1882), I, 1.

P. 198. The enlargement of Eleanor's household at this time is inferred from various entries in the Pipe Rolls, reference to some of which will be made below. Eleanor's visit to Woodstock and her inspection of the apartments there and of the kitchen may be inferred from the following: "And to Ralph fitz Stephen for the queen's allowance from Easter up to the feast of St. John the Baptist (April 1 to June 24) £32. and 14s. by writ of Ranulf de Glanvill." *Et pro .j. plumbo et .ij. caldariis et .vj. patellis et .iiij. trepariis ad coquinam Regis de Wudestoc .xxxv.s. et .vj.d. per breve regis.* (Pipe Roll 30 Henry II, 1183-84, under "Oxfordshire," p. 70). The visit at Sulgrave Manor is suppositious. The visit at Berkhamstead with Matilda and her husband is attested by the following entries: "And in allowance for the queen and the duke and duchess of Saxony £104 by writ of the king. . . . And for clothes for the queen and for wine for herself and the duke of Saxony at Berkhamstead. . . ." (Pipe Roll 30 Henry II, 1183-84, Berkhamstead and *Terra que fuit Henrici de Essex* under "Essex and Hertfordshire," p. 134).

P. 200. The conversation between Eleanor and Richard is suppositious but highly probable.

P. 201. Entries recording purchases of supplies for the Christmas feast are scattered through the Pipe Rolls. The purchase of "entertaining trifles suitable for feasts," etc. is as follows: *Et pro robis ad opus Regis et Regine .xxix.l. et .xx.d. . . . Et pro anulis et lapidibus et firmalibus et aliis jocundiolis ad opus Regis .xxix.m.* [marks] . . . (31 Henry II, 1184-85, Honor of Earl Eustace, under Norfolk and Suffolk, p. 44).

P. 201. *Et pro portandis sellis Regine et puellarum suarum ad Waltham Episcopi Wintoniensis . . .* (Pipe Roll 31 Henry II, 1184-85, under London and Middlesex, 217); under Southampton, 206: *ad procurationem Regine et Ducis Saxonis apud Porcestr' et Portesmuam. . . .*

P. 202. Henry's words to Eleanor at Bayoux are based on Benedict of Peterborough, *Chronicles,* I, 337-38.

P. 203. *Et pro acquietandis pannis Willelmi Angl' filii ducis Saxonie et nutricum suarum et lotricis sue et magistri sui . . .* (Pipe Roll 32 Henry II, 1185-86, under London and Middlesex, p. 49).

P. 204. For Henry's proposal to Philip, see Giraldus Cambrensis, *Opera,* VIII, 231.

P. 205. That Henry had determined to leave Eleanor as regent is only an inference, but, I think, a correct one: there was no one else whom he could have chosen. The Pipe Roll entries seem to indicate that the royal wards were all placed in her household. For one such entry, showing extensive purchases of red and green cloth, hoods, pelisses, and cloaks of squirrel fur, of sable, doe skin, beaver, etc., see 1 Richard I (1188-1189), pp. 223-24. Here Roger de Gruze and Humphrey appear as Eleanor's servants. For Henry's last words, see Giraldus Cambrensis, *Opera*, VIII, 297.

CHAPTER XIX

Kate Norgate in *England under the Angevin Kings,* Vol. II, chap. VII, and in *John Lackland,* (1902) chap. II, gives the fullest treatment of the period covered by this chapter. She has detailed references to the chronicles.

P. 208. For the scene between Richard and William Marshal, see Painter, *William Marshal,* pp. 73-74. For Eleanor's commission as regent, see Painter, pp. 74-76: "Queen Eleanor . . . received from her son the power of decreeing in the realm whatever she wished." See also Ralph of Diceto, *Opera historica,* ed. Stubbs, II, 67-68.

P. 210. The details of the coronation ceremony are given in Benedict of Peterborough, *Chronicles,* II, 78 ff.

P. 213. On Eleanor's journey to Italy: *Alienor regina . . . maris pericula declinavit, transitum habens per montem Jani, per Ytaliae plana, per illos celebres orbis concursus, ad dominum papam Romae.* (Ralph of Diceto, II, 81). For the meeting with Henry VI, see Lionel Landon, *Itinerary of King Richard I* (Pipe Roll, New Series, no. 13, Appendix D, p. 193).

P. 214-18. The best single picture of Eleanor's state of mind and her activities while combating John and Philip is given by Richard of Devizes (Stevenson, *Church Historians of England,* Vol. V, Part I, 278): "Earl John, sending messengers to Southampton, ordered a vessel to be got ready for him, with the intention, as was thought, of going over to the king of the French; but the queen his mother, fearing lest the light-minded youth were, at the instigation of the French, going to form some plot against his lord and brother, anxiously turns over in her mind every art by which she could hinder the purpose of her son. . . . Accordingly, having summoned the great men of the kingdom, first at Windsor, secondly at Oxford, thirdly at London, fourthly at Winchester, she prevailed upon him, after much ado, by her own tears and prayers of the nobles, not to cross the sea at the appointed time."

Imaginative reconstructions are 1) the dialogue between Eleanor and John, 2) the occurrences, and Eleanor's speech, at the council where John demands to be recognized as king. Eleanor's position as queen mother and regent made it possible for her to outface John and to give the barons much-needed leadership. It is also Richard of Devizes (Stevenson, *op. cit.*, p. 277) who gives the picture of Eleanor in her successful efforts to relieve the population of Ely from the horrors of the interdict. Gerviase of Canterbury (*Chronica*, I, 515) says that Eleanor "who then ruled England" gave orders for defense of the east coast.

CHAPTER XX

Miss Norgate's two works already cited, and a third, *Richard the Lion Heart* (1924), give the best account of this period, with full references to the chronicles.

P. 219. I have included the Blondel story, since it may have some basis in fact. Cf. Norgate, *England under the Angevin Kings*, II, 324.

P. 220. The translation of Richard's letter is my own; for the original, see *Chronicles and Memorials of the Reign of Richard I,* ed. William Stubbs, II, 362.

P. 221. That "incomparable woman": the characterization is by Richard of Devizes (Stevenson, *op. cit.*, p. 258). For the chalice incident, see Jocelin of Brakelond's *Chronicle,* trans. L. C. Jane, pp. 74-75.

P. 222. The translation of Richard's song is by Kate Norgate (*Richard the Lion Heart*, p. 278); original words and music are in J. B. Beck, *Les chansonniers des troubadours et des trouvères* (1927), Vol. II, No. 152. Max Meili has made a recording of this song for *L'Anthologie Sonore* (The Gramaphone Shop, N. Y.), No. 18, "French Troubadours."

P. 222. For Philip's warning to John, see Roger of Hoveden, *Chronica,* ed. William Stubbs, III, 216-17.

P. 224-25. For Eleanor's persuasion of Richard to render homage to the emperor and for descriptions of the closing scene of his liberation, see Roger of Hoveden, *Chronica,* III, 202-3, 232; and Ralph de Diceto, II, 112-13. For Adolf's substitution of the introit, see Ralph de Diceto, II, 114.

P. 225. If keys had not at this date been substituted for slides, they were adjusted to the old organ at Winchester probably not very much later.

P. 226. For the reconciliation scene between Richard and John, see Norgate, *John Lackland,* pp. 51-52 and note.

P. 227. For Richard's reformation, see Roger of Hoveden, III, 288-90.

CHAPTER XXI

Fullest secondary accounts of this period are found in Norgate and Richard.

P. 228. For Richard's joking with his guards, see Ralph of Coggeshall, *Chronicon,* (ed. Stevenson, p. 58); as for his geniality in the family circle, the same author says (p. 92): *In triclinio vero, cum privata familia positus, satis, affabilis et blandus esse videbatur, jocis et ludicris cum eisdem animum resolvens efferatum.* Coggleshall describes (p. 97) Richard's delight in leading the choir.

P. 229. For Richard's and Berengaria's visit to Thorée, and their building of a house there, see L. Landon, *op. cit.,* p. 101.

P. 230. Eleanor herself says she was at Richard's deathbed (J. H. Round, *Calendar of Documents preserved in France,* no. 47).

P. 231. Richard of Devizes (in Stevenson, *Church Historians of Eng.,* Vol. V, Part I, p. 258) speaking of Eleanor when ten years earlier she was about to start for Sicily, characterizes her as follows: "Queen Alienor—an incomparable woman, beautiful and modest, influential yet moderate, humble and learned, (qualities which are very rarely found in a woman,) who was old enough to have had two kings for husbands, and two kings for sons, even now indefatigable in any labour, and whose endurance was the admiration of her age—taking with her the daughter of the king of Navarre, a girl more learned than beautiful. . . ."

P. 237. In 1937 there were still some impressive remains of the huge keep and of part of the walls of Mirebeau. My reconstruction of the castle and of many of the battle's details is imaginative.

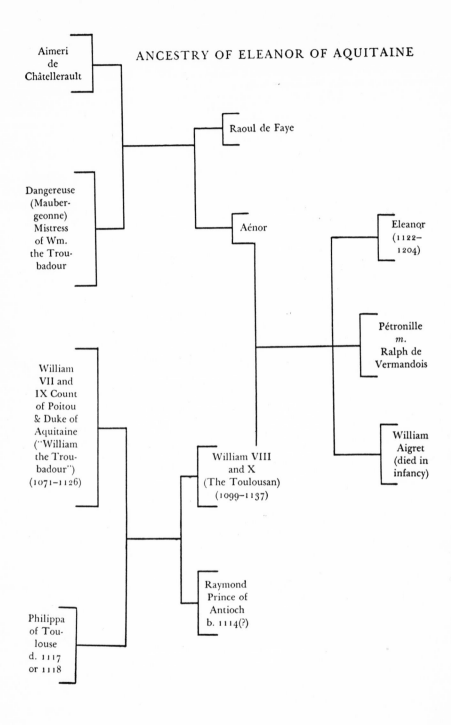

Aimeri de Châtellerault

Raoul de Faye

Dangereuse (Maubergeonne) Mistress of Wm. the Troubadour

Aénor

Eleanor (1122–1204)

Pétronille *m.* Ralph de Vermandois

William VII and IX Count of Poitou & Duke of Aquitaine ("William the Troubadour") (1071–1126)

William VIII and X (The Toulousan) (1099–1137)

William Aigret (died in infancy)

Raymond Prince of Antioch b. 1114(?)

Philippa of Toulouse d. 1117 or 1118

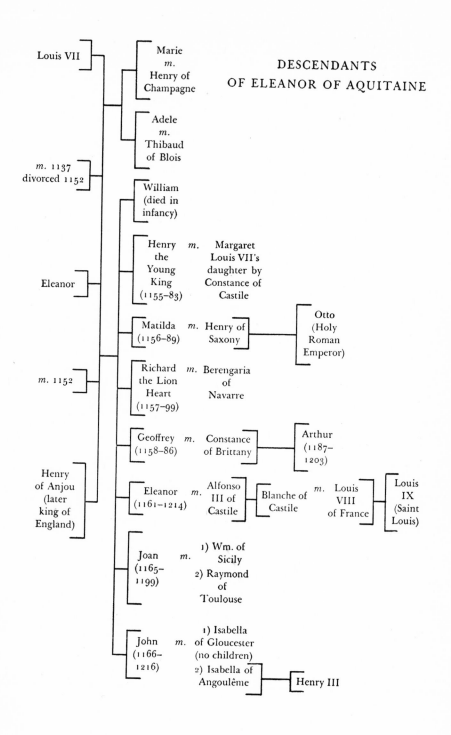

DESCENDANTS
OF ELEANOR OF AQUITAINE

Louis VII

m. 1137
divorced 1152

Eleanor

m. 1152

Henry
of Anjou
(later
king of
England)

Marie
m.
Henry of
Champagne

Adele
m.
Thibaud
of Blois

William
(died in
infancy)

Henry   m.   Margaret
the   Louis VII's
Young   daughter by
King   Constance of
(1155–83)   Castile

Matilda   m.   Henry of   Otto
(1156–89)   Saxony   (Holy
                                Roman
                                Emperor)

Richard   m.   Berengaria
the Lion   of
Heart   Navarre
(1157–99)

Geoffrey m.   Constance   Arthur
(1158–86)   of Brittany   (1187–
                                 1203)

Eleanor   m.   Alfonso   m. Louis   Louis
(1161–1214)   III of   Blanche of   VIII   IX
               Castile   Castile   of France (Saint
                                                         Louis)

Joan   m.   1) Wm. of
(1165–   Sicily
1199)   2) Raymond
               of
               Toulouse

John   m.   1) Isabella
(1166–   of Gloucester
1216)   (no children)
               2) Isabella of
               Angoulême   Henry III

Index

held prisoner at Chinon, 181-82; confined at Salisbury Castle, 184-97; goes to Winchester to see daughter Joan, 191 ff.; reappears before the court, 193; hears of Young Henry's death, 195; freed from Salisbury, 196; tours dowry lands, 198-99; agrees to have Richard return titles to her, 202; at Richard's coronation, 209-10; accompanies Richard to Tours, 211; goes to Sicily, 212; attends consecration of Pope Celestine III in Rome, 213; frustrates John's plans to capture English throne, 214-15; rules during Richard's absence, 214 ff.; has interdicts lifted from Rouen and Ely, 216; sends search for Richard, 217; learns of Richard's capture, 218-19; arranges Richard's ransom, 221-22; at Mainz when Richard is freed, 223-24; returns to England with Richard, 224-25; at Richard's death, 230; attempts to prepare John for duties as king, 231; escorts Blanche of Castile to France, 231-32; defends Castle of Mirebeau, 233 ff.; death and burial of, 238

Eleanor of Castile, daughter of Eleanor of Aquitaine, xiii, 147, 231

Ely, Eleanor has interdict lifted from, 216; archbishop of, see William of Longchamp

Emma, half-sister of Henry II, 140

Enguerrand de Coucy, 31

Ephesus, Turks attack crusaders at, 61

"Eracle," 164

Esnecca, Eleanor's ship, 142, 145, 149, 150, 192, 201

Eudo of Porhoet, 159

Eugenius, Pope, 31, 35, 37, 60, 94-98

Eustace, son of Stephen, King of England, 119, 125

Eustorgius, Bishop, 14

Everard de Barres, Sir, Master of the Templars, 40, 56, 67, 68, 71

Everard de Breteuil, 65

Excommunication, William the Troubadour threatened with, 5; Ralph of Vermandois punished by, 24, 25; of the three bishops in the Thomas Becket affair, 157

"Fair Rosamond." *See* Rosamond

Fitz-Count, Brian, 131-32

"Floire et Blancheflor," 164

Frederick I (Frederick Barbarossa), Emperor of Germany, 34, 58, 61, 149, 199, 201, 212

Fulcher, the Patriarch of Jerusalem, 88

Gaucher de Montjoy, 65

Gautier d'Arras, Sir, 164, 166

Geoffrey, Count of Nantes, brother of Henry II, 110-13, 119-21

Geoffrey, half-brother of Henry II, 140, 175, 208, 218

Geoffrey, son of Eleanor and Henry II, 139, 142, 144, 147, 153, 171, 176-77, 183, 194, 200, 202-3, 213

Geoffrey the Fair, Count of Anjou, father of Henry II, 84, 100, 102, 104, 105, 128, 140, 142

Geoffrey de Lèves, Bishop of Chartres, 17

Geoffrey de Lusignan, 237

Geoffrey de Rancon, 35, 63-7

Geoffrey du Lauroux, Archbishop of Bordeaux, 8-11, 15-16, 18, 116

Geoffrey of Monmouth, 129, 133-34

Gerald of Montreuil-Bellay, 100, 104

Germans, killed at Adrianople, 46; beaten by Turks at Dorylaeum, 58

Girard, Bishop of Angoulême, 8

Godfrey de la Roche, Bishop of Langres, 30, 31, 41, 43, 48, 52, 56, 67, 86

Greek Orthodox Church, conflict between crusaders and, 48, 51-52

Greeks, attack on Louis VII at Cadmos Mountain pass, 64; deceitfully weaken crusaders, 71

Gregory, Admiral of Roger's fleet, 93

Gregory, Bishop, *History of the Franks*, 111

Gualeran, Sir Thierry, 42, 76, 86, 87, 92, 106

Guido of Arezzo, 97

Guy de Lusignan, 204

Harvey the Butler, 166

Helie, Archbishop of Bordeaux, 232

Héloise, 99

Henri, Count of Champagne, 146, 161, 170

Henry, Bishop of Winchester, 130

Henry I, King of England, 75, 100, 128, 138, 148, 198, 210

Henry II, King of England, meets Eleanor, 100 ff.; marriage to Eleanor, 117; forces Louis out of Normandy, 119-20; returns to Eleanor, 121; orders walls of St. Martial torn down, 122;

Otto of Freising, Bishop, 48, 63
Otto of Saxony, grandson of Eleanor, 199
Ovid, 94, 161

Patrick of Salisbury, Earl, 152
Perotin, 20
Peter the Venerable, Abbot, 98
Pétronille, sister of Eleanor, 3, 8, 10, 18, 19, 22, 24-27, 39, 164
Philip, brother of Louis VII, 28
Philip II, King of France, xii, 194, 197, 203-5, 211, 213-14, 216-17, 220, 224-27, 231, 237
Philippa, wife of William the Troubadour, 5, 20
Pierre, chaplain of Eleanor, 4, 113, 115, 140
Pierre la Chatre, 23, 25, 27
Pilgrimage, of William the Toulousan to shrine of Saint James, 9-11; of Henry II to Ste. Marie de Rocamadour, 156; of Henry II to Canterbury, 188; of Louis VII to Canterbury, 194. *See also* Crusades
Poetry, written by William the Troubadour, 5. *See also* Literature
Poitiers, as cultural center under Eleanor of Aquitaine, 122 ff., 151-52, 160 ff.
Porteclie de Mauzé, 175, 178-79

Radegonde, Sainte, 7, 8
Ralph de Hastings, Sir, 136-37
Ralph de Perrone, Count of Vermandois and Seneschal of France, 12, 18, 19-22, 24-27, 39, 99
Ralph of Fougeres, 177-78
Ranulf de Glanville, Sir, 188
Raoul de Faye, uncle of Eleanor, 116, 154-55, 165-66, 177
Ratisbon, reception of Louis VII by Greek envoys at, 43
Raymond, Count of Toulouse, 143-44, 175
Raymond, Prince of Antioch, 74, 75-87, 91, 95, 101, 103
Raymond of St. Gilles, 174
Rhodes, Island of, Greek Navy menaces crusades at, 92
Richard I (Richard the Lion Heart), installed as Count of Poitiers and Duke of Aquitaine, 154-55; at Poitiers, 160-62; in Great Revolt against father, Henry II, 174, 175-77, 182; titles restored by Eleanor, 193-94; disputes with brothers over lands, 199, 200, 202;

joins King Philip II of France, 203-5; appoints Eleanor governor, 208; crowned King of England, 209-10; prepares for crusade, 211; marries Berengaria of Navarre, 212-13; John plots against, 214-16, 217, 222; captured by Leopold of Austria, 216; prisoner in Castle Dürrenstein, 219; sends letter to mother, 220; composes song in prison, 222; liberated, 223-24; returns to England, 225; reconciliation with John, 226; rejoins Berengaria, 227-28; builds Château Gaillard, 229; death of, 230; mentioned, xii, xiii, 139, 140, 144, 150, 164, 171
Richard de Lucy, Sir, 138, 139, 182, 192
Richard of Ilchester, Archdeacon of Poitiers, 155, 191
Robert, Count of Dreux, brother of Louis VII, 25, 31, 44, 49, 55-56, 58, 63, 66, 90, 122
Robert, Earl of Gloucester, 130
Robert, Earl of Leicester, 138-39, 182-83
Robert of Torigny or de Monte, Abbot of St. Michel, 129-30, 133-34
Roger, Archbishop of York, 156-57
Roger, Bishop of Worcester, 155-56, 173
Roger de Gruze, Sir, 185, 187, 193
Roger the Norman, King of Apulia and Sicily, 33-35, 48, 56, 75, 92-94, 96, 190
Roman d'Alexandre, 164
Roman de Eneas, 161
Roman de Troie, 164, 166
Rome, arrival of crusaders at, 98
Rosamond Clifford ("Fair Rosamond"), 159, 198, 203
Rouen, archbishops of. *See* Hugh *and* Walter

St. André, cathedral, scene of marriage and coronation of Eleanor and Louis, 16
St. Denis, abbey church, described, 36; Louis consecrated at, 37
Ste. Radegonde, church of, 7
St. Hilaire, scene of Richard's installation as count of Poitou, 154
St. Martial's, abbey, Henry II asserts authority at, 121-22; scene of Richard's installation as duke of Aquitaine, 155
St. Pierre, cathedral, music at, 7; Eleanor rebuilds, 145
Saintonge, Bishop of, 116
Saldebreuil, seneschal of Eleanor, 116, 166

171 |